DECLINE OF
AN EMPIRE

DECLINE OF AN EMPIRE

The Soviet Socialist Republics in Revolt

Hélène Carrère d'Encausse

Translated
by
Martin Sokolinsky
and
Henry A. La Farge

Newsweek Books, New York

1979 First English Language Edition

Printed in the United States of America

© 1978 Flammarion et Cie
English Translation © 1979 Newsweek, Inc.
Original Edition Published in France
1978 under the title *L'Empire éclaté*

Library of Congress Cataloging in Publication Data

Carrère d'Encausse, Hélène.
  Decline of an Empire.

  Translation of L'Empire éclaté.
  Bibliography: p.
  Includes Index.
  1. Nationalism—Russia. 2. Minorities—Russia.
3. Russia—History—1953 I. Title.
DK274.C2813   323.1'47   79-2293
ISBN 0-88225-280-1

Book Design: Mary Ann Joulwan

TABLE OF CONTENTS
***

TABLE OF CONTENTS

*
**

TABLE OF MAPS AND CHARTS

**
***

MAPS: TRINA MANSFIELD BAYLES

The Federated Republics of the USSR

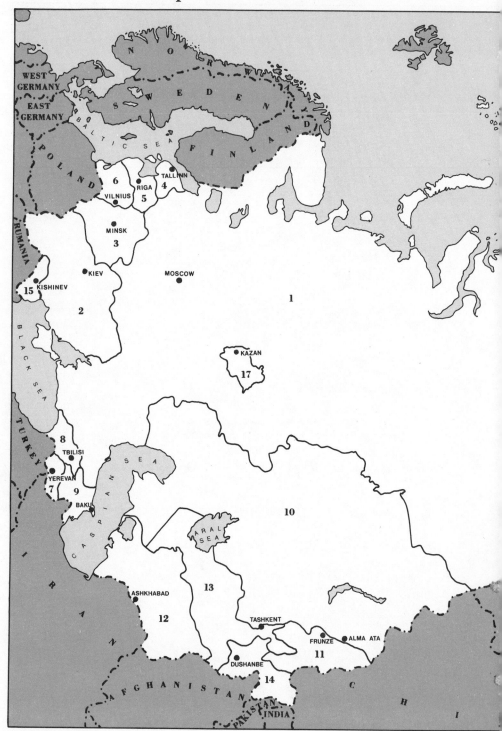

KHABAROVSK

16

O K H O T S K

S E A

ONGOLIA

CHINA

1. RSFSR
2. Ukraine
3. Belorussia
4. Estonia
5. Latvia
6. Lithuania

7. Armenia
8. Georgia
9. Azerbaidzhan
10. Kazakhstan
11. Kirghizia
12. Turkmenia

13. Uzbekistan
14. Tadzhikistan
15. Moldavia
16. Birobidzhan
    autonomous region)
17. Tatar (autonomous republic)

Introduction

The Soviet Union is not a country like others, but almost a continent, where Europe and Asia meet. And it is not a nation so much as an empire, in a world where empires are fading away. In short, it is not the "State of workers and peasants" it claims to be. The truth is that it is primarily a State of nations.

More than a hundred nations and nationalities lie within its borders, speaking more than a hundred languages, with all that keeps them apart: history, race, traditions, religions. The Soviets are in fact a highly diversified people, a mixture of human beings totally dissimilar, both physically and culturally. There are the Balts on the borders of Europe, the Uighurs on the borders of China, and the Russians in between who have undergone the opposing influences of both; there are the Georgians of the south, the Eskimos of the far north, the nomads of the Kazakhian steppes, and innumerable others. A tormented history, comprising invasions, wars, and patient reconquests over the centuries has fashioned this indefinable mass of completely different peoples. One has only to look at the map to comprehend this. In this boundless continent open on every side conquerors have been engulfed and some, like Tamerlane, have made it their final resting place, leaving there their customs, religions and ideas.

Today the descendants of the conquerors and the conquered live side by side. All, according to their passports, are Soviet citizens, children of the Workers' Revolution of 1917. How well has a state, born of a revolution of the working classes and bearer of an ideology that all men are equal as regards work and capital, been able to keep within its borders all those people of vastly different origins and make them live in peaceful coexistence? Has the Marxist ideology of human uniformity gained mastery over this diverse society in which for the first time in history it has taken root and come to power? In other words, is the Soviet Union a workers' State, or does it perpetuate an empire? Has Marxism attained its goal of creating a new society which, by transcending its differences, has realized its communal destiny? Or, on the contrary, has the diversity of nationalities, historic inheritances and mentalities prevailed over an ideology and a government for whom the only reality is the community of workers, with fraternal ties extending across frontiers and ethnic and cultural differences?

The Soviet Union has been in existence long enough to make it possible to assess its development. Two generations have grown up knowing nothing but the Soviet system, which has accordingly had a chance to educate people to its way of thinking. Those are people to whom one should turn to find out whether they are really building a new world, or whether in spite of the radical break of 1917 and the years that followed, the USSR is turning into a society like the one their fathers knew—a society in which national differences always prevail over uniformity of thought.

CHAPTER I

When the "Prison of the Peoples" Was Opened

According to history, the Empire of the czars was a "prison of the peoples" and Lenin opened it. But history is never quite that simple. At the start of the twentieth century the empire was already showing signs of weakness; all its subject peoples were beginning to resent its domination and looking for ways to escape from it. Lenin's genius lies in having grasped the breadth of these desires for emancipation, and in having understood that by utilizing those desires—which had nothing to do with the working class—he could assure the victory of the workers in his own country.

The Russian working class was not large—scarcely 3 million in a population of 140 million people. But Lenin passionately desired a revolution, and he wanted to bring it about at a propitious moment, and not wait until it came of its own accord in time. That is why, in the tumult of the First World War, which was tearing Europe apart, he hurled the countless divisions of nationalities avid for freedom into the revolutionary battle, alongside the small army of the Russian workers.

To the classic Marxist appeal, "Workers of the world, unite!" he added another far more powerful, which still rings today: "Oppressed peoples, rise up!" Actually, the destiny of the peoples he was calling to revolt mattered little to Lenin.[1] They were merely pawns which he was manipulating for *his* revolution. But history plays strange tricks on those who tamper with it. The oppressed heard Lenin's call. The czarist Empire, already shaken by the war, collapsed in the chaos of forces he had triggered. And from the ruins of this once powerful Empire there emerged the Soviet State, the first success of the Revolution.

It mattered little to Lenin that the Soviet State was confined to Russia, while in the former Russian possessions independent governments were being set up—whether Soviet or anti-Soviet. The Soviet territory was still limited, but Lenin thought he would rapidly extend it to Europe. For him the Russia with the dimensions of a continent no longer existed; but soon the Revolution would set fire to another continent, Europe—that was his ambition. For three years, indifferent to the upheavals agitating the peoples formerly tied to Russia, Lenin stood indefatigable watch over the Revolution and waited for the workers of Europe to join and expand the Soviet State.

But in 1920, after a series of abortive revolutions across Europe, he had to face the truth. The European proletariat remained deaf to his appeals and the Revolution remained confined to Russia. It was a revolution restricted to *a single country,* a country limited in terms of territory and population, cut off from its economic base, incapable thus of surviving. What was to be done to save the Revolution? To succeed, it would have to go beyond the framework of one country and spread into a wider sphere.

Like Marx and all those who came after him, Lenin was convinced that to survive, the revolution had to be worldwide or be doomed to perish. Since it was not possible to extend it to Europe, why not profit by the dynamic forces of the oppressed peoples that had insured the triumph of the Russian Revolution? Why not turn to the colonial countries with a renewed appeal for the uprising of the nations? Lenin thought of doing just that. In September 1920 at Baku, under the auspices of the Comintern, he did indeed convene a Congress of Oppressed Peoples of the East, to discuss recourse to a revolution which would be both colonial and social, and which by being extended to the East, would save the Russian Revolution from isolation and defeat. But the Baku Congress had an entirely different outcome.[2] Confronted there for the first time by the view of revolution as conceived by the national Communists of Asia, primarily those of the former czarist Empire, the leaders of the Comintern were seized with panic. What they discovered at Baku in the space of a few momentous days was that the oppressed or formerly oppressed peoples whom Lenin had used to ensure the success of the Revolution no longer wanted to be Bolshevik tools or auxiliaries of the European Revolution. They intended to be masters of their own destiny, and to act in their own interests. Not only that, but from the lips of former subjects of the Russian Empire, obscure men of whom the leaders of the European workers' movement had never heard—Kazakhs or Uzbeks from the far reaches of Central Asia—the Comintern heard strange and disconcerting statements. These men—Narbutabekov, Ryskulov, and a few others whom Stalin was to put to death fifteen years later—stood up to speak to the Europeans in the name of oppressed peoples. What they said was that the Revolution was not "unique" and must not be entirely at the service of Europe and its proletariat. They pointed out that there existed a world of Asian peoples enslaved by Europe; that these people feared being subjugated by Europe's revolution just as they had been subjugated by its imperialism; that for them, revolution and Marxism signified national emancipation, and not class struggle. At Baku the proletariat of Europe saw looming before it—indeed against it—a non-European world which, in the name of Lenin's ideas, was asserting that revolution inside and outside Europe were not one and the same thing; and that *their* revolution was for the worldwide emancipation of dominated peoples.

Before long, other voices in the world of oppressed nations would be heard saying the same thing. The most famous would be that of Mao Tse-tung, whose name at Baku in 1920 was as yet unknown. And Third World ideas advanced by unknown Turkestanis confronted the Bolsheviks with a reality and a dilemma which were unforeseen. To push the Revolution eastward clearly involved creating Soviet states but in no way meant extending the revolution. On the contrary, it meant confronting Russia—the self-styled avant-garde of the European Revolution—with revolutions that would be anti-European and that would make demands on the European workers' movement.

Two concepts of revolution emerged at Baku: that of Marx and Lenin, the revolution of the world-wide proletariat, fraternal, without borders; and the revolution of the oppressed nations which would admit only oppressed nations and for which the European proletariat was primarily European—hence, an oppressor. On the one hand, an internationale of proletarians; on the other, an internationale of oppressed nations. Lenin could not—indeed would not—run the risk of such distortion of the revolutionary idea to which his life was committed. Therefore, having glimpsed the possibility and, he thought, the perils of "colonial" revolutions, he deliberately turned his back on them. He decided to save what he could—the revolution where he had made it, in one country, Russia.

In September 1920 the revolutionary cycle begun in Petrograd three years before came to an end. The Bolsheviks had ceased to expect revolutions which, in Europe, showed little signs of coming and which, elsewhere, seemed more dangerous than desirable. Their task, henceforth, would be to sustain the State of the Soviets, giving it the means to exist in a world that refused to accept it. But this State, as it stood, was not viable. It lacked space, room that would protect it. It lacked the wheat and iron of the Ukraine,[3] the oil of the Caucasus, the cotton of Central Asia.

As early as 1917, the Bolsheviks began setting up normal relations with the nations that had been organized into independent republics. In 1920 the Bolsheviks realized that, to survive, they had to convert those normal relations between good neighbors into contractual relations, then return to the unity lost in 1917.

How could the emancipated nations be "recovered," without at the same time bringing back the "prison of the peoples"? More than Lenin, who was busy governing Russia and later hindered by illness, it was Stalin, the expert on national questions,[4] who was to engineer the reconstruction of a Soviet multi-ethnic state in which the former members of the Empire would wind up side by side.

From Dispersed Nations to the Union of Nations

Looking back at what had become of the Empire by 1920, we marvel at the succession of passing events. For some nations the independence won in the Revolution was an established, durable fact, due primarily to the support that they received from outside. This is the case of the western periphery of the Soviet State: Finland, the Baltic states, and—reunited by the war which had just ended—Poland. And in the Caucasus, mention should be made of Menshevik Georgia, for the time being.[5]

Elsewhere, independent Soviet republics were less certain of their status, either because they had no support from the outside or were suddenly deprived of that support. Such was the case of the Ukraine, Belorussia, Azerbaidzhan, Armenia, the Republic of the Far East, Bukhara, and Khiva. Finally, when the civil war and foreign intervention ended, the Soviet government extended its sphere of authority beyond Russia to territories peopled by the so-called *inorodtsy*, nomads who had special status, generally enjoying autonomy limited to local problems.

How could this heterogeneous whole be made into a viable, governable state? How could the independent Soviet republics be attached to it? By gradually reducing their independence. In 1920–1921 the Soviet State—then in the form of the Federated Republic of Russia—would sign bilateral treaties with all the neighboring Soviet republics, establishing close economic and military ties between the contracting parties and defining common spheres of action within *Commissariats*, placed under the authority of the Republic of Russia. Legally, these treaties were agreements between equals but, among these equals, there was one which, to borrow Orwell's expression, became "more equal than the others": Russia.

This imbalance was particularly evident both in the military sphere, where it confirmed the military unity already achieved by the Red Army, and in diplomatic practice. In the latter domain, law and practice would very soon diverge. By law, each state retained its own organization. In practice, however, only the Ukraine was to keep its own diplomatic representation for a while longer. The outside world looked upon these organizational differences as fictional. The truth became apparent in 1921 when the republics were scarcely represented at the signing of the Treaty of Riga. This was especially striking in 1922 at the Genoa Conference where only the RSFSR (Russian Soviet Federated Socialist Republic) was invited and spoke on behalf of its partners. The Ukraine registered its protest at this slight, making it quite clear that a serious loss of sovereignty was involved.

Simultaneously with this process of consolidation, which included elements of integration, the fate of Georgia was sealed. A republic led by Mensheviks, Georgia was acclaimed by Western socialists as the motherland of "true" socialism. Thus Georgia represented a challenge to the Bolsheviks, who had broken with Menshevism on their own ground. Furthermore, located where it was, right on a strategically important frontier, it seemed to be an advance post of the Entente.* In 1921 this situation was intolerable to the Bolsheviks, and at this juncture, Stalin expressed himself in no uncertain terms: the self-determination offered to the nations in 1917 was an out-moded phase.

---

* TRANSLATOR'S NOTE: Entente, a reference to the Triple Entente originally composed of France, Great Britain, and czarist Russia, but later secretly joined by Italy and Rumania before the end of the First World War.

The time for unification had come and this applied to Georgia. Because independent Georgia seemed viable and uncompromising, she was subjected to unification by force, a procedure that Lenin had always decried. In February 1921, the Red Army invaded Georgia. No doubt, Lenin urged the Bolsheviks who were in the Caucasus to be conciliatory with the Mensheviks and, in a general way, with the Georgian intelligentsia. But his first concern was to limit the consequences of military reconquest to the interior and not to stir up world opinion. On the whole, he seemed to have no doubts about the need for such an operation. On May 21, 1921, Georgia, led this time by Bolsheviks, was ready—like the other republics—to sign a treaty of alliance with the RSFSR.

Thanks to the bilateral treaties, the nations of the former Empire, dispersed for a time, were united in 1921 by a body of contractual links that assured some community of action. Yet these ties did not suffice to provide a unity of spirit that would transcend the differences felt by each nation. Quite to the contrary, both inside and outside the Communist Party, national cadres and national elites rose up against the policy pursued by the leaders of the RSFSR. With growing vehemence, they denounced a policy of domination which, to their way of thinking, was hiding behind the flag of internationalism. Their accusations showed a growing tendency to equate the Soviet State with the imperial state which it had replaced. For the Bolsheviks there could be no doubt that the transitional situation that came into being in 1920, i.e., independent national states linked to the RSFSR by a host of provisions, gave rise to all kinds of resentment and prevented them from building a new nation, one cemented by the social ideal they were appealing for.

That was why, in 1922, the Bolsheviks moved into the second phase of their State's national organization, with the drafting of a plan for federation that would include all the nations. Federation, for Lenin, was a substantial concession. Until 1917 he had constantly opposed federal plans that he claimed would perpetuate national differences. But he began to revise his thinking in 1917, when he perceived the breadth of the centrifugal movements in the former Empire. So as not to unduly weaken Russia, he allowed that the nations not wishing to secede from her could be set up according to the federal principle. Between 1918 and 1921, only the nations enclaved in Russia were affected by this revision, but by 1922 the idea was spreading to all the former possessions. Federal organization was to guarantee equality between the Russian nation and non-Russian nations, and this would make all the difference between the "prison of the peoples" and Soviet egalitarianism.

Yet the Bolsheviks were far from unanimous in the way they pictured federation.[6] Assigned the task of drawing up the constitutional plan, Stalin had very definite ideas on the point. Soviet federation was to be modeled on the RSFSR before becoming a model itself for the worldwide federation of Socialist states of the future. In using the RSFSR as a model, Stalin was unveiling his concept of federation. The Federated Republic of Russia, set up by the 1918 Constitution, did group eight autonomous republics and thirteen autonomous regions, but it was characterized by a high degree of centralization and an almost total lack of local jurisdictional authority. The degree of centralization was such in the RSFSR that a delegate to the Eighth Party Congress, in March 1919, declared, "In England there is a saying: 'Parliament can do anything except change a woman into a man.' In our country, the Council of People's Commissars can do anything, even change a woman into a man."

Under these conditions, proposing the RSFSR as a prototype for federation amounted to advocating centralization extended to a different area. Actually, Lenin had proposed the same concept of federation in 1918 when he said, "The example of the Russian Soviet Republic shows that the federation which we are building will be a step forward toward the unity of Russia's different nationalities in one Soviet State, centralized and democratic."

When the Bolsheviks spoke about federation in the early 1920s, they apparently had a clear plan in mind: an organization of nations that would maintain some degree of national identity, but be controlled by centralized institutions to assure the cohesion of the whole. This rather simple and generally accepted view explains the fact that Stalin played a preponderant role in the commission set up on August 10, 1922, for the purpose of drafting the constitution for the federation. It also explains the fact that the draft worded by Stalin personally is a faithful reproduction of the RSFSR's model.[7] The federation was to be formed by the adherence of still independent republics to the RSFSR. On joining the RSFSR, these republics would enjoy autonomous, not sovereign, status and would accept as organs of federal power those of the RSFSR. Clearly, then, it was a question of a geographic extension of the Russian Republic, and not a new state.

The Leninist Revision
and the Drafting of a True Federal Plan

When submitted to the central committees of the republican Communist parties, Stalin's plan gained acceptance from the more docile Azerbaidzhan and Armenia, but it provoked muffled criticism in the Ukraine, which was holding out for maintaining bilateral relations, and drew open opposition from Georgia.[8]

The crisis with the Georgian Communist leaders turned out to be especially serious inasmuch as bilateral treaties still governed relations between the RSFSR and its allies. When Stalin announced coldly to the Georgian leaders that the decisions made by the supreme authorities of the RSFSR were to be applied without discussion in the independent republics, the Georgians had the feeling that the era of relations by force had returned; and they were subsequently to show that they were determined to defend their independence— by any means. Neither the Georgian opposition nor the Ukrainian hesitation sufficed to block the plan adopted by the constitutional commission—on which Stalin had a majority of supporters. But this draft would be doomed when Lenin studied it.

In the autumn of 1922 Lenin was already gravely ill. At the end of 1921, exhausted, he had been forced to withdraw from public life for several weeks. When he returned, his capacity for work was limited and his condition steadily worsened. On May 25, 1922, he had suffered a terrible stroke. His right side paralyzed, unable to speak for a time, he had to wait until the autumn to resume his work. But he was—and would remain—a mere shadow of the fighter who had stirred Russia to revolt. People who saw him at the Fourth Comintern Congress in November 1922, a month before a new attack was to force him out of politics for good, were astonished at the change that had come over him. Yet, in the last few weeks of an active life that was now slowing down, the national question would be one of his major concerns, and he perceived the problems looming ahead with clearsightedness and despair.

After some delay, the draft constitution was submitted to the convalescing Lenin, and he found it alarming. He knew the opposition that the plan had encountered. He realized that this draft, far from contributing to internationalism, would actually stir up national passions. Furthermore, Lenin was attached—as he had been all his life—to an internationalist view of the Soviet State. He wanted to go beyond nations into a new community—not crystallize nationalism. Finally, the Revolution and the ensuing years had shown him irrefutably that social awareness evolves at its own pace, according to its own laws, not by force nor by institutions which are foreign to its aspirations.

In four years, the headstrong Lenin had discovered that the naked will of a party, even the party of the proletariat's avant-garde, was not enough to change ways of thinking. Circumstances had favored this will for a while, enabling him to exploit the chaos on behalf of the Revolution. But once the Revolution had been carried out, the Bolsheviks and the State that they had created found themselves far ahead of a social conscience that aspired to land, civic peace and national independence. As early as 1921, Lenin perceived that only long years of teaching could alter ways of thinking. And that making national awareness international called for a great deal of time, a great deal of trust, a great deal of tact.

Stalin's dictatorial plan had the effect of a bombshell on Lenin, whose essentially pedagogic view of change had been further deepened by illness and isolation. Reports of opposition convinced Lenin that national mentalities had to be taken into account and not shoved aside, something that could actually solidify national differences. For this reason, Lenin—with all the might left in him—opposed this draft constitution which, he wrote, "would be grist for the mill of the independentists." He reproached Stalin for "being too impatient," for ignoring the real feelings of people.

He countered this draft with another, one that would spare minority sensitivities. This State of the Soviets would have a new structure which would unite, on the basis of equality, all the republics, the Russian Republic along with all the others. Equality, then, was the master-word of Leninist thought. Resentment and national differences could only be abolished by an equality guaranteeing to each nation that there subsisted none of the former domination based on inequality.

This shows how events had ripened Lenin's thinking since 1918. True to himself, he never struggled against an obstacle that he encountered but tried to go around it. In 1922 that obstacle was the differences between the nations. That is why he attached so much importance to them, for he realized that the immediate choice would determine all future relations of the Soviet nations. Moreover, this choice would determine the revolutions of the future insofar as, with the Revolution receding everywhere, the Soviet State alone offered a model for those aspiring to revolution.

Lenin was not alone in thinking that the problem was crucial. Stalin, who had kept in the background until then, rebelled. Speaking to the members of the Politburo, he criticized Lenin's position and accused him of "national liberalism." But this revolt was short-lived. Seeing that he had no followers, Stalin yielded, and prepared a new draft in keeping with Lenin's wishes, which he distributed as if it were in no way the outcome of a serious conflict.[9] The draft, thus corrected, was adopted by the national Communist parties, with the exception of the Georgians, who were fighting tenaciously so that their entry into the federation might be on the fundamental basis of true equality.[10]

The struggle merged with the one that would suddenly pit Lenin against Stalin. The latter had yielded on the federation's juridical organization, but he had no intention of yielding on its actual implementation. In the conflict which would, right to the very end, set him against Stalin—a conflict over the real application of the egalitarian principle between nations—Lenin, rendered acutely sensitive by illness, perceived the basis of the relations that had developed between the central government and the republics. Clearly, it was nothing short of domination and Russian chauvinism. It was at this point that Lenin perceived the extent of the impending setback. His closest co-workers had been corrupted by power; his party had become a mafia; on all sides, chauvinism had revived, encouraged by the insolence of the most powerful of all, Russian chauvinism.

In the last weeks that remained before a new stroke isolated him completely from the world of the living, Lenin wrote a text which reveals his clearsightedness regarding the national problem—and his despair of a solution. His text is, first of all, a confession: "I am much to blame before the workers of Russia for not handling with sufficient energy the famous question of 'autonomization', officially called the Union of Soviet Socialist Republics." Yet this text was written on December 30, 1922, coinciding with the date of the draft constitution adopted, which represented the triumph of his ideas. Why, then, did he feel guilty? Because he was aware of the ambiguity of the situation he would be leaving behind him.[11]

On December 30, 1922, the Third Congress of the Soviets adopted the Treaty of Union forming the USSR (Union of Soviet Socialist Republics), concluded between the RSFSR and the Soviet Republics of the Ukraine and Belorussia, and, finally, the Federated Republic of Transcaucasus that had been imposed by force on the Georgians. This treaty established the fundamental provisions that were to become the 1924 Soviet Constitution. The federation which emerged was indeed the new juridical community as desired by Lenin; its institutions were specific—different from those of the RSFSR.

But Lenin clearly saw that the legal provisions were insufficient to offset the weight of actual fact. Stalin also had understood this discrepancy between *law* and *fact*, and this explains why, after a fit of temper, he converted his plan for autonomy into a federal one. For Stalin, the reality of the existing situation was easy to decipher. There was no denying the RSFSR's primacy in terms of population and politics. Its ability to control national territorial formations through diverse institutions—the Party, economic organs, the Army—was obvious. Stalin undoubtedly believed that the ideal legal situation would be the one reflecting this reality—hence, his plan for autonomization. But compelled by Lenin to give it up, he did so without too much grumbling, for he firmly believed that fact would prevail over law. Whether the federation was egalitarian or not hardly mattered; the RSFSR would be the heart of it. Lenin was aware of this inescapable consequence of the imbalance between reality and professed law. But he attributed it to a specific cause: "This one hundred percent Russian product, the Great Russian chauvinism that characterizes the Russian bureaucrat." And the Russian bureaucrat, Lenin sensed, pervades the Communist. That was why he scarcely believed in the merits of juridical texts, for, he wrote, the solution arrived at "reduces the freedom of exit from the Union, with which we justify ourselves, to a scrap of paper."

In this last fight against Stalin, Lenin sized up the national problem, its extent, and his failure. But had he changed his views fundamentally? Not at all. His ultimate goal remained the fading away of the nations in favor of a new human community united by class solidarity. Only the methods and tempo had changed. He hoped this new community would be achieved in time through education, equal rights, trust. Stubborn determination yielded to a concern for reality, haste yielded to patience. Clearsightedness, since it was a matter of seeing the depth of national awareness, overcame obstinate fidelity to an ultimate vision in which the problem of nationalities would no longer exist. This conflict explains why Lenin's last directives led only to deadlocks.

The Dialectic of Equality and Control

According to the December 1922 Treaty of Union, the Soviet structure instituted that year was a federated state. But this same treaty emphasized chiefly what was *common*, i.e., jurisdiction and institutions, relegating what was strictly republican to the background.[12] Yet the equality of peoples, affirmed in the Treaty of Union, which represents one of the two basic components of Soviet law, was not just a hollow phrase. At that time, the desire for equality marked Soviet doctrine on the relations between nations. And while Lenin and Stalin hardly agreed on political equality, Stalin would nevertheless bring it into the sphere of the USSR's national policy. Like Lenin, he knew that the solution of the national problem lay in appeasement, which implied that concessions would be made to the nations incorporated in the USSR.

While Stalin's political solution was basically centralist, it was in the context of an egalitarian ideology and a series of provisions intended to prove that the USSR was based on equality between national units.

Egalitarian ideology was affirmed by constitutional law. Federation gave way to highly complicated statutes which responded in principle to highly varied situations. Some nations were organized into sovereign states, i.e., the national federated republics. Smaller nations or those not meeting all the prerequisites for sovereignty nevertheless had a state structure, although not actually sovereign, and were called autonomous republics. Finally, nationalities—ethnic units less clearly defined than nations—also enjoyed recognition of their specific culture and had the status of autonomous regions or national districts that guaranteed them their own cultural rights. Thus Soviet internal organization reflects the ethnic complexity of the society and the existence within it of groups whose political and cultural development is far from uniform.

The republics are legally equal, united only by their will to live together and free to secede at any time. While none then undertook to test the right to secession—Georgia's experience had shown that unification was a categorical imperative—the equality of national minorities nevertheless had a political and cultural side.

The political aspect is reflected in the watch-word: "indigenization" of cadres everywhere and at all levels.[13] The national republics had to be led by their own cadres. The Communist Party imposed this line of action on the whole Union, both to combat national bit-terness, and because it was a necessity. The revolution had deprived Russia of its former elites. The Soviets could not guide and make this vast country function with only the newly organized Russian cadres. The scarcity of qualified Russian leaders, added to political difficulties, prompted Lenin's successors to follow the course that he had charted. It was not an easy one. The border republics and the autonomous entities located in the RSFSR experienced the same leadership difficulties as RSFSR itself. Where were they to find the personnel for the Party's cadres, for the administrators, for educa-tion, for the economy?[14] They had little choice. There was only a handful of veteran Communists. That left only the old national elites or else semiliterate peasants unfamiliar with Bolshevism and its aims. The new elites which would provide the leadership included all three of these elements. In Russia, the working class, its ranks thinned by the civil war, could still manage to supply the necessary cadres, but in the national states the new regime had to accept any-one willing to help.

This policy of all-out "indigenization" had two consequences: it induced the promotion of national cultures and required the con-stant control of cadres of diverse origins. The promotion of national cultures is unquestionably the most original and the most fascinating aspect of Soviet policy in that period. Here, too, doctrine and neces-sity had combined to produce such a solution.

The USSR of the 1920s remained marked by a revolutionary uto-pia—a fact which must not be overlooked. Despite blows struck at this utopia—the forced incorporation of nations was a major blow—the Bolsheviks as a whole remained attached to an egalitarian con-cept of society. And the equality of nations, once it had been initiat-ed politically, carried over into the cultural domain.[15] Earlier in the century, Otto Bauer—determined to maintain the cohesion of the Austro-Hungarian Empire—had seen that the primary concern of nations was to preserve and develop their own cultures, particularly their languages. This explains why the national program of the 1920s stressed the promotion of *all* national cultures on an equal ba-sis, and first of all the promotion of national languages.[16]

The cadres required for the "indigenization" policy had to be na-tionals because they would be the bearers of their nation's culture. As it turned out, this policy had its ludicrous side. Sometimes a na-tion—such as it was defined in the plan of statehood in the 1920s—

had no real language of its own or, perhaps, was accustomed to speaking another. Yet the Soviets insisted that each national administrative unit have a language and use it. Thus, in the framework of the Belorussian Republic, where several languages were used concurrently, an official Belorussian language was imposed by the government, even if most of the population had to go to school to learn it.[17] More ridiculous still, linguistic scholars were called in to transform dialects spoken by groups of a few hundred persons into languages for litarary use.[18]

Despite its poverty, the Soviet state devoted great effort and considerable sums of money to this promotion of cultures—even to making some up. When there was a crying need to stamp out illiteracy quickly and simply, a tremendous amount of time and energy went into printing alphabets and books that would have only a few hundred readers, and into the training of teachers capable of teaching these future readers.[19] But the Party "line" allowed for no deviation. Each national group was entitled to *its* culture and, hence, to *its* language. All the same, the egalitarianism underlying that line was coupled with political aims.

The equality of cultural rights given to each nation would also make it possible to break up some large groups united by special factors. Such was the case for the Moslem peoples of the Caucasus and Central Asia,[20] who ever since the beginning of the century had been trying to unite around common languages.[21] Within established borders, each nation had to use a language of its own. The cultural egalitarianism thus put an end to pan-Turkish or pan-Moslem dreams which would have pitted dangerously unwieldy communities and civilizations against the policy of centralism.

At the same time, the promotion of national cultures presented serious drawbacks. Purely national education could only reinforce national feelings and run counter to the ultimate unifying goal. National culture was therefore a double-barreled concept, one that was perfectly defined by Stalin. These cultures were to be national in *form*—principally as to language. But at the same time they were to be socialist in *content*.[22] What these national languages were to transmit was not each nation's own heritage, but a new heritage shared by all—socialism, its values and ultimate goals. Only when seen in this light could the national cultures perform the function expected of them. They placated and satisfied national feelings. But at the same time, they induced the nations to move gradually toward a new awareness, common to all. Lenin would not have repudiated this cultural compromise framed by Stalin. Actually, it combined the demands of the present—satisfying local national feelings and breaking up any large pan-national solidarity—with the future goal, the gradual acceptance of a common political culture. Here, force yielded to education and, once again, Stalin heeded Lenin's warnings.

Nevertheless, this cultural egalitarianism was not to be established without a system of controls. In principle, the local national cadres and cultures were supposed to satisfy nationalist demands and gradually reduce them. But these concessions could also lead to a result diametrically opposed, i.e., an intensification of nationalist feelings. In order to limit the egalitarian concessions to their pedagogic function, the Soviets, from the 1920s on, began coupling them with multiple controls. Various checks were instituted: control by the internationalist Party over the nationalist-minded state; primacy of the federal State over the federated units; economic control increasing the ties between the center and the periphery; and particularly, cultural control. The latter was exerted by the centralized Communist Party over cultural activities, and by the substitution of a common system of values—centrally defined—for the systems of values and rules governing each particular society.[23] With a mixture of liberalism and controls, the USSR's national policy of the 1920s sought to forge a new community, a Soviet proletarian nation which would demonstrate that class solidarity could prevail over national consciousness.

Stalinist Federalism: Control without Equality

The equality of peoples, the basis of federal equilibrium in the 1920s was intended to build the "friendship of peoples" living together. This equality was also to lead to the creation of a new elite which, like its culture, would be national in form, but which would be the same from one republic to another: it would be a Soviet elite devoted to the system which had promoted it, and serving as a bridge between different traditions and a common future.

By 1930, however, it became apparent that the results of this cultural revolution within the USSR were more ambiguous than its promoters had expected. On all sides, new elites were springing up, gradually replacing the old ones steeped in nationalism. But at the same time, these new elites, pushed forward by the Communist Party, became imbued with the very nationalism which they were to have stamped out. The most flagrant case was that of the Belorussian elite.

To bind the people of Belorussia to their language, the regime had been forced to demonstrate real tenacity. Notwithstanding this, the 1926 census showed that, out of four million Belorussians, a quarter still considered the Russian language as their mother tongue.[24]

Here, where the penetration of Russian culture was strong, the elite affirmed that there was no room for the class struggle. They maintained that the characteristic feature of the Belorussian nation was the absence of any bourgeoisie. Here, Westernized ideas were developing and, along with them, the refusal to belong to the Eastern Slavic world.

In the early 1930s Moscow discovered that the Belorussian elite had formed a national center whose aim was to get Belorussia out of the federation.[25] Whether or not this center carried on activities dangerous to Soviet unity was incidental. The mere fact that it existed was important. It showed the elite's deep attachment to traditional values—ones foreign to Soviet society. This situation was all the more disquieting because, in other regions, too, the Soviets could see the drawbacks involved in salvaging national elites that had played a role before the revolution.

In Central Asia a former leader of the local nationalist movement, Faizullah Hodjaev, promoted to the summit of the Communist hierarchy, was doing his best to hinder the region's economic integration into the Soviet Union, while acting the part of a national leader won over to Communism. In that same region the Soviet regime was bogged down in the insidious war waged by the Basmachis, Moslem guerrillas who resisted for nearly ten years with the tacit support of the population.[26]

By the early 1930s Stalin, having rid himself of all his adversaries, could finally impose his own thinking on the national problem. His approach was multi-faceted. From previous experience he retained the cultural compromise and the federalism that he was to improve.

Unlike the Fundamental Law of 1924, the 1936 Constitution was truly federal. National formations were increasing in those days, and the hierarchy of nations and nationalities, with their inherent theoretical rights and jurisdictions, had been clearly established.[27] But alongside of this theoretical respect for the federal structure, Stalin plunged into a cataclysmic operation aimed at transforming society. In so doing, he believed that nationalism would lose all reason for being.

The nations in the Union were essentially peasant nations, and some were still nomadic. Collectivization for all and "sedentarization" for nomads would have a twofold effect on the country as a whole: first, it would eliminate the peasant and his individualism, his system of values so foreign to the new society; and secondly, for the non-Russians it would eliminate all roots of traditions peculiar to each people, traditions which rural life tends to foster. At the national level this attachment to typically non-Russian values had given desperate strength to the people's resistance to collectivization.

Everywhere in the USSR, social change—one aim of which was the eradication of all national peculiarities and particular ways of living—went hand in hand with violence, a violence which was characteristic of the Stalinist approach to the problem. Lenin's confidence in the teaching of internationalism never tempted Stalin. In the early 1930s he replaced education with naked violence. After destroying the traditional conditions of life for society as a whole, he went on to purge all the national elites of the 1920s. Their unpardonable crime: returning to the springs of national fidelity. While Stalin's purges seemed to strike blindly throughout the USSR, they had a deliberate purpose in the borderlands, making possible the systematic destruction of both the old elites and the new ones established in the 1920s.

On the eve of the Second World War, the consequences of the purges were clear: Stalin had made room for a new elite that would embody a new concept of relations between nations of the USSR, a concept that was patently unegalitarian, borrowed from the imperial past. This concept of a federation of unequals did not emerge officially until 1945. But by the end of the 1930s, harbingers had announced its coming. First of all, the Cyrillic alphabet was universally imposed. In the 1920s many of the Soviet languages using different alphabets such as Arabic and Mongolian, or those lacking any alphabet at all, had been provided with the Latin alphabet.[28] The demands of a rapid method of universal education coupled with Soviet poverty justified this step. The Latin alphabet, which was not used in Russia itself, offered the additional advantage of not giving this change of intellectual traditions an imperial stamp. At the end of the 1930s the very rapid replacement of the Latin alphabet by the Cyrillic alphabet[29] revealed an effort to bring diverse languages closer to

Russian—at least, as regards the written language. It also suggests that a general process of cultural Russification had begun.

In like manner, toward the end of the 1930s, the history of the Russian Empire began to be revised in a direction that stressed the persistent inequality of the nations. Immediately after the Revolution the Bolsheviks had proclaimed the hateful nature of imperial domination, condemning everything connected with it. They maintained that the resistance of the conquered nations to the Russian invader had been a "progressive" historical act, regardless of whether the leaders had been religious chiefs like the Imam Chamil in the Caucasus, or tribal chiefs like Khan Kennesary Kasymov who had been the implacable foe of the Russians on the Kazakh plains a century before. On the eve of the Second World War, the cleavage between the Imperial Russian domination and legitimate movements for national independence no longer seemed quite so pronounced in the interpretation of history.[30]

The 1936 Constitution already revealed this change of attitude. The Soviet State implicitly declared itself the heir, territorially and historically, of the Empire.[31] Under Stalin's orders the historians rediscovered the positive historical role played by the "land-gathering" princes, by the Orthodox Church, by monasticism, that bearer of Byzantine civilization.

While deploring the authoritarian character of the Empire of the czars, historians in the 1930s began to uncover the good side of that Empire. For them the first of these positive traits was the power of the state which had enabled Russia to become the rampart of Europe against the invasions from the east. Little by little, Russian history was vindicated,[32] not only that of the people, but also that of the sovereigns who had forged the nation against the foreign enemy. The cinema lent assistance to this new awareness of history, glorifying Peter the Great and especially Alexander Nevsky. Along with the rulers, the military leaders were celebrated—especially those who had fought against Napoleon, and could be evoked in the commemoration of the Battle of Borodino. Thus the Russian people began to regain a past which they had become accustomed to repudiate since 1917.

But this rehabilitation of Russian history raised a serious problem as regards the histories of the other peoples of the Soviet Union. Here, too, the view of history accepted since the Revolution would gradually be reversed. The revolutionary egalitarianism led to glori-

fying all movements of national resistance to oppression, which was considered as an "absolute evil." In the mid-1930s the historians began to wonder. Undoubtedly the czarist oppression had been condemnable; but hadn't its effects been beneficial? Thanks to colonial domination, the peoples of the Empire had rallied to the Revolution at the same time as the Russian people, leaping over that painful historical phase—capitalism. Hadn't the ultimate benefits of colonialism been at least as great as the drawbacks? Thus colonialism, regarded as an "absolute evil" up until then, was toned down by postrevolutionary history and became a "relative evil."

Gradually, the reasoning developed still further. Soviet historians found that, for many peoples subjugated by Russia, the choice had not been between colonization or liberty, but between two colonizations. For instance, Georgia had been threatened on the one hand by Turkey, which would have destroyed its culture; and on the other by Russia, which had preserved the culture and opened the way to socialism. Consequently, colonization became the "lesser evil."[33] Seen in this light, the national movements of resistance to colonization seemed to foster outmoded sentiments rather than to further the national interest of the peoples concerned. The history books were full of new heroes. To the wise rulers of Russia—who certainly had been autocrats, but who had been forced by history into their roles—were added the heroes of the national histories who had understood the need for union with Russia, the need to accept that "lesser evil." Actually, there was only a handful of them. On the eve of the Second World War the only historical figure of any real stature meeting these conditions was Bohdan Khmelnitskii,[34] who in the sixteenth century had signed the agreement uniting the Ukraine with Russia.

These changes were still unclear until 1941. Soviet society, as it emerged from the nightmare of collectivization and purges, could not yet see the implications of this new history of the peoples forming the USSR. It was the Second World War which would give a definitive meaning to the Stalinist version of "the friendship of the peoples." What the war showed, first of all, was the precariousness of this multinational structure. The lightning speed with which the German armies rolled across Soviet soil stems, in part, from the fact that those armies were crossing territory that was not inhabited by Russians, but by peoples who grudgingly accepted incorporation in the Soviet state; some only a short time before, such as the Baltic states. The Ukrainian attitude to the advancing German troops revealed the depth of this national bitterness which was fostered to some extent by German policy in Soviet territory.[35]

Before June 22, 1941, a fantastic plan for the dismemberment of the USSR had been devised by Alfred Rosenberg, author of *The Myth of the 20th Century*. Aware of the volatile nature of a multinational state, the only one still surviving in Europe, Rosenberg proposed that Germany exploit the nationality problem to destroy the USSR. His plan called for reducing Russia to a vassal-state turned toward the East. Russia would be encircled by a network of national states created by and subordinate to Germany.

In certain cases the actual implementation of the Rosenberg plan compounded the military problems of the Soviet government, for it stirred up nationalist feelings. The Caucasus was the prime target for the experiment, and the German Army backed national governments which sprang up in the wake of the Red Army's retreat. Such was the case for the Karachay national government led by a peasant, Kadi Bairamukov, who began to restore traditional social and religious structures, as well as to decollectivize rural life.

Had the German Army extended the Caucasian experiment to all the occupied territories, the Soviet federation would have been reduced to nothingness. But Rosenberg's ideas were atttacked from two sides. On the one hand, they were opposed by a part of the German military establishment led by General Jodl, for whom backing dispersed nations meant provoking the opposition of the most important nation—Russia. According to Jodl, Germany should appeal to the Russian nation and separate it from its leaders, thereby destroying the Soviet state from within. At the other extreme was the Hitlerian plan, which was just as negative. This called for colonizing all Soviet soil indiscriminately. The creation of national governments would only mortgage the future and complicate the task of German colonists. To Hitler, all citizens of the USSR, whether Ukrainians or Russians, were *Untermenschen* (inferior race). So why bother to discriminate among them?

This resistance from German leaders paralyzed Rosenberg's plan for backing Soviet nationalities and had the effect of actually pushing them back—disillusioned and horrified by German violence in the East—toward federation.

But the Germans' isolated experiments in the Caucasus had several consequences. They proved to Stalin that the federal state, as it stood, was very fragile, and that new elements would be needed. Under the pressure of the German Army, these elements had to be concessions, on a short-term basis, to local national sentiment. In this way, Stalin could beat the Germans to the punch whenever they tried to exploit the nationality problem. As a result of the Soviet military collapse in June 1941, it became clear that merely appealing to Communist values was not enough, but that the names of heroes who had defended their country in the past proved infinitely more effective in rallying the people than those of Marx or Lenin. On a long-term basis, Stalin was to formulate the whole balance between the nations along new lines.

The application of Rosenberg's plan had a second consequence: the Second World War fostered—or rather freed—local nationalist sentiments that the tragic period of the 1930s had relegated to the background. The war years seemed to re-create nationalistic tensions like those which had led to the breakup of the Empire, despite nearly a quarter century's socialist training and federalism.

The war had also proved to the central government that the borderlands were vulnerable, and that this vulnerability, in a tense international situation, might threaten the entire system with death. Also, Stalin had observed the weak response to appeals for international solidarity and decided it was necessary to replace them with an appeal for another kind of solidarity, one involving history, the nation, religion.[36] In so doing, he introduced new elements into Soviet ideology, elements which would profoundly modify it.

The Rehabilitation of the "Elder Brother": a New Imperial System

Victory revealed the extent of the change that war had brought to the USSR, and the lessons that Stalin drew from it. In this country of exacerbated nationalisms he would completely renounce prewar egalitarianism, establish levels of priority for local nationalist sentiments, and raise the Russian nation to the top rank, exalting its traditions and culture. The war had provided him with an excellent pretext.

As soon as the German armies retreated from the national territories in which autonomist tendencies had appeared, Stalin moved in ruthlessly. Between October 1943 and June 1944, the peoples of six small nations were accused of treason, ripped from their native soil, and deported to Central Asia or Siberia. They suffered the same fate as the Volga Germans who had been deported in 1941. At least a million people—in 1939 there were 407,690 Chechens, 92,074 Ingush, 75,737 Karachays, 42,666 Balkars, 134,271 Kalmyks, more than 200,000 Crimean Tatars, and 380,000 Volga Germans—were accused of a collective crime, one that was attributed to entire nations.[37] In 1946 a decree would specify that these measures called for the dissolution of the national territories of the Chechens, the Ingush and the Tatars. And for ten years these national groups would have no legal existence, no representative to the Soviet of Nationalities, and no mention anywhere.

By attacking entire nations in this way—and not simply individuals—Stalin was doubtless trying to make examples of them. But mainly he was following a clear-cut program, trying to assign different levels to national responsibilities in Soviet life. There were bad nations; there were also some exemplary ones; but of them all, the most exemplary was the Russian nation. The message was clear.

When he celebrated victory on May 24, 1945, Stalin toasted the *Russian people*—not the Soviet people. He declared that "Russia is the leading nation of the USSR," and that "in this war she had won the right to be recognized as the guide for the whole Union." He defined her dominant traits as "intelligence, perseverance and patience." In contrast to the other peoples that had shown their weaknesses in the war, the Russian people had demonstrated where it belonged—in first place. Thus the officially professed egalitarianism vanished, yielding to a community of nations that would be organized around an "elder brother," the Russian people, in charge of all and a guide for all.[38]

The light of the present now illuminated the past. Russia had succeeded in its Revolution in 1917 because everything in its past had predestined it for this vanguard role. As early as the Kievan era in the ninth century, Russia was as developed as the Carolingian State and exerted a real influence on Western Europe.

In the nineteenth century—and here Stalin corrected Engels—far from being a bastion of reaction, Russia was moving toward revolution. Consequently, for the conquered peoples, Russian domination—once an "absolute evil," then a "relative evil," then the "lesser evil,"—now became an "absolute good."[39]

This position was clearly expressed by the main Communist leader of Azerbaidzhan, Baghirov, who wrote in 1952: "Without underestimating in any way the reactionary nature of czarist colonial policy, it must be borne in mind . . . that Russia's annexation of the peoples was the only answer for them and had a highly favorable effect on their future."

Since conquest was an "absolute good," those who had fought against it no longer possessed any claim to fame. Accordingly, all national heroes who had led movements of resistance to colonialism were damned by history. Despite the love of national elites for their heroes—such as Iman Chamil—such resistance was condemned as a display of feudal obscurantism. The non-Russians were urged to recall from their national histories only those events which had brought them closer to Russia. Thus stripped of their own past, they had only to identify historically with the Russian people, just as Baghirov urged them to do: "The leading force that unites, cements and guides the peoples of our country is our big brother, the great Russian people. . . . Its virtues deserve the trust, respect and love of all the other peoples."

In 1918 the *de facto* inequality of the Soviet federation stemmed from the numerical weight of the Russian people, from its central position, from its head start on most of the peoples around it. After the Second World War, this inequality, justified by ancient and modern history, was set up as a basic principle for relations between the nations. The federation, like the Empire before it, grouped many peoples around one guiding people.

Coupled with the historical legitimization of the leading role henceforth assigned to the Russian nation was an attempt at cultural assimilation in the same period. This move marked a complete break with the earlier cultural compromise.[40] National cultures were suddenly denounced, both because they divided the various points of view instead of bringing them closer together, and because they represented for Stalin symbols of a reactionary past.

All the monuments of national cultures—sagas, ballads, legends— were subjected to merciless attack and were banned. But Stalin did not stop at the literary monuments of the past. He attacked and suppressed any expression—even the most modern—of national culture. Literature everywhere was accused of transmitting antiquated words and concepts. Singing the praises of roses in imitation of the medieval Persian Poet Saadi, even in a Soviet novel, became an intolerable display of nationalism. The minority languages were intended to elucidate the world of socialist realism—the technology of tractors and milking machines. Under no circumstances were those languages to be used to convey traditions peculiar to a given people. What this cultural revision forced the nationalities to do was copy a single cultural model, retaining only words as a national form. If the national languages lacked technical words, they had only to borrow them from Russian. If their grammatical and syntactical forms were ill-suited to such rigidity, they could pattern themselves after Russian.

While minority cultures were thus reduced to a mere shell of words, Russian culture flourished and prepared to replace the doomed cultures. In contrast to minority epics—such as the Azeris' *Dede Korkut* or the Uzbeks' *Alpamysh*, such monuments of Russian culture as the *byliny* (long narrative poems) and *The Song of Igor's Campaign* were elevated to the level of a legacy intended for the whole human race. Non-Russian peoples were urged to adopt this heritage and use it to inspire their future creations.

Lenin had imagined that some day the non-Russian peoples would voluntarily adopt the Russian language for the sake of ease and because they had been left free to develop their own cultures. But in 1952 the community of Soviet nations had to turn to Russian culture, for it no longer had any other choice.

Often indifferent to its minorities, the czarist Empire had never tried to carry out such a systematic Russification of its subjects. Nor did it ever have a clear imperial doctrine applicable for the entire area that it covered. The Soviet federation in 1952 was a real empire, one in which the preeminence of the Russian people was justified—as in the colonial empires of the past—by a superior civilization and the progress toward which it led its subjects. The "prison of the peoples" no longer existed. But the federation was a perfectly unegalitarian community, where the "elder brother" dominated and sought to assimilate others. Stalin responded to the outburst of nationalism in the war years by imposing a brutal solution on the nations: rapid Russification.

After Stalin: a Return to Utopia

Stalin's legacy is without ambiguity. He always believed in the permanence of nations. To reduce national antagonisms within his country, he could imagine no other solution than the domination of one nation over the others. This was also his view at the international level. That is why after the war, whenever he could foment revolutions outside the USSR, he transferred his solutions to the new socialist states of Eastern Europe—notably, Soviet control and the systematic elimination of local national leadership. The East European bloc is an almost exact copy of the Soviet monolith.

But Stalin's death marked a radical break for the nations. His successors were unable to follow the course he had charted. They sensed their country's weariness, the need to find new answers; they perceived outside the USSR a changed world, one to which they would have to adapt. By 1953 the trail had been blazed for a total revision which was actually begun in 1955, and became definitive at the Twentieth Congress.

To an extent, the struggle for Stalin's succession gave the needed impetus for this change. Among Stalin's possible successors, Beria was the most formidable. To stand up to Stalin in the last few months of the dictator's life and to fight his rivals after March 1953, Beria tried to manipulate the Communist organization of Mingrelia in Georgia—in other words, his own compatriots. Stalin had understood the move and had dismantled this organization in 1952, a policy which his successors sought to carry on collectively. But the lesson had not been lost. Everyone remembered the war and sensed that the calm reigning in the non-Russian borderlands was only an illusion.

Foreign policy would also help tip the balance in favor of a revision of the relations between the Soviet nations. Here, too, succession and political choices were closely intertwined. In 1955 Khrushchev went to Belgrade to put an end to the conflict which, since 1948, had separated two great socialist states, the USSR and Yugoslavia. He thought that making this obvious peace gesture of going to his adversary's country would be enough to settle all problems. But what was to have been a pardon generously granted by Moscow turned into humiliation.

So that his trip might bear fruit, Khrushchev acknowledged that the USSR had abused its power and had confused socialist solidarity with a striving for domination. He had to admit that each socialist nation was free to choose its own path. Thus, National Communism—so long opposed in the Soviet Union—had received startling approval. No doubt, Yugoslavia had always been independent of the USSR, and the principles henceforth governing its relations with Moscow were not transferable to the Soviet domestic situation. But the meaning of this change was perceived in the USSR.

The message was clear. It meant the rehabilitation of nations and of equal relations between nations—even at the stage of socialism. It was also Moscow's tacit renunciation of the thesis of its own infallibility and primacy. But while the full consequences of Khrushchev's trip to Belgrade were not immediately apparent, they were present—latent forces in a fantastic upset of the socialist world.

Internal change would also come for reasons outside the socialist world. In 1955 Stalin's foreign policy—one of withdrawal and distrust—had led the Soviet Union into a true state of siege. At its borders or at the frontiers of the socialist domain, the United States, which was becoming increasingly powerful, had set up a network of alliances aimed at containing the USSR.

By 1952 Stalin had sensed the changes wrought in the world, the stabilization of capitalism and the need for his country to adapt by moving into a policy of peaceful competition. While Stalin had been unable to make this perception a concrete reality, Khrushchev intended to do just that. He sensed that the prime targets for Soviet intrusion could be neighboring areas, namely India and the Middle East. He also perceived that such intrusion might find allies in the nationalist movements springing up everywhere. On this point, Khrushchev's thinking coincided with that of Lenin in 1916. The latter had considered nationalist forces in the nonindustrial world to be historical forces at work. But, like Lenin, Khrushchev knew that a policy banking on national forces abroad cannot accommodate itself to crushing nations at home without facing domestic crises of unforeseeable dimensions.

These ideas were developed and presented at the Twentieth Congress. The USSR, which officially professed its support of Third World national movements, declared itself a model of national emancipation at home. Khrushchev denounced all the crimes Stalin had committed against the non-Russian nations: the liquidation of minority leadership; excessive centralization; the striving for Russification; the rehabilitation of colonialism; and the setting up of new, unequal relations.

In place of Stalin's imperialistic policy, Khrushchev urged the nations to resume their cultural rights and enjoy once more their own traditions. The provisions making it possible to gauge the extent of the change then increased by leaps and bounds. The classification of the nations at the end of World War II, according to their respective degrees of adherence to the Soviet Union, was largely abolished by the official rehabilitation (in the decree of the Supreme Soviet of January 9, 1957) of five nations deported for treason after the war, and by the restitution of their territories.

While the Chechens, Ingush, Karachays, Balkars and Kalmyks thus gained the right to return to their homes, two other nations which had shared the same fate, the Volga Germans and the Tatars, were excluded from this rehabilitation. The causes and consequences of this selective admission of injustice will be discussed in a later chapter.

The nations of the USSR also regained possession of their pasts. The Communist Party of the Soviet Union was doubtless very cautious when it came to specifying Stalin's crimes. In a general way, while the Party admitted the destruction of national elites, it tried not to stir up the memory of particular national leaders, probably in order to forestall any serious discussion of centralizing options vs. national options. It also sought to avoid giving the nations models for national Communist heroes. This explains the fact that so few individuals were rehabilitated and that the privilege was reserved for those who had not defended subversive ideas.

It was chiefly the distant, colonial past that regained its right to a place in history. Once more, Soviet historians were asked to rewrite history, but now rather more subtly shaded than in the 1920s, thereby breaking with Stalinist history. This of course meant breaking with the justification for Russian domination which became an evil once more. It also meant assigning a place in history to those who had defended national independence, and the symbol of this revision would be the Imam Chamil, who became the focal point for all the great debates of the 1950s.[41] This choice sheds light on the meaning of the revision and its limitations. The Imam Chamil epitomized the struggle of Islam against the infidel. Here, nationality and religion were closely intertwined. This explains why a debate on the Chamil movement was opened after the Twentieth Congress, pitting local national historians against the Soviet academic community. It also explains why this debate, which the minority elites followed closely, took place in an intellectual climate that alternated between open-mindedness and withdrawal.

While the intelligentsia in the Caucasus hoped for a recognition of the absolute legitimacy of the Imam Chamil's resistance to Russia, the Party's theoretical organs attempted to solve the problem by a partial rehabilitation. It was said that national resistance was undoubtedly legitimate in its time, but that this legitimacy should not conceal the fact that the Imam Chamil was head of a politically reactionary movement whose victory would have cut the Caucasus off from historical progress.

This quarrel gave rise to an ambiguous theory.[42] The colonial evil at least had been mitigated, if not actually offset, by post-revolutionary history. While restoring history and honor to the nations, the USSR's new leaders refused to let the past serve to fire a new nationalism. Nearly forty years of communal life under the banner of socialism had to be recognized in bringing into being a new human community, a Soviet people.

In this respect, Khrushchev—like Lenin—showed some optimism. He believed in the pedagogical value of concessions which, in his time, came under the heading of a break with Stalinist policy. But he refused to give up what he regarded as part of a long history in common—one not limited to what had happened since 1917. He believed that there was consciousness of a common destiny in the Soviet nations, and for that reason he would not accept a pure and simple condemnation of unification with Russia. For Khrushchev historical continuity was a factor in improving ways of thinking.

After the rehabilitation of peoples, history, and culture, there came a revision of the practice of federalism. To give new life to the Soviet system, to make it rational, Khrushchev strove to decentralize the Soviet economy, thereby linking all territorial and national communities in a new organization. The reform of the *Sovnarkhozes* (regional economic councils) stemmed from this desire to decentralize powers.[43]

On May 30, 1956 the process began with a joint decision of the Party's Central Committee and the USSR's Council of Ministers. By this decision a number of enterprises which until then had been subordinated to federal ministries were transferred to the federal republics. In February 1957 the republics' powers with regard to judicial organization and legislation were considerably bolstered. Finally, the USSR Council of Ministers, On August 29, 1957 and June 22, 1959, issued decrees enhancing the powers of the councils of ministers of the federal republics.[44]

Here, too, Khrushchev was following in Lenin's footsteps. To make reform meaningful, a real place had to be given to the national cadres—hence, a return to the policy of "indigenization" practiced in the 1920s. At every level, in every sphere, the late 1950s were marked by an increased number of indigenous cadres and by a decline in the representatives of the central government. Furthermore, representatives of the national elites were sometimes involved in Soviet foreign policy. Until 1956 this involvement was limited to representation of two national republics, the Ukraine and Belorussia, in the international organizations. But the presence of these two republics alongside the Soviet Union in international affairs did not grant them special privileges at home. Yet, after the end of World War II, the 1936 constitution was amended by two articles, 18a and 18b, in order to justify the seats at the United Nations demanded by the Ukraine and Belorussia. These articles gave the republics the right to have their own armed forces and diplomatic representation.[45]

In 1956, when the Soviet Union embarked on an active policy in the Third World and especially in the Middle East, it called on its national elites to a limited extent. By 1955 Khrushchev and Bulganin were being accompanied on trips to India by representatives of the Tadzhik and Uzbek peoples. The following year a Soviet delegation in Damascus included the spiritual leader of the Central Asian Moslems, who spoke to his hosts in Arabic on behalf of their Moslem brothers in the USSR. A few diplomats—mainly natives of the Moslem borderlands—were posted in Soviet embassies in the Middle East, and their coreligionists took part in Moscow's technical assistance programs in neighboring countries.

In countries where he backed national governments, Khrushchev aimed to picture the USSR as a multi-ethnic society where the nations lived together in equality.

At the time, the concessions and decentralization of powers created such a climate of euphoria that the Soviet Union opened its frontiers just wide enough for guests from young nations who came to Central Asia or the Caucasus to see a model of modernization combining a respect for culture and traditions with access to technology and material progress.

A few signs nevertheless suggest that de-Stalinization was encouraging local nationalist demands rather than leading to internationalist progress. On August 21, 1956, for instance, the Supreme Soviet of Azerbaidzhan proclaimed that, henceforth, Azeri would be the only official language of the republic. The coexistence of local national cultures with Russian culture seemed in jeopardy once more.

In the economic sphere as well, limited conflicts revealed that the local national authorities wanted more than the concessions they had been granted. At the Twenty-first Congress in 1959, Khrushchev pointed to these demonstrations of what he termed "local chauvinism" and was disturbed by them.[46] De-Stalinization was to have promoted a common consciousness. This resurgence of local nationalistic feeling, encouraged by Soviet concessions and a foreign policy that supported nationalist movements, prompted Khrushchev to disrupt the evolution of Soviet society and return to the idea of the internationalist utopia.

Administrative-Territorial Distribution of the Nations and Nationalities of the USSR

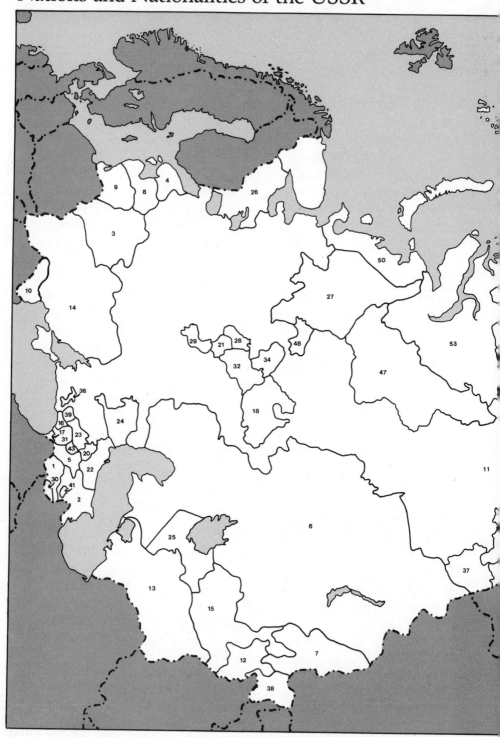

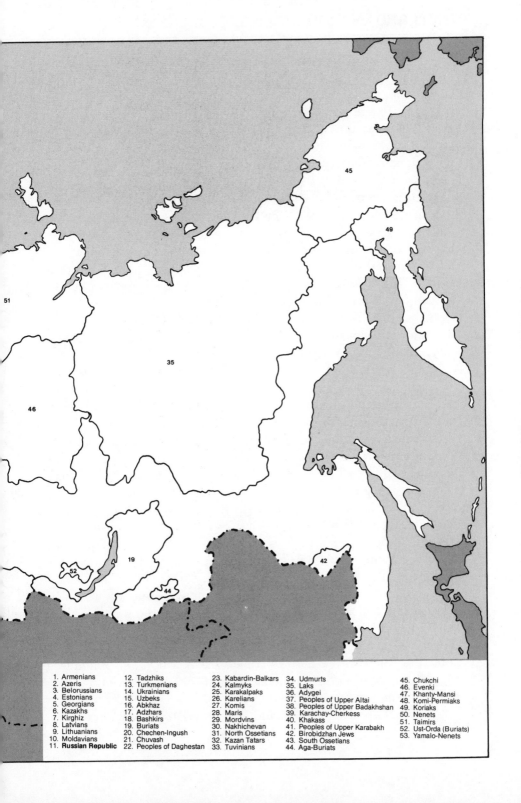

1. Armenians	12. Tadzhiks	23. Kabardin-Balkars	34. Udmurts	45. Chukchi
2. Azeris	13. Turkmenians	24. Kalmyks	35. Laks	46. Evenki
3. Belorussians	14. Ukrainians	25. Karakalpaks	36. Adygei	47. Khanty-Mansi
4. Estonians	15. Uzbeks	26. Karelians	37. Peoples of Upper Altai	48. Komi-Permiaks
5. Georgians	16. Abkhaz	27. Komis	38. Peoples of Upper Badakhshan	49. Koriaks
6. Kazakhs	17. Adzhars	28. Maris	39. Karachay-Cherkess	50. Nenets
7. Kirghiz	18. Bashkirs	29. Mordvins	40. Khakass	51. Taimirs
8. Latvians	19. Buriats	30. Nakhichevan	41. Peoples of Upper Karabakh	52. Ust-Orda (Buriats)
9. Lithuanians	20. Chechen-Ingush	31. North Ossetians	42. Birobidzhan Jews	53. Yamalo-Nenets
10. Moldavians	21. Chuvash	32. Kazan Tatars	43. South Ossetians	
11. **Russian Republic**	22. Peoples of Daghestan	33. Tuvinians	44. Aga-Buriats	

The Twenty-second Congress, held in 1961, gave him the opportunity he needed. He announced a new Soviet society for all the nations, namely Communism.[47] Could Communism still adapt to a society divided into local national groups faithful to traditions that belonged to the past? Khrushchev's response to this question was clear. Soviet society, which was striding toward what Marx had described as the kingdom where need would no longer exist, had nothing in common with the multi-ethnic society of 1917. The Soviets had profoundly changed and the changes served to unify rather than differentiate them.

New developments had been brought about by cultural and economic progress. The people of Soviet society in the 1960s was highly educated, having mastered two languages: their own national one, learned in childhood, and Russian. This language, henceforth common to all and spoken so fluently that it resembled a second mother tongue, was a powerful cement for unity.

The second factor in the qualitatively changed status of the non-Russian nations was economic progress. It had unified Soviet territory, creating migratory currents by making jobs accessible to everyone. As a result of educational progress and the mastery of the common language, everyone could fill these jobs. Seen in this new light, the national territorial divisions had only nostalgic value; population mobility and fusion represented the trend of the future.[48]

Khrushchev outlined the history of the Soviet nations and the work accomplished by the regime in three points: (1) The egalitarian course charted by Lenin had led to the "flowering" of national consciousness and national cultures; (2) economic and cultural progress, as well as the trust generated by Lenin's policy, had produced the "rapprochement" of the nations; and (3) this stage of the march toward Communism would also lead toward the "fusion" of those nations, creating a new type of community in which the memories of past inequality or injustice would disappear.[49]

Just what the legal framework for this new community would be Khrushchev did not explain; but his plan as a whole suggested that the framework itself would be new. From 1961 on he was asserting that the nature of the Soviet State had changed and that it had become the "State of the Entire People." Furthermore, he announced that a new constitution was being drafted, one which would reflect the profound changes of society.

Clearly, this constitution would also reflect the USSR's transition from a multi-ethnic society attached to its national characteristics to a society undergoing ethnic fusion. Cultural differences would fade behind the unity of political culture, a common language, and increasingly loose ties between the individual and his native soil.

In 1961 all of Khrushchev's pronouncements suggested that Lenin's belief in the primacy of social solidarity over national loyalties was being realized. Everything pointed to the national policy proposed by Lenin in 1922, namely that the development of the nations and egalitarianism had created the conditions necessary to transcend prejudice and strong nationalist feelings. At least, that was Khrushchev's conviction, and one that would be shared by his successors.

Between 1917 and 1964 the national policy of the USSR did not follow a uniform course. Circumstances and leaders dictated so many shifts and ruptures that it is hard to fathom Soviet aims. Yet, by examining this complex period, which historians generally forget is a decisive part of overall Soviet history, several constants can be found. First of all, every policy after 1917 was marked by an underestimation of the national problem and an inadequate knowledge of the facts involved. Lenin, so close to the events and so aware of the weapon that the freedom-hungry nations offered him, was nevertheless optimistic enough to think that he could master "the chaotic forces" he had unleashed against the czarist regime. Indeed, he had seriously underestimated the autonomous strength of the national movements, not to speak of the strength of Russian nationalism, which would not allow Russia to be reduced to the rank of a state like the ones she had dominated until then.

This underestimation can be ascribed mainly to Lenin's lack of real concern for the nations. He was only interested in the nation as a tool to be added to his arsenal of revolutionary means, and not at all for its own sake. He knew nothing of the realities in the Russian borderlands, of the actual conditions of coexistence between different communities. In many cases, this ignorance explains the errors of judgment and tactics committed by the Bolsheviks.

Stalin, unlike Lenin and the others, was keenly aware of the overwhelming difficulty of the national problem, but he had only a limited understanding of it. Looking at it in terms of force, Stalin thought that the power of the central government would prevail; and, if the problem were not actually solved, at least it would cease to hang as a threat over Soviet political life. Here, too, the facts refuted this approach. When war broke out, the national borderlands would prove to be the weakest link in the Soviet system.

Trying to return to a more egalitarian concept of national problems, Khrushchev—like Lenin—would find that, while national feelings were invariably stirred up by injustice and violence, they were also fostered by concessions. Thus, after trying to respond to national tensions by returning to the egalitarianism of the 1920s, Khrushchev turned to a utopian solution—to transform the whole Communist society in a very short time—without taking into account the realities of life.

Thus we see what has been common to the Soviet leaders since 1917. Primarily, they have all seen the national problem as a legacy from the past or the result of political errors. They all turned to solutions they believed would enable them to eliminate this problem for good. Then they realized its real dimensions and the lasting threat that it posed for the whole Soviet system.

Another trait shared by all the Soviet leaders has been the belief that the only solution to the national problem lies in eliminating national differences. Only the methods have changed. Lenin relied on education to reach this goal; Stalin on violence; Khrushchev on breaking with Stalinist methods and seeking political and economic rationality. But the passage of time had brought about one important difference: Lenin and Stalin realized that they had done nothing to ease inter-ethnic relations, that the difficulties persisted, threatening the whole system. On the other hand, Khrushchev—ousted from power—was to leave his successors facing a situation apparently simpler than the one Lenin and Stalin had confronted. The fruits of the Revolution seemed to have ripened at last. Nearly a half century had elapsed since 1917, almost two generations that had known nothing but the Soviet system, its ideology and institutions. This explains why Khrushchev said that nothing remained of the past. The federation had finally taken on its full meaning and had accomplished the historic task assigned to it, i.e., of erasing every trace of the unegalitarian relations inherent in the "prison of the peoples," which the Bolsheviks had opened. It was up to Khrushchev's successors to do their utmost so that the new community of people, the socialist community, might develop in place of dispersed and divided ethnic groups. The era of a *Soviet people* had begun.[50]

CHAPTER II

A Soviet People? Or Soviet Peoples?
The Demographic Revolution

T he Soviet people constitutes a significant human community, numbering 261.2 million in 1978.[1] Until the last few years the Soviet government considered the demographic evolution of this community in the light of two assumptions. First of all, that it was a united community whose trends, behavior, and demographic options constituted one inseparable whole, one in which—as in any society—regional variations did exist, but where economic and intellectual development assured the drawing together of demographic trends—not constant differentiation. Secondly, that socialist societies are the only ones able "to assure regular population growth, because planned economic development makes it possible to raise the economic potential to the optimum level necessary for that regular growth." Coupled with these two beliefs is a conviction that Soviet leaders have held for decades, namely, that the USSR has been making constant demographic progress and therefore has been shielded from population problems affecting the industrial societies since the First World War.

Notwithstanding this, the history of the Soviet population has been eventful and tragic. There have been natural phenomena, such as the high rate of infant mortality, epidemics, famines; there have been political disturbances, war, collectivization, purges; and there have been territorial changes. Among the latter were the various territorial reductions after the treaty of Brest-Litovsk, and the extensions during the Second World War. If to all this is added a cataclysmic process of change in the 1930s that was characterized by very rapid industrialization and urbanization, and the dwindling of rural life, the magnitude of the blows suffered by the Soviet population and the difficulty of precisely tracing demographic trends can be imagined.

Basile Kerblay, noted authority on the USSR, emphasizes that, on a long-term basis, Soviet demographic history resembles that of the large human communities which began to register accelerated growth in the eighteenth century and especially at the end of the nineteenth century. In Russia he found fairly rapid growth, 0.8% per year for the eighteenth century and most of the nineteenth century, then a population boom of 1.7% yearly between 1897 and 1913, followed by a certain slowdown after the Revolution.[2]

Everything suggests that even today the USSR is following more or less the same patterns as Western societies, i.e., a declining birth rate offset by a rapid reduction of infant mortality and an increased life expectancy. The 1970 census, tremendously important because it establishes the demographic facts for the first extended period of total peace that the USSR has ever known, shook all the Soviet leaders' convictions and the general trends previously attributed to the Soviet Union. This census shows that the USSR does have population problems, that the socialist system is not so well equipped as it imagined to assure regular, planned population growth. Most of all, the 1970 census reveals that the Soviet community is not a single homogenous nation, but that national cleavages are perpetuated in demographic cleavages, creating imbalances which may cause significant problems in the near future. The national question which Khrushchev claimed had been resolved has now become a demographic question.

The Population of the USSR
from One Census to Another

It is not easy to follow Soviet demographic trends owing to territorial variations and the heterogeneous nature of existing information. What are the yardsticks at our disposal?

Three complete censuses—1897, 1959 and 1970—are extraordinarily rich in information. For the intervening years there are incomplete censuses that were interrupted by war (1913) and by the Soviet leaders' bewilderment at the discrepancy between their forecasts and actuality (1937), and partial censuses for the cities in the early

1920s, for birth and death rates in 1950, etc. In addition, census data have on occasion been corrected *a posteriori* (1926, 1939).[3] Finally, the questions asked have varied from one census to another.

It is therefore impossible to put implicit trust in the figures, and they should rather be taken for what they are—indications of trends. As such, the figures are quite revealing. They reflect exceptionally difficult times and accentuate the extent of changes that occurred in the last period, 1959–1970, because this is the first break in an im-

Table 1
Population of Russia, later the USSR [4]

Year	Source of data	Population
1897	Census	125,000,000
1926	Incomplete census	167,676,000
1939	Incomplete census	193,077,000
1950	Partial data	181,700,000
1959	Census	208,827,000
1970	Census	241,720,000

Table 2
Population Growth Rates

Period	Characteristics of the period	% of growth for the period	Annual growth rates
1897-1926 = 30 years	Russo-Japanese War World War I Revolution Civil War	34.1	0.98
1926-1939 = 12 years	Collectivization Industrialization Urbanization Purges	15.1	1.19
1939-1950 = 12 years	World War II and reconstruction	-5.9	-0.49
1950-1959 = 8 years	Continuation of reconstruction	14.9	1.76
1959-1970 = 11 years	Period of complete peace	15.8	1.34

mense collective tragedy. For greater clarity, the attempt has been made in Tables 1 and 2 to use the same territorial base and to view population changes over significant periods, marked off by decisive events.

These two tables describing the general trend of the Soviet population call for several observations. First of all, the period subsequent to 1917 can be interpreted both in terms of demographic deceleration and dynamism. (Compared to the trend in the United States, whose population jumped from 76 million at the start of this century to over 200 million at the start of the 1970s, the population growth of the Soviet Union seems negligible.) During this whole period the Soviet population made significant gains compared to that of Western Europe.

But a true picture of Soviet demography can be obtained only by taking population losses into account. Can those losses be estimated with any accuracy?[5] The most contradictory and, often, wildly fanciful figures have been advanced. It is difficult to reach serious conclusions when statistical differences often run into the millions. On the other hand, it is possible to make an approximate estimate by breaking down the causes for this loss of lives, i.e., wars, famines and epidemics, purges, the decline in the birth rate resulting from these drains on the population, birth control legislation, etc.

In the first place, wars have caused increasingly heavy losses of life. While the Russo-Japanese War cost the Empire only 46,000 dead, the death toll in the First World War was about 3 million (1 million soldiers and 2 million civilians), and the Second World War cost the Soviet Union 20 million dead, 7 million of them soldiers. In addition to these formidable losses are the various slaughters in the years 1918–1936. The civil war alone accounted for 7 million civilian deaths. In 1921 famine resulted in the loss of 5 million lives. If to this stark toll are added the 2 million emigrés who fled the Revolution, with a resultant loss of 8.5 million potential births, the population losses as of 1921 for the past seven years of war stood at 26 million.[6]

While the relatively peaceful years of the New Economic Policy in the 1920s gave the USSR a breathing spell, the early 1930s ushered in a new phase of torment. Khrushchev estimated that 10 million Soviet lives were lost during the latter period, but the actual figures without doubt surpass that estimate. The 1937 census revealed that there was a gap of 16.7 million lives between the USSR's real population on January 1, 1937 and the population forecast by the Second Five-Year plan.[7]

The statistical disappearance of 16 million people is relatively easy to explain. Forced collectivization led to the deportation and, often, the death of an as yet undocumented number of peasants. Basile Kerblay rightly emphasizes that, even now, historians know more about the losses of Soviet livestock than about the number of people who were liquidated as kulaks or, later, as opponents of the regime.[8]

But partial figures give us an insight into the overall picture. The 1933–34 famine alone killed more than 3 million infants. The so-called "sedentarization" which accompanied the collectivization of the nomadic peoples cost the Kazakhs alone 1 million people—or a quarter of their total population. To this list of dead must be added the countless deportees who died of malnutrition in the camps or work sites where their labor, virtually free of charge, brought about the success of Stalin's five-year plans. In addition, there are the peasants who were sacrificed to this enormous effort at transformation and, in particular, the most vulnerable—the children and the elderly. Lastly, there are those who were liquidated with varying degrees of legality in the course of blind repression.

To the death toll should be added the reduction of demographic growth, the low birth rate resulting from First World War casualties and the legalization of abortion. The losses in the Second World War were offset by territorial annexations which brought the Soviet Union an additional 20 million inhabitants in 1945.

Notwithstanding these acquisitions and a policy that promoted a higher birth rate, the Soviet population did not return to its prewar level until 1955. Thus, between 1914 and 1946 the demographic deficit of the USSR would have been approximately 60 million, or one-third of the postwar Soviet population, had not the country's borders been extended with the incorporation of the Baltic States, Bessarabia, Karelia, Bukovina, and Polish territories. Even if this figure is lowered to 40 million by taking into account the territorial annexations, and even if this deficit is minimized by considering that it reflects not only human lives that were snuffed out but also the lack of any growth in the birth rate, the figure expresses the frightful tragedy that befell Soviet society as a whole.[9] But the increase in population from 1946 to 1949, especially considering the progress accomplished during the difficult years of reconstruction, offers ample evidence of the vitality of this society.

Current Soviet Demographic Trends

The population gains referred to above took place essentially before 1959, when the relatively high birth rate made it possible to offset the terrible losses in the past. This is particularly apparent for the period that followed the Second World War, but also holds true for the years from 1926 to 1939.

On the other hand, the most recent period has been marked by an obvious decline in the Soviet birth rate. The figures must not conceal this decline. The population increase between 1959 and 1970 is roughly comparable to that achieved between 1926 and 1939. But considering that in this period the Soviet Union enjoyed absolute peace for the first time, that this period marked the first improvement in living conditions, and that progress in medicine and education had begun to bear fruit, we can only conclude that the Soviet population has entered a phase of regression which has been accelerating constantly since 1959. In this respect, the comparison of birth rate gains registered each year is particularly revealing, as shown in Table 3.

Table 3
Birth Rate Trend

Years	Soviet population (millions)	Annual increase (percentage)
1959	208.8	—
1960	212.3	1,68
1961	216.2	1.83
1962	220.0	1.70
1963	223.4	1.56
1964	226.6	1.43
1965	229.6	1.30
1966	232.2	1.13
1967	234.8	1.10
1968	237.1	0.95
1969	239.4	0.97
1970	241.7	0.94

In 1976 the population of the USSR rose to 255.5 million,[10] representing an increase of 13.8 million in six years, or an annual growth rate of slightly under 0.93 percent. The chief consequence of this Soviet demographic trend is to change the age pyramid. The aging of the population shows up quite clearly in the statistics. This holds true whether the present situation is compared to the one prevailing under the czars or, for that matter, to the darkest years of Stalinism, as shown in Table 4.

Table 4
Age group Percentage Compared to Total Soviet Population

Age group	1897	1939	1959	1970
0-19 years	48.4	49.3	37.4	38.0
20-59 years	44.8	44.0	53.2	50.0
60 years and over	6.8	6.7	9.4	11.8

To understand this increase in aging the comparative trend of births and deaths for the period as a whole must be considered. Here too, the juxtaposition of figures reveals serious imbalances. To begin with, one tends to attribute simple trends to any country undergoing modernization, i.e., a drop in the birth rate offset by a constant decline in the death rate and, primarily, infant mortality. In the case of the USSR it is clear that the terrible years of collectivization, famines, and wars drastically reduced the most vulnerable segment of the population, i.e., the elderly and children in periods when the country was beset by material difficulties, and young men during wartime. Table 5 (see p. 54) bears out these tendencies but also shows some special trends.

First of all, the table reveals that the economic turning point of industrialization and urbanization in 1929, as elsewhere, was followed by a steady decline in the birth rate. This index kept on dropping until 1969, but seems to have stabilized since then. During the years between 1930 and 1960 the Soviet population growth rate does not seem affected by the declining birth rate. This is due to a significant drop in the death rate, primarily that of infants. Right after the war, we see that the Soviet government's efforts aimed at protecting infants were fruitful. This increase was to continue steadily until the early 1970s, when infant mortality leveled off to a very low rate.

On the other hand, the death rate of the population as a whole reached its lowest point at the end of the 1950s, whereupon it began to rise once more.[13] This upswing, which the statistics fail to indicate

Table 5
**Birth, Death, Natural Growth Rates
of the Soviet Population**

Year	Per 1,000 inhabitants			Infants dying before age 1, per 1000 births
	Births	Deaths	Natural Increase	
1913 a) within pre-1939 borders	47.0	30.2	16.8	273
b) within present-day borders of USSR	45.5	29.1	16.4	269
1926	44.0	20.3	23.7	174
1928	44.3	23.3	21.0	182
1937	38.7	18.9	19.8	170
1938	37.5	17.5	20.0	161
1939	36.5	17.3	19.2	167
1940	31.2	18.0	13.2	182
1950	26.7	9.7	17.0	81
1955	25.7	8.2	17.5	60
1956	25.2	7.6	17.6	47
1957	25.4	7.8	17.6	45
1958	25.3	7.2	18.1	41
1959	25.0	7.6	17.4	41
1960	24.9	7.1	17.8	35
1961	23.8	7.2	16.6	32
1962	22.4	7.5	14.9	32
1963	21.1	7.2	13.9	31
1964	19.5	6.9	12.6	29
1965	18.4	7.3	11.1	27
1966	18.2	7.3	10.9	26
1967	17.3	7.6	9.7	26
1968	17.2	7.7	9.5	26
1969	17.0	8.1	8.9	26
1970	17.4	8.2	9.2	25
1971	17.8	8.2	9.6	23
1972	17.8	8.5	9.3	24
1973	17.6	8.6	9.0	26

until the end of the decade, actually began a few years earlier. The decline in infant mortality, which is still continuing, must be borne in mind when discussing this period. The reason is apparent. As the population of the USSR ages, people die in greater numbers despite advances in medicine and a generally longer life expectancy.

This unfavorable trend in Soviet demography was one of the surprises that emerged from the 1970 census. Soviet demographers, basing their figures on the 1959 census, had forecast a different curve.[14] They expected a population of more than 250 million, but the census figure fell short of this by nearly 10 million. Can this trend be corrected? Considering the progress in the area of public health and the aging of the population, demographic gains can only result from an improved birth rate, not from decline in the death rate. This improvement in the birth rate will have to be lasting, indeed, to offset a rising death rate, one that promises to continue for a good many years to come.

To what extent does the age-sex ratio of Soviet society make it possible to expect real progress in demographic trends? Two factors must be taken into consideration when answering this question: (1) the number of women of child-bearing age (16–49 years, average period of fertility, as shown in Table 6), and particularly of women under forty; (2) the number of married women in the population (Table 7; see p. 56.)

Table 6
Women of Child-bearing Age [15]
Percentage of the Soviet Population

	Number of Women (million)			Percentage of the Soviet population		
	1939	1959	1970	1939	1959	1970
Total number of women 16-49 years	48.4	58.5	60.8	25.4	28.0	25.2
of which: age 16-29	24.3	26.9	23.9	12.7	12.9	9.9
age 30-49	24.1	31.6	36.9	12.7	15.1	15.3

Table 7 clearly shows a factor that would promote a higher birth rate: the increased number of married women of child-bearing age. This trend reflects the fact that the male-female ratio is slowly coming back into balance. The Second World War had decimated the Soviet Union's male population, particularly the young men, and thus reduced the chances for a spectacular demographic recovery. Notwithstanding this drain of the male population, there was a relatively high growth rate for postwar births. The women who were between 35 and 50 years of age in 1959 are precisely the ones who far outnumbered the men surviving the war. At that time, those women were between 20 and 35. Compared to women in the same age brackets in the 1970s, they were in a much more unfavorable

Table 7
Number of Married Women (per 1000 women)[16]

Age bracket	1939	1959	1970
From age 16 and over	605	522	580
16-19	140	112	105
20-24	614	501	559
25-29	787	759	827
30-34	818	776	853
35-39	800	725	839
40-44	759	623	790
45-49	688	549	719
50-54	593	483	603
55-59	497	433	501
60-69	363	361	371
Age 70 and over	168	169	196

position; nevertheless, their fertility was much greater than that of married women today. The same table indicates another tendency that keeps the birth rate down: Soviet people are marrying later, thus reducing the period of fertility.

But it is chiefly Table 6 that explains the demographic problems of the USSR. The proportion of women of child-bearing age has remained constant since 1939 at 25% of the population. Here, too, the general aging makes itself felt. The number of women between 16 and 30, the most favorable ages for maternity, is declining compared to the overall Soviet population, and compared to the whole female population as well. In 1926, 56.7% of Soviet women were between 16 and 29; in 1939, their share dropped to 50.2%; in 1959, to 46%; in 1970, to 39.3%.

Fewer young wives, later marriages, a reduced number of children per family are the three factors that explain why Soviet population has not grown in keeping with initial forecasts. To what extent can the Soviet government offset these unfavorable tendencies with policies aimed at promoting a higher birth rate?

By 1936, Stalin had felt the need to encourage women to have more children, thus repudiating the total freedom of choice women had won in this respect after the Revolution. Since then, Soviet political culture, while constantly extolling women's role in society, has been glorifying the image of the mother, the woman whose vocation is childbearing. In concrete terms this upgrading of maternity has been translated into legislation that seems extremely meager compared with the social benefits in the West, particularly in France since the Second World War.

Of course, decorations are awarded to mothers of large families, in the form of "medals of maternity" or titles, such as "heroine-mother" or "glory of motherhood." Prenatal allowances, rather insubstantial family benefits, and longer-term assistance to mothers of large families are supposed to encourage the birth rate. But neither high-sounding titles nor absurdly low allowances are able to compensate for the difficulties of existence.

In the cities the shortage of apartments and day-care centers, coupled with the growing aspiration of Soviet citizens for a better life, tends to keep family size down. In rural areas, where women are apt to have more children, the living conditions of women scarcely promote large families.

To understand the problem, one need only read the account given by the Soviet writer, Ivan Belov, in *An Ordinary Occurrence.*[17] This book was published legally in the USSR and can be presumed free of any anti-Soviet bias. The heroine, living on a *kolkhoz* (collective farm), has a large family. This poor woman rises before dawn, goes to bed late at night, works until the day she gives birth, then goes back to work on leaving the hospital. She dies at work on the day after the birth of her last child.

The numerous children of this "heroine-mother" then shuttle back and forth between a grandmother and the drunken father, barely escaping starvation. We glimpse the absolute misery of the female condition and the acute problem of paternal alcoholism in this officially published account of everyday life in a *kolkhoz.* The picture has its counterpart in the image of the harassed city-dweller, the woman constantly on the run from her job to crowded food shops with their interminable waiting-lines and to a home where children—often unattended—await her return. Understandably, this kind of motherhood has little appeal for the Soviet woman.

This may explain why Soviet demographers have become more cautious in their predictions, and have lowered their estimate for the Soviet population for the year 2000 from 350 million citizens—often forecast by the press before 1970—to a modest 300–310 million.[18] The pessimism pervading these forecasts is obvious. Far from contemplating an upswing in the Soviet birth rate curve or even a stabilization, the demographers expect the current downward trend to accelerate.

At the same time Soviet leaders maintain that they need a policy more conducive to demographic growth. There is a clear-cut divergence between a political approach to the demographic problem and a more scientific one. To understand the causes behind this divergence, the Soviet population should no longer be regarded as a homogeneous unit, but as a disparate entity with significant differences in behavior, depending on the region. In other words, these differences depend on the nations involved and, in all likelihood, on their cultures.

Two Demographic Worlds:
the Soviet Europeans and the "Others"

The most important revelation from the 1970 census concerns the demographic differences between various regions as they relate to birth rates and growth rates, but not to death rates, which show an increasing tendency toward uniformity from one region to another. Considering the results of the 1970 census and comparing them with the results of preceding censuses, we find: (1) an increasing differentiation between various national regions; (2) a reversal of the traditional demographic trends that prevailed in the czarist Empire and in Soviet territory up to the late 1950s; and (3) a complete alteration in the human balances of the country.

These changes stem from two apparently contradictory demographic processes. On the one hand, certain Soviet nations that formerly had fairly divergent demographic behavior now tend to draw closer together. On the other hand, one group stands out in the Soviet population for its totally different behavior, producing completely opposite trends in the two groups. The general results of the census make this contrast clear, as shown in Table 8.

One thing becomes obvious on reading this table. The line of cleavage in Soviet demography now becomes clear-cut. Except for Moldavia, all the western republics, comprising the Slavic group (Russia, the Ukraine, Belorussia) and the Baltic group (Latvia, Lithuania, Estonia), during the last period have experienced a lower growth rate than the average for the USSR as a whole. The western part of the Soviet Union appears as a demographically declining, albeit strongly homogeneous, area. This fact becomes apparent when we consider that in all these republics the growth index for 1959–1970 falls between 111 and 113 (100 in 1959). In contrast, the eastern USSR—

Table 8

Population Trends in the Republics [19]
(present borders of the USSR)
(in thousands)

Republics	1913	1939 estimates	1959	1970	1970 % compared to 1959
USSR	159,153	190,678	208,827	241,720	116
RSFSR	89,902	108,377	117,534	130,079	111
Ukraine	35,210	40,469	41,869	47,126	113
Belorussia	6,899	8,912	8,056	9,002	112
Uzbekistan	4,334	6,347	8,119	11,800	145
Kazakhstan	5,597	6,082	9,295	13,009	140
Georgia	2,601	3,540	4,044	4,686	116
Azerbaidzhan	2,339	3,205	3,698	5,117	138
Lithuania	2,828	2,880	2,711	3,128	115
Moldavia	2,056	2,452	2,885	3,569	124
Latvia	2,493	1885	2,093	2,364	113
Kirghizia	864	1,458	2,066	2,933	142
Tadzhikistan	1,034	1,485	1,981	2,900	146
Armenia	1,000	1,282	1,763	2,492	141
Turkmenia	1,042	1,252	1,516	2,159	142
Estonia	954	1,052	1,197	1,356	113

Central Asia and the Caucasus—forms a second homogeneous unit characterized by a rapidly growing population.

If we now take up the ethnic groups themselves, and not the republics whose multinational make-up, like that of the whole USSR, distorts our view of the demographic changes, we gain a better idea of the changes that each group has undergone, both on a long-term basis (1897–1970) and during the last period (1959–1970).

Table 9 reveals that from 1897 to 1959 the population of the Russian people alone steadily increased in proportion to all the peoples that it dominated. All the other ethnic groups went through phases of regression either continuously or sporadically. Now, the latest census reveals a departure from this longstanding trend in a way which relates adversely to the Russian people, whose population, proportionate to that of the whole country, has begun to decline, even if they do remain in the majority.

The figures also show that other peoples—Slavs, Europeans, Jews, and Finns—continue to decline or stagnate; whereas the contrary is true of the Moslem peoples, all of whom registered a spectacular upswing in 1959.

Table 9
**Percentage of Ethnic Groups
Compared with Total Population** [20]

Ethnic groups	1897	1926	1959	1970
Russians	44.4	47.5	54.6	53.4
Ukrainians	19.4	21.4	17.8	16.9
Belorussians	4.5	3.6	3.8	3.7
Tatars	1.9	1.7	2.4	2.5
Turko-Moslems	12.1	10.1	10.3	12.9
Jews	3.5	2.4	1.1	0.9
European peoples (Georgians, Armenians, Latvians, Estonians)	3.9	3.6	3.8	3.8
Lithuanians	1.3	1.2	1.1	1.1
Finnish	2.3	2.2	1.5	1.4
Moldavians (Rumanians)	1.0	1.2	1.1	1.2

To what extent can these differences be explained by classic factors? Can they be attributed to the high degree of urbanization in the western USSR? Or is it the more rural nature of the eastern USSR coupled with factors peculiar to the rural, less-developed world, such as a high rate of infant mortality and a higher birth rate? Certainly gains in urbanization loom large here. But while it is true that the western part of the USSR is more urban, it would be a mistake to underestimate the trend of city/country ratios for the Soviet Union as a whole. This trend appears in Table 10.[21]

This table shows clearly that urbanization is greatest in the RSFSR, along with Estonia and Latvia. Russian population growth is also lowest. But even with rising urbanization in Armenia, Kazakhstan and Azerbaidzhan, it appears that these republics have very high birth rates, whereas Lithuania, with a similar urbanization rate, has a birth rate slightly below the national average. Turkmenia, which presently shows a higher rate of urbanization than the other Moslem republics, generally reflects the same growth in terms of population; while Belorussia, which is less urbanized, has a particularly low birth rate. These differences make it necessary to alter the classic idea that urbanization has an immediate impact on demographic behavior. The divergences also make it advisable not to rely solely on raw statistics, but rather to examine in detail the situation of the main national groups to try to grasp the essential elements in their recent demographic history.

The decline of the Russian group is without doubt the most spectacular fact uncovered by the latest census.[22] Spectacular not only because this human group dominates the whole Soviet Union with its numerical and political weight, but also because this decline, although still slight, contrasts with a constant demographic trend. The fact is that numerically the Russians have been growing more steadily and more regularly than all the other ethnic groups living with them. It is, however, hard to evaluate the statistical data, since the criteria that assign an individual to a nationality vary from one census to another.

In 1897, during the census which serves as a basis for all comparisons, the nationality of citizens in the Empire was not recorded; only the mother tongue records enabled census-takers to measure the size of the various national groups. In 1926 on the other hand, the census included two distinct questions along these lines, one on mother tongue, the other on *nationality.* The results showed that the mother tongue and the nationality did not always coincide. More than 6 million people who claimed a nationality other than Russian (essentially, Ukrainian Jews and Belorussians) nevertheless designated the Russian language as their mother tongue.

We can deduce from this that in 1897 some 5 to 6 million persons

Table 10
Proportion of Urban Population

Republics	Proportion of Urban Population in the total population as %	
	1939	1970
USSR	**32**	**56**
RSFSR	33	62
Ukraine	34	55
Belorussia	21	43
Uzbekistan	23	37
Kazakhstan	28	50
Georgia	30	48
Azerbaidzhan	36	50
Latvia	35	62
Moldavia	13	32
Lithuania	23	50
Kirghizia	19	37
Tadzhikistan	17	37
Armenia	29	59
Turkmenia	33	48
Estonia	34	65

were improperly counted as Russians, and were to be placed in other groups in subsequent censuses. Thus, by subtracting this number from the 89 million Russians counted in 1897, the annual growth for Russians from 1897 to 1926 becomes 1.5% instead of 1.2%. In addition, this revision shows that the increase in the Russian population until the beginning of the 1960s was even greater than official estimates would indicate.

Throughout the twentieth century the Russians suffered considerably greater losses of human life than most of the other national groups. The First World War hit the Russians hardest of all; the famine of 1921 caused the largest number of victims in the Volga region, inhabited mainly by Russians. The price paid by the Russian people in the Second World War was considerable. Yet despite these constant losses, the fact that the Russian group increased by 1.2% annually (an official figure that must be corrected upwards to roughly 1.5%) between 1897 and 1926, during a period when the country's total population grew by only 0.98%, and that from 1926 to 1959 the Russian growth rate was 1.1% annually for a general rate of 0.7%, bears witness to the exceptional dynamism of the group. But at the same time this considerable discrepancy between Russians and non-Russians gives rise to another question.

To what extent is Russian dynamism the result of an assimilation of non-Russian peoples? The ambiguities of the 1897 census distorted some of the data in determining the respective sizes of the various nations. The fact that subsequent census questionnaires carefully separated language and nationality gives a clearer idea of the development of national consciousness in the individual, and enables us to gauge the capacity for assimilation in certain large nations, particularly Russia. Assimilation may also reveal both Russian dynamism and the decrease, if not the actual disappearance, of some national groups.

The Ukrainians likewise raise a serious problem insofar as their growth rate was low in the period 1897 to 1960 and in the last period as well. Here also the substantial losses in human life suffered by this group should be borne in mind. While Ukrainian losses in the First World War were not exceptionally high, the civil war, which was fought chiefly in the Ukraine, proved murderous. So did the great famine of 1921 which ravaged the southern Ukraine and the Crimea, as well as the famine of 1932–1934. Finally, in the Second World War the region bore the brunt of the fighting, and the Germans deported considerable numbers of men and women of child-bearing age.

As hard-hit as the Russians by the events that have ravaged the Soviet population for nearly a half century, the Ukrainians have at no time demonstrated the same demographic vitality as the Russians. Moreover, everything points to the fact that their demographic stagnation covers the whole period in question. The gains made between 1897 and 1926, when the Ukrainians climbed from 19% of the total population to 21.4%, are due mainly to the census distortions previously mentioned. The Ukrainians were underestimated in 1897, while in 1926 part of the demographic progress recorded must be attributed to the transfer of Russian-speaking Ukrainians from the Russian group to the Ukrainian.[23]

The Belorussians have suffered the same massive population losses as the other Slavic peoples. Having borne the brunt of two world wars, they have registered their best growth rate during the last period of peace, which clearly indicates the impact of wars on the evolution of this group. Less urbanized than Russia and the Ukraine, Belorussia now has a birth rate that is slightly higher than theirs.[24]

These three peoples in the Slavic group have lived through the same tragedies and have shown fairly similar trends. The Second World War killed off a generation, and the impact of this destruction of the Slavic population is still being felt in Soviet society. Yet the demographic weakness of the Slavic peoples is not so much attributable to these immense losses as to their attitudes toward having children.

The situation of the Baltic peoples is even more disturbing than that of the Slavs. The proportion of their population to that of the whole country has been shrinking steadily since the beginning of the century. However, this calls for comment. The decreasing Baltic population is not a trend at all but rather a situation that developed quite early. By 1897 these peoples had the lowest birth rate in the Empire. Separate consideration should of course be given to Catholic Lithuania, where the decline in the birth rate began just after the turn of the century, but was more gradual and moderate than in the Protestant Baltic countries. The religious factor probably led to different behavior patterns, as well as to a different socio-economic trend. Less urbanized and less educated than the Estonian and Latvian populations, the Lithuanians were relatively slow in lining up with the other two, but this has now come about and the Baltic countries as a whole are approaching zero population growth.[25]

In certain cases the raw figures conceal much more complex situations, particularly in regard to the Jews and the Georgians. The Jews have undergone a drastic reduction of population both in actual numbers and compared to the rest of the USSR. Between 1897 and 1970 the Jewish population decreased by 50%, from 4,308,460 to 2,151,000. For the most part, the causes are well known. Before the First World War more than a million Jews left the czarist Empire, disheartened by a harsh policy of segregation and terrified by the pogroms—the most notorious being the Kichinev pogrom in 1903, which revealed the government's responsibility for the growing wave of anti-Semitism at the time. During the Second World War occupied Soviet territory witnessed the massacre of Jews, the extent of which has never been accurately determined, but which can be estimated at a minimum of 2.5 million persons.[26]

While these figures explain the long-term decline in the Jewish population, they do not fully account for the group's evolution between the two censuses. Nor does the emigration which has been accelerating since 1970—about 150,000 Jews have been authorized to leave the USSR in the past few years—account for the decrease. A low birth rate is characteristic of the Jewish community's demographic behavior. It is a pattern in keeping with the fact that Jews are urban dwellers living primarily in the western part of the USSR, and their birth rates are comparable with those of the general population living in the same conditions.

Nevertheless there are certain indications that the image of Soviet Jews which emerges from the census is somewhat distorted. First of all, according to the statistics, the Jews in the USSR are much older than the population average. In 1970, people over 60 years of age made up 12% of the Soviet population, but 26% of the Jews residing in the RSFSR, or 38% of the total Jewish population, seem to have passed that age. At the other end of the age pyramid the situation of the Jews also seems abnormal. At the last census, children under 10 years of age represented 18.6% of the Soviet population, whereas only 6% of the Jewish population falls into that age bracket. The difference between the age structure for the whole Soviet population and the Jewish population is too great to be accurate, since there is no real explanation for it.[27] This suggests that the Jewish community has been subjected to a fairly thorough process of assimilation. Those who remain Jewish are the ones who opted for this when their identity papers were issued, at a time when they might have believed that anti-Semitism no longer existed in the USSR. This would explain the sizable proportion of Jews in the highest age brackets. On the other hand, the younger generation who are the offspring of mixed marriages probably tend to choose the nationality of the non-Jewish parent. The high number of mixed marriages involving Jews would seem to reinforce this hypothesis.

Furthermore, it is reasonable to assume that the census underestimates the Jewish community simply because of inaccurate replies. The person answering census questions decides on his or her reply, and no proof of the veracity of statements is required. While it is reasonable to suppose that a member of a nationality enjoying all the rights inherent in this status would readily declare his national affiliation, it is equally reasonable to suppose that a Jew, especially one living in a non-Jewish environment, might be reticent about confessing his Jewishness. Thus it is altogether likely that tens or even hundreds of thousands of Jews should be added to the figure furnished by the census.[28]

Exactly the opposite problem is raised by the Georgians, who were probably overestimated or, rather, enjoy a certain ambiguity owing to the status of their republic. This is due to the fact that the Georgian SSR encompasses within its borders two autonomous republics, the Abkhaz ASSR and the Adzhar ASSR, as well as an autonomous region, the South Ossetian Autonomous Oblast—all three of which are inhabited mainly by Moslem nationalities. Thus the Georgians, who are of Christian origin and made up 66.8% of this republic's population at the 1970 census (64.3% according to the 1959 census), live side by side with ethnic groups having Islamic affiliations and cultures far removed from the Georgian. These minorities belong to the great Turko-Moslem group more than to the republic in which they are included. The relative weight of the Georgian group within the republic has undoubtedly increased from one census to the other. But Georgian demographers acknowledge that while the Georgian birth rate was high at the turn of the century, even before the Revolution it dropped below the Russian level, then really tapered off in the 1950s. It can be estimated that the republic's demographic progress stems chiefly from the birth rate of other nationalities,[29] and that the Georgians' growing weight in the republic is more the effect of migratory movements than that of a gain in their own birth rate. Despite average demographic growth, which happens to be the lowest in the Caucasus, Georgia must, for the time being, be classed among the declining western nations.

The Armenians on the other hand seem closer to the eastern pattern, despite their vigorous economic development and high degree of urbanization and education. In the first large-scale studies devoted to the Soviet Union's postwar population, the exceptionally high birth rate of the Caucasus was revealed. The Soviet Armenians undoubtedly benefited from added population during the First World War, when nearly half a million Armenians fled from Turkey. But this nation's demographic gains stem primarily from a consistently high birth rate, and are further accentuated by a drop in the death rate. Here, unlike Georgia, the high birth rate must be attributed to the Armenians themselves, who in 1970 comprised 89% of the population of their republic. The youthfulness of the population suggests that Armenia will maintain its high birth rate in the coming years along with a much lower death rate than the USSR's general average of 5.1 per thousand in the 1970 census. (In 1972, the general average reached 8.5 per thousand; the death rate in Estonia and Latvia climbed to 11 per thousand.[30])

But it is the Moslem peoples of the USSR which show the most favorable demographic situation and the one that is in sharpest contrast to the previous trend. From 1917 to the end of the 1950s, these peoples had made little headway, considerably less than that of the Russians.[31] Many reasons can be advanced for this phenomenon. The Kazakh nomads, for example, suffered serious human losses in the rebellion of 1916, followed by collectivization for which they paid an exceptionally high price. More than a quarter of the population was physically eliminated. If we consider the anticipated growth of the Kazakh population between 1926 and 1936, it is safe to say that this people lost 1.5 million persons out of the 4 million counted in 1926.

Likewise, the number of Bashkirs was reduced by roughly one-third as a result of the war with the Soviet government in 1920, which led to the suppression of Bashkir as an independent state. Since then, despite a higher birth rate than those of neighboring populations—the Bashkirs live in an autonomous republic incorporated in the Russian Republic—the Bashkirs have not yet caught up to their prerevolutionary levels (1.5 million in 1897; 1 million in 1926; 954,800 in 1959; 1,181,000 in 1970).

To the list of decimated peoples should be added those deported by Stalin during the war—including the Chechen, the Ingush, the Karachays, and the Balkars of the Caucasus, all of whom suffered considerable losses of population. Yet some idea of their destiny can be gathered by analyzing the trend of the Chechen group which had 408,000 members in 1939 and 419,800 in 1959. Rehabilitated after the Twentieth Congress and authorized to return to their territories, these peoples have made a rather spectacular recovery since then. The Chechen have increased from 408,000 to 581,800; the Ingush from 56,000 to 137,000. The other deported peoples have followed the same trend.

The Crimean Tatars, who were deported by Stalin, have not yet been granted permission to return to their national homeland. Their territory was eliminated under the law; and the Tatars, despite their vehement protests, have been compelled to remain in the places to which they were deported. But somehow they have managed to make up for the loss of life suffered at Stalin's hands. In spite of unreliable statistical data covering this group, we know that there were 179,094 Tatars in the republic of Crimea in 1926. Their numbers can be estimated at 230,000 before the Second World War. While the cost of their deportation is not known with any certainty, we can presume that it was heavy. It is hard to measure the actual gains made by this group since the war, inasmuch as census figures for the number of Tatars in Central Asia include both the Crimean Tatars and the Volga Tatars—both those long settled in the region and those who emigrated there in recent years. We can nevertheless estimate that the Crimean Tatars have a demographic trend similar to that of the surrounding Central Asian peoples.

Central Asia, along with Moslem Transcaucasia, is the major zone of high birth rate. The remarkable feature in the evolution of this population is the fact that it does not represent a steady trend, but rather a sudden jump in fertility, coinciding with economic and intellectual progress which has already taken place. The consequences of this change are manifold. First of all, in purely demographic terms, the weight of the Moslem peoples in the Soviet State has increased both numerically and proportionately. The Moslem population has climbed from 24 million to 35 million within a decade.

Furthermore, the age and sex ratios of the Moslem population is beginning to diverge from that of the USSR's western population. In a still basically youthful Soviet population, the Central Asian and

Chart I
Demographic Geography of the Soviet Population —
Births per 1,000

Situation on 1940

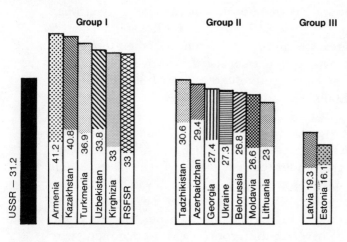

Group I

Group II

Group III

Group I > USSR average
Group II < USSR average but still assuring increased fertility
Group III < USSR average and below the level of increased fertility

USSR — 31.2

Armenia 41.2
Kazakhstan 40.8
Turkmenia 36.9
Uzbekistan 33.8
Kirghizia 33
RSFSR 33

Tadzhikistan 30.6
Azerbaidzhan 29.4
Georgia 27.4
Ukraine 27.3
Belorussia 26.8
Moldavia 26.6
Lithuania 23

Latvia 19.3
Estonia 16.1

Situation in 1960

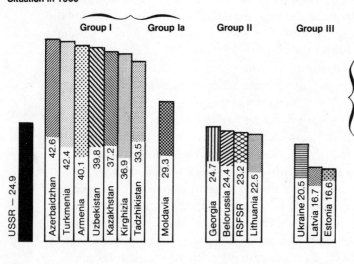

Group I

Group Ia

Group II

Group III

Group I > USSR average
Group Ia > USSR average but < 1940 USSR average
Group II < USSR average but assuring increased fertility
Group III < USSR average not assuring increased fertility

USSR — 24.9

Azerbaidzhan 42.6
Turkmenia 42.4
Armenia 40.1
Uzbekistan 39.8
Kazakhstan 37.2
Kirghizia 36.9
Tadzhikistan 33.5

Moldavia 29.3

Georgia 24.7
Belorussia 24.4
RSFSR 23.2
Lithuania 22.5

Ukraine 20.5
Latvia 16.7
Estonia 16.6

Situation in 1970

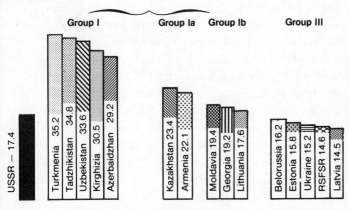

Group I > USSR average and 1960 USSR average
Group Ia > USSR average but < 1960 USSR average
Group Ib > USSR average but not assuring increased fertility
Group III < USSR average and < the level of increased fertility

Situation in 1974

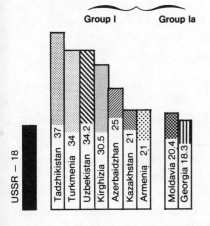

Group I > USSR average
Group Ia > USSR average but not assuring increased fertility
Group III < USSR average, not assuring increased fertility

Caucasian population is particularly youthful,[32] and the balance between men and women is more even there than anywhere else.[33] These factors also contribute to maintaining high birth rates.

A new geography is emerging for the USSR (Chart 1), in which the divisions seem almost biological. On the one hand, the western part of the country seems to have had its vitality sapped by its repeated and fearful trials. On the other hand, the eastern part, which is better preserved even though it has had its share of common disasters, is where living conditions tend to be more comfortable (this will be discussed later on), and where the high birth rate reflects exceptional vigor and probably greater confidence in the future. Furthermore, the contrasts between the two areas occur at both ends of life—in the number of offspring and in the number of people who reach an advanced age. The eastern region, with the most youthful population, also has the greatest number of persons who live a hundred years or more. It is true that the RSFSR breaks all longevity records in absolute numbers, with 8,366 centenarians according to the latest census. But their proportion in the population falls far behind the republics of Central Asia and the Caucasus, the proportional record being held by Georgia and Armenia.[34] Admittedly, these longevity records must be taken with a grain of salt, in view of birth records dating back to pre-Revolutionary times, and the fact that a civilization of "elders" has prevailed in Central Asia and the Caucasus. The prestige attached to age (the authorities in Central Asian villages are called the *Aksakal*, or "white-beards") has certainly encouraged some elderly men to add a few years to their real age. But this longevity also bears witness to a certain biological strength and ability to survive.

Russian Dispersion and Migratory Currents

The national states created by the Bolsheviks were only intended to be temporary formations. They were expected to provide the framework for a national life and, as meeting places for different ethnic groups, eventually to lose their very reason for being. This expectation was not so utopian as it might seem, since the movements of populations on imperial soil had proved that economic demands could produce considerable migratory currents. To what extent was this expectation realized? To what extent have recent demographic upheavals affected this plan for transcending national differences?

Here again any understanding of the Soviet Union's human evolution must be based on the 1897 census.

First of all, the censuses indicate that the Russian people is pre-eminently a nomadic people. In 1897 the Russians were concentrated in six great regions: Center, Central Chernoziom, Ural, Volga, Northwest, and Volga-Viatsk. These regions formed a compact bloc in the western part of the imperial territory. By 1926 the main lines of the migratory movements in future decades could be discerned.

In spite of the rapid industrialization of the western regions (Center, Volga, Ural, Northwest), the Russian population began migrations to the east, a movement that was to continue right into the early 1970s. Western and eastern Siberia, the Far East, Kazakhstan, and Central Asia were the destinations for constant streams of Russians, whose proportion in the population of the eastern USSR rose from 10% to 20% in those decades. A glance at a demographic map reveals this continuous spread of the Russian population and its march to the east. This trend raises two questions: (1) Have the massive migrations of Russians deeply affected the structure of the various Soviet national states? (2) Have these movements been matched by a corresponding spread of non-Russian peoples?

The answer becomes apparent by comparing the last two censuses. This comparison is particularly meaningful since the censuses were carried out in periods of total domestic peace. In addition, the comparison is significant because the population movements were no longer connected with external constraints but were more or less voluntary. To understand these migratory currents and their consequences, it is necessary to examine the population breakdown of the republics and compare the evolution of the official nationality with that of the other ethnic groups living in a given republic.

Generally speaking, it is found that next to the official nationality, the group which is second in order of importance is the Russian.[35] A few exceptions must be emphasized immediately. In Kazakhstan the official Kazakh nationality is outnumbered by the Russian group. In Georgia the Armenians constitute the second national group. In Moldavia the Ukrainians come second, ahead of the Russians. In Tadzhikistan the Uzbeks come after the Tadzhiks, which is only logical since the republic was formed on the basis of the eastern region of the old Uzbek emirate of Bukhara. Finally, in Armenia the Turkish-speaking and Moslem Azeris surpass the Russians in number. Everywhere else, the Russians rank second. Lastly, in the republic of Rus-

Dispersion of Russians in USSR in 1970

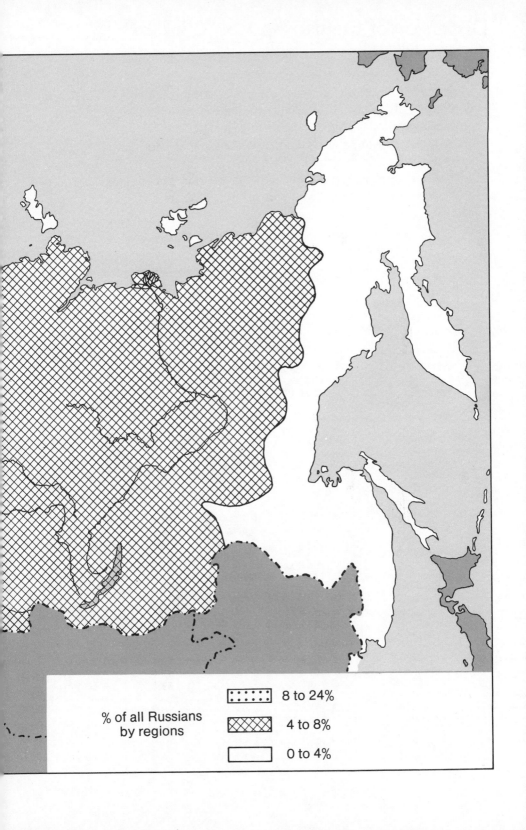

% of all Russians
by regions

8 to 24%

4 to 8%

0 to 4%

sia (RSFSR), the Tatars—Turkish-speaking Moslems—come just after the Russians. How do the official nationalities fare within their own republics? Table 11 shows this clearly.

By juxtaposing the situations of the official nationalities in their own republic during the last two censuses, the same trends appear to characterize the nations during that period. The demographically weak nations of the western part of the USSR are also growing weak

Table 11
Comparative Size of Official Nationality by Republics,[36] 1959-1970

Republic and official nationality	1959	1970	1959 percentage of republic's population	1970 percentage of republic's population
RSFSR	**117,534,000**	**130,079,000**		
Russians	97,864,000	107,748,000	83.3	82.8
Ukraine	**41,689,000**	**47,126,000**		
Ukrainians	32,158,000	32,284,000	76.8	74.9
Belorussia	**8,056,000**	**9,002,000**		
Belorussians	6,532,000	7,290,000	81.1	81.0
Uzbekistan	**8,110,000**	**11,800,000**		
Uzbeks	5,038,000	7,725,000	62.1	65.5
Kazakhstan	**9,295,000**	**13,009,000**		
Kazakhs (official nationality)	2,787,000	4,234,000	29.8	32.6
(Russians)	(3,972,000)	(5,522,000)	42.7	42.4
Georgia	**4,044,000**	**4,686,000**		
Georgians	2,601,000	3,131,000	64.3	66.8
Azerbaidzhan	**3,698,000**	**5,117,000**		
Azeris	2,494,000	3,777,000	67.5	73.8
Lithuania	**2,711,000**	**3,128,000**		
Lithuanians	2,151,000	2,507,000	79.3	80.1
Moldavia	**2,885,000**	**3,569,000**		
Moldavians	1,887,000	2,304,000	65.4	64.6
Latvia	**2,093,000**	**2,634,000**		
Latvians	1,298,000	1,342,000	62.0	56.8
Kirghizia	**2,066,000**	**2,933,000**		
Kirghiz	837,000	1,285,000	40.5	43.8
Tadzhikistan	**1,981,000**	**2,900,000**		
Tadzhiks	1,051,000	1,630,000	53.1	56.2
Armenia	**1,763,000**	**2,492,000**		
Armenians	1,552,000	2,208,000	88.0	88.6
Turkmenia	**1,516,000**	**2,159,000**		
Turkmenians	924,000	1,417,000	60.9	65.6
Estonia	**1,197,000**	**1,356,000**		
Estonians	893,000	925,000	74.6	68.2

within their own republics. Conversely, the demographically dynamic nations of the eastern USSR are stronger now than in the past. This is particularly significant in the case of the Kazakhs, who were long in the minority in their own land and are now registering an upswing. Although not spectacular, this population increase suggests a real break with the past, when the numerically declining Kazakhs barely justified their recognition as a national state. These figures clearly show two contrasting situations in the USSR, as can be seen in Table 12.

Table 12

Nationalities Declining in Their Own Republics		Nationalities Increasing in Their Own Republics	
Estonians	-6.4%	Armenians	+0.6%
Latvians	-3.2%	Lithuanians	+0.8%
Ukrainians	-1.9%	Georgians	+2.5%
Moldavians	-0.8%	Kazakhs	+2.6%
Russians	-0.5%	Tadzhiks	+3.1%
Belorussians	-0.1%	Kirghiz	+3.3%
		Uzbeks	+3.4%
		Turkmenians	+4.7%
		Azeris	+6.3%

These gains by official nationalities in their own national territories have gone hand in hand with a decrease on the part of the Russians, as shown in Table 13. As a general rule, this situation stems from the vigorous demographic trend of the indigenous population. Only in Georgia is the downward swing of the Russian group the result of a decrease in the actual number—not the relative weight—of Russians living in the republic. Between 1959 and 1970 the Russian community in Georgia shrank by 11,000, or roughly 0.3%.

The relative downswing of Russians in the eastern regions nevertheless should not hide the actual trend of the Russian group residing outside its own republic. If we consider the number of Russians residing outside the RSFSR and not their relative proportion in local populations, we find that Russian dispersion which has characterized the past two decades has continued to the present (see Table 14).

First of all, this table shows a very irregular trend for the Russian group. Generally speaking, it appears that Russians have increased numerically more outside the RSFSR than within their own repub-

Table 13
**Comparative Trend of Russians
and Official Ethnic Groups
in the Various Republics, in percentages**

Republics	Russians in %			Official Ethnic Group
	1959	1970	Difference	Difference between 1970 and 1959
Estonia	20.1	24.7	+4.6	-6.4
Ukraine	16.9	19.4	+2.5	-1.9
Belorussia	8.2	10.4	+2.2	-0.1
Moldavia	10.2	11.6	+1.4	-0.8
Latvia	2.9	4.0	+1.1	-3.2
Lithuania	8.5	8.6	+0.1	+0.8
Kazakhstan	42.7	42.4	-0.3	+2.6
Armenia	3.2	2.7	-0.5	+0.6
Kirghizia	30.2	29.2	-1.0	+3.3
Uzbekistan	13.5	12.5	-1.0	+3.4
Tadzhikistan	13.3	11.9	-1.4	+3.1
Georgia	10.1	8.5	-1.6	+2.5
Azerbaidzhan	13.6	10.0	-3.6	+6.3
Turkmenia	17.3	14.5	-2.8	+4.7

lic. Whereas, in the RSFSR they increased by only 10.1%, elsewhere, the increase was 37.4%, the group's overall increase being 14%. This difference stems both from the continuing nature of Russian migrations and from Russian demographic behavior which varies with their place of residence.

With regard to migratory currents, Table 14 shows that the Russians are now moving along two axes. They emigrate massively into the western regions with the exceptions of Lithuania, where they have made very weak gains, and the Ukraine, where they have made only moderate gains. Central Asia, with the exception of Turkmenia, continues to attract the Russians. The Caucasus, on the other hand, seems gradually to be losing its appeal; in Armenia the Russian population registered only a slight increase, less than half its average growth outside the RSFSR.

These differences are the more interesting in that they reveal that Russian demographic behavior is influenced by the given environment. Their birth rates in Central Asia and in the Caucasus, regions where the small family is looked on with disfavor, have risen sharply. It can therefore be concluded that the gains of the Russian popu-

Table 14
Number of Russians Living in the Republics

Republic	1959 Census (thousands)	1970 Census (thousands)	Change (%)
Ukraine	7,091	9,126	+28.7
Belorussia	660	938	+42.1
Uzbekistan	1,092	1,473	+34.3
Kazakhstan	3,972	5,522	+39.2
Georgia	408	397	- 2.7
Azerbaidzhan	501	510	+ 1.8
Lithuania	231	268	+16.0
Moldavia	293	414	+41.3
Latvia	556	705	+26.8
Kirghizia	624	856	+37.2
Tadzhikistan	263	344	+30.8
Armenia	56	66	+17.9
Turkmenia	263	313	+19.0
Estonia	240	335	+39.6

lation in the western republics are due to rising immigration, while in the eastern republics these upward trends can be explained by a higher birth rate. Finally, the Russian downswing in the Caucasus can be attributed to a drop in immigration and to the fact that the Russians have actually been leaving, as is the case in Georgia. The dispersion of Russians therefore has largely changed direction. After the stampede to the east in the years 1926–1959, it is now a stampede to the west, toward republics that lie on the edges of the Western world. The causes for this profound change in Russian migratory currents will be taken up later.

The Soviet Population in the Year 2000

Russian primacy was taken for granted for a long time, in the czarist Empire and the Soviet State. The dynamic nature of Russia made her the heartland of this great living space. But the figures compiled on the basis of the 1970 census call for careful consideration. Dynamism is no longer an exclusive attribute of the Russians. Other ethnic groups are gaining in size and influence. Moreover, the population of Russia itself is decreasing. Finally, the weight of the Russians outside the RSFSR tends to decline, and their dispersion seems to be less significant.

The essential problem no longer has to do with the past or the present, but the future population of the USSR. It is of course hazardous to project present trends into the future. Nevertheless, considering the trend in recent years, the structure of the population of different ethnic groups in terms of age and sex, and the attitude prevailing in the ethnic groups with regard to problems of having children, it would seem possible to make some cautious hypotheses.

The main question is as follows: can two very different demographic trends—one suited to highly developed societies, the other to less developed ones—subsist in the Soviet Union? Or is this demographic difference attributable mainly to a gap in development which will quickly be reduced? In other words, is it a question of inherited situations in the process of change, or of specific problems which must be handled individually and not in the light of general demographic tendencies?

After some hesitation Soviet demographers have admitted that regional variations in birth rate represent a key factor in Soviet demography.[37] But the conclusions that they draw from this are not uniform. Some believe that the differences will be lasting;[38] others that the study of data subsequent to the census seems to indicate a drawing together of national behavior patterns.[39] This rapprochement, they maintain, results from a very slight rise in the lowest birth rates, and a gradual downswing in the highest birth rates. In this way the most prolific nations are gradually evolving their demographic behavior from "the biological maximum to conscious regulation of family size." To support this theory the experts compare the birth rate calculations supplied by the 1970 census with rates based on partial data gathered in 1971 and 1972 (see Table 15).

A comparison of the figures does enable us to draw several conclusions. First of all it is evident that there has been a general decline in the birth rate throughout the USSR since 1960, even though the rate of that decline varies according to region. Everywhere, including the regions with a high birth rate, a certain lowering of the birth rate can be seen, except in Tadzhikistan where demographic gains have been a constant factor since 1940. A slight recovery in the birth rate is indicated for the RSFSR—14.6 per thousand in 1970, 15.3 per thousand in 1972, and 15.6 per thousand in 1974. A similar recovery in the birth rate appears to a lesser degree in Moldavia—19.4 per thousand in 1970, 20.6 per thousand in 1972, 20.4 per thousand in 1974. All the other European groups, including the Ukrainians, continue to show a tendency toward lower birth rates. However,

Table 15
Birth Rates by Republic per 1,000 Inhabitants

Republic	1940	1960	1970	1972
USSR	31.2	24.9	17.4	17.8
RSFSR	33.0	23.2	14.6	15.3
Ukraine	27.3	20.5	15.2	15.5
Belorussia	26.8	24.4	16.2	16.1
Uzbekistan	33.8	39.8	33.6	33.2
Kazakhstan	40.8	37.2	23.4	23.5
Georgia	27.4	24.7	19.2	18.0
Azerbaidzhan	29.4	42.6	29.2	25.6
Lithuania	23.0	22.5	17.6	17.0
Moldavia	26.6	29.3	19.4	20.6
Latvia	19.3	16.7	14.5	14.5
Kirghizia	33.0	36.9	30.5	30.5
Tadzhikistan	30.6	33.5	34.8	35.3
Armenia	41.2	40.1	22.1	22.5
Turkmenia	36.9	42.4	35.2	33.9
Estonia	16.1	16.6	15.8	15.6

caution should be exercised in drawing conclusions because the last four-year period is far too short to permit any definitive judgment. Variations from one year to the next may often indicate slightly conflicting tendencies.

A second conclusion seems called for, namely, that in spite of a gradual leveling of behavior patterns, the Soviet Union's demographic structure will continue for several decades to shape the balance of the various populations by the beginning of the twenty-first century. Furthermore, some Soviet demographers have rejected the generally accepted thesis of gradual leveling and stress the persistence, if not the actual development, of differences in birth rate behavior, even when the economy and the culture are unified. Therefore, what really counts in evaluating future trends of Soviet demography is to analyze the main factors in human behavior and their respective weight.

Isn't the economic factor a fairly decisive one? The family income has a decided effect on demographic behavior. But do income and birth rate levels always follow the same curve everywhere? Unfortunately, there is no entirely homogeneous source of information covering the whole USSR that enables one to compare income and birth rate for all types of Soviet populations. But by juxtaposing two surveys carried out in 1972—one in both the cities and countryside of the western regions, the other in only the countryside of Central

Asia, Azerbaidzhan and the Caucasus—the results shown in Table 16 are obtained.[40]

This table shows clearly that families have two different reactions to their economic status. In the case of families in the western republics, the influence of economic status on family size is undeniable. Even though the rural population, given the same income, has a higher number of children, income has a decided effect on demographic behavior both in the cities and in the country. In the eastern re-

Table 16
Average Number of Births per Woman

Monthly family income (rubles)	Western Republics		Moslem Republics
	Blue- and white-collar workers	Kolkhoz and sovkhoz workers	Kolkhoz and sovkhoz workers
150 or less	1.77	2.22	3.88
151-210	1.69	2.37	4.16
211-300	1.72	2.51	4.12
301-450	1.79	2.67	4.21
451-600	1.88	2.89	4.12
601-900	1.96	3.04	4.17
901 and over	2.08	3.23	4.22

publics, on the other hand, family size is no more than moderately affected by income. In fact, only the poorest families here show a lower birth rate than the others, and this is for special reasons which will be discussed later on.

Education may be an even more important factor. A survey carried out in 1972 in an urban setting in the western republics[41] showed that the birth rate is practically unaffected by income in families where the educational level does not exceed elementary or, at best, incomplete secondary school training. Furthermore, incomplete schooling is more frequent in the rural setting. At the other end of the scale, income scarcely affects couples who have had a higher education.

On the other hand, among families with average education—ten years' elementary and secondary education, vocational and technical schooling—the correlation between family income and birth rate is very close. These tendencies prevailing in families in the west appear to only a partial degree among families in the east. There is no question that in the republics with high birth rates the higher the married couple's educational level, the more the family tends to space and control births.

Table 17, analyzing data on the education-birth rate correlation in the western and eastern republics, suggests extremely interesting conclusions for the Soviet Union's demographic future. It is based not on the real number of births but on the births planned by the women.

What can be concluded from this table? First of all, that education has a pronounced effect on demographic behavior patterns, both in the USSR's western societies and in the eastern. Secondly, that there is an important difference in the two types of societies with regard to the decisive factor in behavior change. In the eastern societies the woman's education may lead to real changes. Thus, the table shows that when the spouses have different levels of education, an educated husband has an infinitely more conservative attitude than an educated woman. The birth rate differential between a couple in which both spouses have a higher education and one in which the woman has little schooling is almost as large as the difference between a couple having a higher education and one with little education.

When only the wife has a higher education, a couple's birth rate is quite similar to that of the couple in which both spouses are equally educated. In the western family, on the contrary, the difference lies in the couple's educational level taken as a whole, while the variations are negligible if only one spouse's education is considered.

Table 17
Planned Number of Children[41]

Wife's education	Nationalities with low birth rates		Nationalities with high birth rates	
	Husband's education			
	Secondary and higher	Below secondary	Secondary and higher	Below secondary
Secondary and higher	1.89	2.06	4.76	5.34
Below secondary	2.15	2.41	6.73	7.03

From this it can be seen that women's education in the eastern republics is one of the decisive factors in Soviet demographic policy. As long as the men there are better educated, they will impose their views on the society, and these views are markedly conservative and tend toward a high birth rate.

Finally, urbanization, which varies appreciably from one region to another, affects human behavior in a way often considered decisive.[42] In all human societies the development of cities has brought about considerable changes in demography. Obviously, there will be fewer births. But often better living conditions serve to offset to some extent the reduced size of families by lowering the infant mortality rate.

Do the demographic differences in the USSR vary with each region's degree of urbanization? And can urban populations with similar behavior patterns be contrasted with rural populations characterized by large families? Actually, the situation is not that simple. The western part of the USSR is certainly much more urbanized than the Central Asian periphery; yet these borderlands are far from being without urban life.

Even the 1897 census listed 56 cities in Central Asia, with 26 in Uzbekistan alone. The census found that 15 percent of the population were city dwellers, and that there were urban activities in the form of small-scale commerce and cottage industries which had been developing during the nineteenth century. Nevertheless, the great economic revolution of the 1930s did little to change these peripheral regions, whereas it totally upset the structure and lifestyle of the Russian and Ukrainian populations. No region in the USSR was unaffected by this radical change, but the extent of the change varied from one region to another. In places where this change was greatest, the economic revolution not only gave urban life primary importance, it separated the city from the country and created two different ways of life.

This dualism made the city and its culture a pole of attraction and a model on which the peasant society would try to pattern itself. Elsewhere, despite the gains in urbanization, this process went on without breaking up the unity of the society. The population of cities and rural areas remained one, bound to a single cultural model in which tradition prevailed. In the early 1960s, when it became possible to take stock of social changes made since 1930, three distinct societies could be discerned within Soviet society:

(1) People who had begun to move from a rural type of population to an urban type, among whom the most involved from the demographic standpoint were the Russians, Ukrainians, Belorussians, and Balts. Their behavior was characterized by a lowered birth rate both in the cities and in the countryside, where the urban model had penetrated. Other peoples like the Tatars, Udmurts, and Moldavians were tending in the same direction but to a lesser degree, inasmuch as the birth rate of their urban populations was dropping without the countryside following suit. But the process of change had also clearly begun for these peoples.

(2) At the other end of the scale of demographic behavior during this period was a compact group of peoples in Central Asia, part of Daghestan, Azerbaidzhan, and elsewhere who were still untouched by the change. For these peoples urbanization brought no reduction in the birth rate, so that urban and rural behavior patterns in this area remained very similar.

(3) Between these two contrasting groups, a third can be distinguished—the Armenians, Yakuts, and Bashkirs—whose birth rates remain high both in the city and in the country. Nevertheless, there are some indications that these peoples are about to adopt the urban demographic pattern.

Since the end of the 1950s the USSR has changed a great deal and urbanization has spread particularly in places where it had seemed to be stagnant. But the most important social change lies neither in the development of cities nor in their increase in number, but rather in a kind of urbanization of the countryside. The irreversible nature of this sociological phenomenon, which has been stressed by Basile Kerblay,[43] is the result of the city's value systems and lifestyles penetrating into rural society and shaping it. The family has felt the repercussions of this change, and the urban family—a couple with a small number of children—is becoming the model in rural areas.

The drop in birth rate revealed by the 1970 census is primarily the result of the obliteration of behavioral differences between city and country. While in the past the countryside dictated the Soviet Union's demographic situation, the cities now take the lead, because the city dweller has become a model for the farmer, a model notably more alluring with the development of the communications media. In the years 1930–1950, city and country represented two distinct environments moving away from each other; but today the better educated farmers are permeated by urban culture through their newspapers and television sets. The USSR having desperately sought to become an industrial society, it comes as no surprise that in interpreting modernization in terms of urbanization and the rejection of rural life, the Soviet Union is losing the family values that country living had succeeded in preserving for a time, and it pays the price for this demographically. Yet, this trend characterizing Soviet society as a whole is not totally applicable to the Moslem societies where urbanization has nevertheless progressed.

The 1970 census, which generally reflects the standardization of Soviet society, also reveals the distinctive nature of these borderland peoples. Here, city-country demographic behavior, far from drawing together, has diverged more than in the past. Table 18 bears witness to these different trends among the peoples.

Table 18
City-Country Differences [44]
(Urban Demography = 100)

Nationalities	1958/1959	1969/1970	Nationalities	1958/1959	1969/1970
Russians	155	129	Armenians	128	154
Ukrainians	144	126	Uzbeks	122	136
Belorussians	143	129	Kazakhs	111	140
Georgians	156	132	Kirghiz	111	137
Moldavians	148	136	Tadzhiks	77	106
Latvians	138	128	Turkmenians	90	116
Estonians	150	135	Azerbaidzhans	149	139
Lithuanians	130	145			

How can these differences be explained? Although the second group has a lower degree of urbanization than the first, it has made undeniable gains. Yet in this group it is the countryside that dictates demographic progress and from every indication preserves its demographic standards, its own value system, and its own behavior patterns, instead of conforming to the urban model. There are several explanations for this.

First of all, the Soviet Union's economic policy has determined geographic priorities which have turned the Moslem borderlands primarily into an agrarian zone. The economic development of Central Asia had been geared to big harvests, thus preserving the rural population there. The last few years have been marked by the development of cities and their population; but these urban centers have accommodated a population foreign to the region, rather than native farmers converted to urban living. This point will be discussed at greater length in the next chapter.

In addition, Central Asian cities—at least the medium-sized ones—often differ from the European cities by their proximity to the countryside and the ties that have been retained. These ties are primarily those of the family, which is rarely dispersed. Children residing in the city remain physically and emotionally close to relatives living near them in a rural environment. There are also the bonds of work. In these regions the urban population is often employed in agricultural tasks in the nearby countryside. At times the percentage of these agricultural workers runs as high as 40 percent of the city's active population. This explains the continuance of the rural culture even in the cities. It also explains why the countryside—without being the demographic model for the city—does at least preserve its behavioral autonomy. Despite its development, the Central Asian city remains an island in a peasant civilization and population. It goes without saying that the large cities are autonomous, unlike the small and medium-sized urban centers which are connected physically and culturally to the neighboring countryside.

Is one to conclude from this that the differences in Soviet society remain irreducible? Certainly not. The nations of the Soviet Union's southern borderlands have scarcely begun the transition to an urban civilization of the classic type. In the long term, the development of industrialization, the improvement in women's education, and above all the extensive migratory currents should alter the culture and behavior patterns of these peoples. But the process will be slow. Naturally, brutal economic measures like those of the 1930s could shorten the time required. Actually, the Stalinist revolution spared the southern periphery of the USSR to some extent, and a second revolution as violent and ruthless as the first hardly seems possible in the Soviet Union of today. We may therefore conclude that a few years will not suffice to unify Soviet society, and that right up to the turn of the century its evolution will be marked by geographical and cultural lags.

Is it possible, then, to attempt any forecasts for the year 2000? Despite the advent of unforeseeable external events, famines, and epidemics, which can speedily wreck the most cautious speculations, one can nevertheless try to imagine the USSR at the turn of the century on the basis of the 1970 census. The year 2000 is justified be-

Chart II
Soviet Population Trend between 1970 and 2000

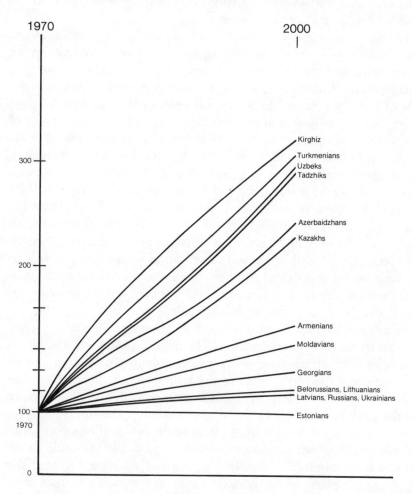

cause 30 years, or one generation, separates it from the census serving as the basis for our projections.

Adhering strictly to the data supplied by the census without making corrections, highly divergent population trends can be predicted. These forecasts range from the pure and simple continuance of the 1970 level—as is the case for the Estonians—to the tripling of the population in Central Asia. These diverse situations appear in Chart II.

This chart is based mainly on the present situation, namely the

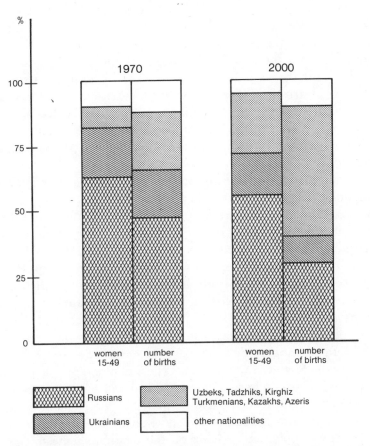

Chart III
Foreseeable trend in the ratio between the number
of women from 15 to 49 years of age and the number
of births, by national groups (in percentages)

Russians

Uzbeks, Tadzhiks, Kirghiz
Turkmenians, Kazakhs, Azeris

Ukrainians

other nationalities

age-sex structure of the different national groups. This structure leads us to believe that, if the reproductive capacity of all the national groups were to decline at a given moment, the future would be dictated largely by the different moments when population structure will affect demography. The rapid weakening of the Russo-Ukrainian group stems from the fact that the impact of age-sex structure made itself felt by 1975. But for the Armenians, Moldavians, Belorussians, and Georgians, this factor will not become decisive until about ten years later. Meanwhile the peoples with high birth rates will not feel the effects of the age-sex structure until about 1990.[45]

Is it possible to go beyond these rather general predictions, and try to estimate the future population of the USSR? On the basis of the current situation and trends, estimates have been attempted both in the USSR and in the Western world. They lead us to conclude—with varying degrees of caution—that a new balance can take place between the diverse nationalities of the Soviet Union. Chart III shows this new balance, based on the attempt to forecast the comparative trend for the female population of childbearing age and the birth trend for the various national groups.[46] The new balance appears very clearly in Table 19, which focuses on only three geographic regions—Russia, Central Asia, Transcaucasia—in other words, on the future of the Russian people and the Moslem peoples.

What value can one assign to this table?[47] What lessons can be drawn from it?

Basile Kerblay rightly recalls that in 1900 the great Russian scientist Mendeleyev predicted that, in the year 2050, his country's population would stand at 800 million.[48] This calculation is quite justifiable for its time if we bear in mind that, at the turn of the century, the population of the czarist Empire had doubled in forty years. Compared to the current state of the Soviet population, this calculation serves to emphasize the unreliable nature of any predictions.

If, however, we assume that the present growth rate is maintained until the year 2000—a hypothesis which forms the basis of the forecasts offered here—it is clear that this growth could only be continued with the demographic support of the eastern Soviet nations. Inasmuch as the Soviet Union cannot expect demographic gains much below those indicated here without major drawbacks for its economic development and security, and inasmuch as there can be no other source of demographic gains on a short-term basis than the eastern regions, Soviet policy must bank on the continuing dynamism and particularism of these peoples, and not on the standardization of the Soviet population's behavior patterns. This means that Soviet progress is linked with the growth of population imbalances, and not on restoring those balances.

Just exactly what do these imbalances signify? The demographic rise of the Moslem peoples has often led observers to conclude hastily that the Soviet multi-ethnic society was undergoing total revolution. Yet, the figures in Table 19 prompt us to be more circumspect. In spite of the changes that have occurred and will occur, and even

Table 19
Population of USSR 1950 to 2000 (in thousands)
(Russia, Central Asia, Transcaucasia)

	1950 Total	1950 %	1960 Total	1960 %	1970 Total	1970 %	1980 Total	1980 %	1990 Total	1990 %	2000 Total	2000 %
USSR	**180,075**	**100**	**214.329**	**100**	**242,756**	**100**	**267,057**	**100**	**292,324**	**100**	**312,215**	**100**
RSFSR	102,191	56.7	119,906	55.9	130,360	53.7	138,842	52	145,686	49.8	147,335	47.2
Central Asia	**17,499**	**9.7**	**24,402**	**11.4**	**33,187**	**13.7**	**42,449**	**15.9**	**55,742**	**19.1**	**71,903**	**23**
Kazakhstan	6,628	3.7	9,850	4.6	13,116	5.4	15,710	5.9	19,038	6.5	22,328	7.1
Kirghizia	1,740	1	2,172	1	2,968	1.2	} 26,739	} 10	} 36,704	} 12.6	} 49,575	} 15.9
Tadzhikistan	1,532	0.9	2,082	1	2,943	1.2						
Turkmenia	1,210	0.7	1,594	0.7	2,190	0.9						
Uzbekistan	6,383	3.5	8,704	4.1	11,970	4.9						
Caucasia	**7,777**	**4.3**	**9,921**	**4.6**	**12,393**	**5.1**	**14,649**	**5.5**	**17,660**	**6**	**20,671**	**6.6**
Armenia	1,354	0.8	1,867	0.9	2,518	1	} 14,649	} 5.5	} 17,660	} 6	} 20,671	} 6.6
Azerbaidzhan	2,896	1.6	3,894	1.8	5,166	2.2						
Georgia	3,527	2	4,160	1.9	4,709	1.9						

though it may be plausible to assume that the Russian percentage of the total population may dip below the 50 percent mark, the Russian people at the end of this century will still be the most numerous in the USSR. By then the Central Asian peoples will represent at best a quarter of the Soviet population—or a third if we add the peoples of the Caucasus, two of which are Christian and traditionally hostile to Islam and the Turkish civilization. The gains made by the Turko-Moslem peoples are considerable; within half a century their weight altogether has more than doubled. Nevertheless, their progress does not imply that the Russian people will be submerged by them or deposed from its position of predominance.

The problem resides less in the gross figures than in the new situation being created. First of all, the consciousness that dynamic peoples have that they hold the key to the overall progress of Soviet society may lead them to demand that their role be expressed in terms of new political responsibilities. Secondly, these new population balances raise economic problems such as employment and regional development—which may give rise to serious disturbances if not settled. Thus we see that the problems arising from these new balances must be studied in order to understand their range and potential.

Finally, there is one question underlying all the analyses that can be made here. Is it a question of regional or national imbalances? If Soviet society is moving toward a growing integration and if national differences show a tendency to fade away, then it hardly matters whether demographic growth stems from the dynamism of one people or of another. In the final analysis, it is the whole Soviet nation that is expanding. If, on the contrary, Soviet society is not moving toward integration, then the imbalances between the diverse national groups may in time be dangerous for the whole country and its unity. The imbalances could then encourage tendencies toward divergence, adversely affecting conditions which might foster integration. Accordingly, demographic changes and future prospects have meaning only when considered in the light of two fundamental problems:

(1) Which tendency is now dominant in Soviet society? The tendency toward integration, or the tendency toward consolidation of differences?

(2) What role will the demographic differences play? Will they help integration or will they be the ferment for differentiation—or even for disintegration?

CHAPTER III

Demographic Changes and Economic Conflicts

Demographic trends are not isolated phenomena in the life of a country. Nor is their impact limited. They go on shaping the human community for a long time, determining its relationships with the environment. On one specific point, recent demographic changes may have considerable impact on the USSR: manpower is going to become scarcer.

This may not seem catastrophic at first sight. Industrial societies today are more likely to be confronted with problems of unemployment and utilization of increased leisure time than with recruiting labor. The USSR, however, in spite of its high degree of industrialization, is facing a crisis stemming from an insufficient work force, unequally distributed over a vast territory. For the Soviets this is a new problem that conflicts with long-standing habits of the State and the individual. It demands wide-ranging solutions, none of them crystal clear or easy to implement.

From Waste to Scarcity:
Soviet Labor at the Turn of the Century

In every country economic development depends on manpower, and this is true for the USSR more than anywhere. The abundance of seemingly unlimited labor contributed decisively to the transformation of the country. For decades the rural areas supplied industry with as many workers as were required—and under the most favorable conditions. The State, master of the whole economy, was also master of the men necessary for its development. The State could decide on the quantities of workers needed, distribute them as it saw fit and pay them very little.

In the gigantic effort toward economic change undertaken in the early 1930s, the State drew heavily on this quasi-limitless human reserve totally in its power. Even though the end of the Stalinist period saw labor becoming less malleable or more independent, the economy was still based largely on the abundance of manpower. Despite appeals for greater productivity and for improved quality of work, the Soviets continued to rely on the number of workers more than on the development of individual effort to reach goals set in every sphere. The squandering of the Soviet labor force has been an economic rule for almost half a century. Demographic changes now demand that the rule be broken for the maximum utilization of the labor henceforth available. Has the problem become acute? Has it become urgent?

Emphatically, yes. The data makes that plain enough. In 1970 the USSR had a potential labor force of 130.5 million persons in a total population of 241.7 million. It was a potential labor force because the figure covers the able-bodied population, comprising males between sixteen and sixty years of age, and females between sixteen and fifty-five. This potential labor force was not totally used, however, since the census showed 115.2 million persons actually employed, including 2.6 million in age brackets above the normal working age. Those outside the labor force included a great many students (8,627,000 males and females between sixteen and nineteen), housewives, the military and the police (3.2 million), and the incapacitated.[1]

Nevertheless, the number of active workers in the USSR must be raised to include those independently engaged in private work, chiefly in rural areas. On this basis the present size of the Soviet labor pool can be estimated at 125.6 million persons,[2] which is very close to the potential active population.

The impact demographic changes will have on the active work force in coming years is obvious in Table 20.[3]

This table clearly corresponds with the trend of the Soviet population as a whole. The drop in births recorded in the early 1960s is reflected in a reduction of the work force by the late 1970s, culminating in all likelihood around 1990. Only then can the trend begin to change, and an increase in the work force be anticipated. But this is

Table 20
**Estimated Increase in the Potential Active Population
of the Soviet Union between 1971 and 2000
(in thousands)**

Years (by 5-year plans)	Total increase	Average annual increase	Average annual growth rate in %
1971-1975	12,963	2,593	1.9
1976-1980	10,378	2,076	1.4
1981-1985	2,664	533	0.3
1986-1990	2,630	526	0.3
1991-1995	3,291	658	0.4
1996-2000	8,101	1,620	1.0

contingent on the continuance of the slight demographic upswing currently taking place, with no spectacular drop in the dynamic growth rate of the USSR's southern nations. For it is the problem of nationalities which has a bearing on the stagnation of the active work force. Any increase in the work force, as opposed to a drastic reduction, can be attributed to the vitality of the borderlands. Employing the same data as in the foregoing table, but breaking them down into the various Soviet demographic regions, the impact of diverse birth trends on the future work force becomes infinitely clearer. (See Table 21.)

This table[4] calls for several observations. First of all it demonstrates the special importance the non-Russian peoples' demographic development has for the future of the USSR. Although their relative weight in the Soviet population has increased considerably, the non-Russians are still in the minority. Nevertheless it will all depend on them whether or not the Soviet Union's active work force in the years 1980–1995 remains at its present level, when even now, Soviet leaders[5] say, the economy is facing a manpower shortage. In the years when the labor shortage becomes critical, Central Asia and Kazakhstan will be the sole manpower reservoir on which the economy can draw to meet its needs.[6] The economic role of that area will consequently far surpass its human weight in the Soviet Union as a whole. At the start of the next century, when the situation becomes more favorable and better balanced, Central Asia will still account for more than half of the increase in the active work force.

By comparing the trend in these three regions with the trend for

Table 21
**Estimated Increase in the Potential Active Population
of the USSR by Region, Between 1971 and 2000
(in thousands)**

Years (by 5-year plans)	R.S.F.S.R.			Central Asia and Kazakhstan			The Caucasus		
	Total increase	% of USSR increase	Average annual growth rate	Total increase	% of USSR increase	Average annual growth rate	Total increase	% of USSR increase	Average annual growth rate
1971-1975	6,039	46.6	1.6	3,089	23.8	3.7	1,059	8.2	3.3
1976-1980	3,928	37.8	1	3,444	33.2	3.5	1,142	11	3
1981-1985	-813		-0.2	2,773	104.1	2.4	690	26.1	1.6
1986-1990	-880		-0.2	2,880	109.5	2.2	514	19.5	1.1
1991-1995	-425		-0.1	3,361	102.1	2.4	548	16.7	1.1
1996-2000	1,964	24.2	0.5	4,380	54.1	2.7	954	11.8	1.8

the overall active work force we can reach two conclusions: first, all the other peoples of the USSR will be in a position at least as unfavorable as Russia's; and secondly, those peoples will not compensate for the shortages in Russian labor. By 1980 these shortages in the labor force will affect all the republics other than those of Central Asia, Kazakhstan, and the Caucasus. Apparently, this trend will make itself felt in the Baltic republics mainly after 1990.

This split in the demographic trends of the USSR will be reflected in a similar split in the development of its active work force in the decades to come.

Finally, by relating the demography of the USSR to its economy, it becomes easier to understand why the uneven gains in population present a real challenge to the future of the economy. The main factor behind this threat is the lack of workers. The shortage centers chiefly in those areas where the demand for labor is greatest, namely in the more industrialized, more urbanized regions. The greatest industrial complexes are found in Russia and, to a lesser extent, in the Ukraine. The development of resources in Siberia and the Far East also demands sizable human investment. For this reason, all Soviet economic projects will run into the demographic problem and its consequences for the work force. How can the government deal with this problem? It must be borne in mind that, given the Soviet Union's present situation, the government will have to attempt to increase the supply of manpower available, and adjust its allocation according to the geographic distribution of resources and industries.

Is a general labor policy possible in the USSR? Several solutions are possible and some have already been implemented to some extent. First of all, the State can try to extend the active working years at both ends. The span of working years in the USSR is in fact shorter than in the United States, due to increasingly longer compulsory education and two years' required military service, while retirement comes earlier, at age fifty-five for women and sixty for men.

The question is whether the Soviets can reduce compulsory education and, hence, the number of students who are unavailable for work during the years they are receiving intellectual or vocational training. The reduction of compulsory education is unlikely; the Soviet State makes education one of its prime goals. At the present time compulsory education covers only the first eight years, but there are plans for universal ten-year education. This insistence on schooling stems both from the Soviet's strong attachment to intellectual progress and the country's need for trained workers. When labor is in short supply, the quality of the available work force becomes a very important factor for the economy. Thus, rather than reduce the length of compulsory schooling, the government is trying to encourage technical education. Often, this policy has an adverse effect on higher education where a strict selection system makes it possible to limit admissions.[7]

At the other end of the working life, the retired workers are a constant temptation for the government. In fact, they have been brought back into the active work force to a large extent, as is revealed by the 1970 census. In addition, various measures aimed at inducing retirees to return to work have been adopted.[8]

On this score, however, the government has run into strong opposition. There is no question that the number of retirees who keep their jobs or who return to work has been increasing. In 1960 only 11% of Soviet pensioners had employment; but in the 1970 census, 19% were back in the labor force, and five years later their proportion jumped to 24.3%.[9] It is nevertheless doubtful that the manpower shortage can be solved by an ever-increasing dependence on those who have reached retirement age. In addition, the people grow alarmed at infringements on their pension rights. To satisfy the rural labor force in 1968, the Soviets had to bring the *kolkhoz* retirement age into line with that of blue and white-collar workers in the State sector, and even more favorable legislation had to be passed for certain categories of rural workers.[10]

In this respect there was obvious public pressure when the new Constitution came under discussion. Newspaper accounts of this debate at the grass roots reveal that there was significant popular interest in working conditions and retirement. Soviet citizens feared that the Constitution might entail the raising of the retirement age. They insisted that the pensionable age be stated in the country's Fundamental Law, in the section pertaining to pension rights. The heated discussions that took place in this connection show how hard it is to take a step backwards.

Unable to make changes in the pension system, can the Soviet government siphon off rural labor for industry? Here, too, it seems that the possible solutions have already been exhausted. In 1950 the active work force employed in agriculture still represented 50 million persons, but in 1970 there were only 37 million, and in 1974 just 35 million. Furthermore, by recruiting rural labor for work in industry, the government was tapping the youngest segment, mostly men. As a result, the countryside now has an older population than the city, with a greater proportion of women. The rural population is also less educated, and consequently less dynamic. This explains why the countryside has become increasingly unattractive for young people, whose exodus to the cities has been an unalterable factor in Soviet history over recent decades. Yet farm production—at least the way it is organized in the USSR—requires many hands, preferably ones that are still strong. The problems of Soviet agriculture have compelled the government to consider the human factor as well, in an attempt to reduce the migration from rural areas. Thus any solution to the labor shortage must lie elsewhere.

Reducing the manpower of the armed forces or the length of military service raises questions for the army's integrative function in Soviet society, which will be discussed later. Moreover, this reduction would hardly help matters inasmuch as recruits are largely employed on civilian projects, such as the construction of the Baikal-Amur railroad.[11]

It is apparent therefore that the means of bolstering the deficient labor force are very limited. The only answer lies in allocating manpower according to the needs of the economy. Here again, the situation would seem to call for simple solutions. Economically developed and industrialized regions are already up against a labor shortage; soon, they will feel the pinch even more. On the other hand, regions devoted chiefly to farming, where the nature of the soil and the climate prevent unlimited expansion of agricultural space, have an abundant supply of labor that will become surplus in time.

These imbalances coexist in a single state where people have received the same education, using a common language—Russian. Khrushchev had not yet foreseen the argument of underemployment here and a shortage of workers there when he announced that the Soviets showed an increasing tendency to move in keeping with the country's economic needs. Now that those needs have become critical and will affect the future of everybody, can Khrushchev's solution—migration—be implemented? Can we imagine the massive arrival of Uzbeks in the industrial cities of Russia or the new towns of Siberia?[12] To attempt to answer this question, it is necessary first to glance at the past and the present, and see to what extent such a trend in the geographic distribution of populations fits into spontaneous, organized movements already in process.

Civilizations Unwilling to Migrate

Theoretically Central Asia, the potential labor pool, should lend it-self to migration. At least the past would make this seem plausible because some of the higher civilizations that flourished in this region were nomadic, and for centuries the roads of Central Asia were rut-ted by the hooves of pack camels. Even at the start of this century, the boundary between nomadic and sedentary peoples was often hard to draw. The Soviet government broke up what remained of nomadism and replaced it by organized, limited transfers of popula-tions wherever required by the economy.

About this time, Stalin put a new kind of migration to work for in-dustrialization, uprooting masses of peasants from their homes and dumping them into remote labor camps. The peoples of Central Asia also had to pay their tribute to these murderous forced migrations.

Since Stalin, however, his successors have tried to govern to a cer-tain extent on the basis of the people's consent, and the days of those great migrations are over. To attract workers to the construction sites of the Far North, they must be paid higher wages than the oth-ers. The question is whether the incentives used to draw labor to deficit areas—special pay scales for inhospitable regions, the attrac-tion of big cities, the chance to give children a better education—are sufficient to lure the Central Asian peoples away from their native land. This question cannot be answered without placing the migra-tion problem within the overall context of the USSR and comparing the behavior patterns of all the peoples living there.

Prior to the 1970 census the lack of detailed statistics prevented a clear picture of population movements. Since then, however, a growing body of information has enabled us to gain a better under-standing of the scope and direction of those movements over the past twenty years.[13] Essentially, the Soviet population is moving along four axes: (1) from the country to the city; (2) from the city to the country; (3) from one rural area to another; (4) from one city to another. These migrations also occur within a single region, or from one region to another.

When we consider the diverse directions taken by the migrants, we find that, on the whole, the Soviet population moves a great deal. Every year at least 15 million persons change their place of resi-dence.[14] These movements take place chiefly from city to city (38.1%), country-city (31.4%), country-country (17.8%) and city-country (12.7%).

The figures reveal that the center of attraction is certainly the city and that the rural areas are being depopulated. In addition, surveys have shown that the slight city-country movement involves primarily older people who leave the cities as they finish their active work lives. But these figures are only averages, concealing important variations from one republic to another. The migrations from one city to another are particularly large in Central Asia and the Caucasus, where they represent a considerable share of the migratory flow: 58.7% in Turkmenia, 50.6% in Azerbaidzhan, 41.5% in Armenia, 40.6% in Uzbekistan, 40% in Tadzhikistan, and everywhere else, 30% to 40% of the flow. At the other end of the scale, in Moldavia, city-city migration accounts for 25.4% of the total.

By contrast, country-city movement affects Central Asia and the Caucasus less than other republics with two exceptions: Armenia (33.5%) and Kirghizia (33%). But this trend is strong in Moldavia (43.3%), Belorussia (42%), and the Ukraine (33%). Lastly, Georgia (31.3%) stands exactly at the national average.[15]

Coupled with differences in the structure of migratory flows are differences in the size of those flows. The republics most affected by migration are the RSFSR (17,395,000 persons in 1968–1969), the Ukraine (4,385,000), Kazakhstan (2,073,000). Elsewhere, we find fewer than a million migrants; the lowest figure was recorded by Uzbekistan (289,600 entries and 372,300 exits in 1968–1969). The Uzbek example illustrates another peculiar feature of Soviet migratory flows, i.e., the contrast—despite fairly universal mobility—between republics receiving added population (the RSFSR, the Ukraine, Belorussia, Lithuania, Armenia, Estonia) and those lacking immigration, which is the case for all of Central Asia and the Caucasus excepting Armenia, and which is now beginning to characterize Moldavia.[16]

Whether Soviet populations migrate more or less, and whether the migrations within the respective republics occur more from one city to another, or from country to city, these differences in the extent and direction of migratory flows must not conceal the very general nature of the population movements. The USSR is in constant movement. But does this perpetual movement drastically alter the national distribution of each republic? Does it disperse all the national groups evenly? Does it likewise prepare those groups for subsequent dispersals? Our first answer can be found by analyzing the distribution of national groups in their respective republics and outside, between 1959 and 1970 (see Table 22).

Contrary to the illusions formerly cherished by Khrushchev, this table shows that migratory flows and national dispersion are far from coinciding. Except for the Russians and Belorussians, all the national groups were more heavily concentrated in their respective republics in 1970 than they were ten years before. This process of group concentration within national boundaries is particularly noteworthy in the case of one nation with a very sizable diaspora, Armenia, and in the case of low-birth nations like the Baltic ones. This change in the situation of the Armenians was probably due to demographic behavior differences between Armenians of the republic (who have a very high birth rate) and those of the diaspora who seem to adopt the demographic behavior of the locality in which they happen to reside. In the case of the Balts, we see a clear-cut return of dispersed Balts to their own republics.

Despite this sizable difference between nationalities which are dispersing and nationalities which are gathering together, our first impression from the foregoing table is one of uniformity. The proportion of members of one national community living within its borders compared to the total group varies relatively little from the one group to the other. With the exception of some particularly concentrated nations (Georgians, Balts, and Turkmenians) almost all the national groups have about 80% to 85% of their members in their republic, and some 15% to 20% are dispersed. What are we to conclude from this? Is there a comparable situation everywhere with a relatively stable proportion of members cut off from their group, living in an alien setting, and hence easier to assimilate?

In other words, are all the national groups being dispersed at random throughout the entire Soviet Union, or are there different situations for the diasporas? As already noted, the Russian dispersion is a traditional factor characterizing the history of both the Empire and the USSR. The Russians are represented everywhere; but clearly the direction of their movements has changed.

What we see between 1959 and 1970 is an emigration of Russians from Georgia, expressed as a reduction in their number, and in addition an emigration from Azerbaidzhan and Armenia, while their number increases everywhere else. In the same way, the Ukrainians, of whom 5.5 million live outside the Ukraine, "received" about 1 million Russians[18] between 1959 and 1970, while during the same period they bolstered their numbers in every Soviet republic, with the exception of the RSFSR.[19] Their most sizable gains were chalked

Table 22
**Proportion of the Official Nationality Living
in its Own Republic Compared to the Total
Nationality Group in the Whole USSR**[17]
(in percentages)

Nationality	1959	1970
Russians	85.8	83.5
Ukrainians	86.3	86.6
Belorussians	82.5	80.5
Uzbeks	83.8	84.0
Kazakhs	77.2	79.9
Georgians	96.6	96.5
Azeris	84.9	96.2
Lithuanians	92.5	94.1
Moldavians	85.2	86.2
Latvians	92.7	93.8
Kirghiz	86.4	88.5
Tadzhiks	75.2	76.3
Armenians	55.7	62.0
Turkmenians	92.2	92.9
Estonians	90.3	91.8

up in Kirghizia (+87%), Latvia (+82%), Estonia (+85%), Turkmenia (+66%), and Belorussia (+43%). Like the Russians, the Ukrainians are beginning to withdraw from Georgia.[20] The great spread of Belorussians—one-fifth of this ethnic group—is headed mainly for the other Slavic republics (964,000 Belorussians live in Russia), Kazakhstan, and the Baltic republics.[21] Thus, the migratory flows of the Slavs are carrying them to all the republics in the Soviet Union.

Does this situation hold true for the Central Asians or Caucasians living outside their respective republics? Are they following the same course as the Russians and Belorussians but just the other way around? The position of the official nationalities in the five large republics of Central Asia is summarized in Table 23, which shows quite clearly that the migrations of the Central Asian peoples cannot be compared to those of the Slavic peoples. The peoples of Central Asia are emigrating toward neighboring republics that share the same civilization. Only the Kazakhs have a large community in European Russia. But for all the other peoples, the share of those leaving the region is negligible; they are composed mainly of persons attached to central political and cultural organs whose presence in the federal capital attests to the existence of federalism.

The situation of the Caucasus is slightly different, but at the same

Table 23
Geographic Distribution of the Peoples of Central Asia [22]

Nations	Total Number	Kazakhstan	Uzbekistan	Kirghizia	Tadzhikistan	Turkmenia	Elsewhere
Kazakhs	5,299,000	**4,234,000**	476,000	22,000	8,000	69,000	468,000 (RSFSR)
Uzbeks	9,195,000	216,000	**7,725,000**	333,000	666,000	179,000	76,000
Kirghiz	1,452,000		111,000	**1,285,000**	35,000		21,000
Tadzhiks	2,136,000		449,000	22,000	**1,630,000**		35,000
Turkmenians	1,525,000		71,000			**1,417,000**	37,000

time it is far removed from the Slavic model[23] (see Table 24). While the Azerbaidzhanis and Armenians have emigrated rather freely into the neighboring republics, the Georgians are more concentrated. Furthermore, within the three groups the share of nationals residing in the RSFSR is much larger than the share for peoples originally from Central Asia. The weight of the past explains this orientation toward the capital, as well as the longstanding role played by the Armenians and Georgians in the central government and in the diverse institutions surrounding it. Their traditional, historical ties with Russia and their high level of culture have contributed to this leaning.

Table 24
Geographic Distribution of the Peoples of the Caucasus

	Total number	Armenia	Azerbaidzhan	Georgia	Elsewhere
Armenians	3,559,000	**2,208,000**	484,000	452,000	414,000 (299,000 in RSFSR)
Azeris	4,380,000	148,000	**3,777,000**	218,000	237,000 (96,000 in RSFSR)
Georgians	3,245,000			**3,131,000**	114,000 (69,000 in RSFSR)

This brief incursion into the national makeup of the states and of neighboring regions serves to emphasize the contrast between the two parts of the USSR. On the one hand, there are peoples who have been dispersing continuously, mingling with all the other peoples of the Soviet Union in distant migrations. On the other hand, there are peoples concentrated in the region where their civilization is predominant. These peoples move readily from one republic to another, but always within their own cultural area. On balance, their ties with the other peoples of the Soviet Union are very weak or dependent on the presence of others on their soil. Their attachment to their background is only one of the features that makes them different from the rest.

In addition to these purely regional migrations, mention should be made of a behavioral difference between city and country dwellers of this general area, compared to the behavior for the same categories in the rest of the USSR. It has already been noted that, on the whole, migratory flows result mainly in the movement of country dwellers to the cities. That these migrations adversely affect the rural areas is easy to understand in a country where urbanization and industrialization have been going on constantly since the turn of the century, and where the great migrators are primarily those from rural areas.

On this point Central Asia and the Caucasus represent exceptions to the rule prevailing in the rest of the country. The farmers stay in the country and are infinitely less migratory than city dwellers. The inhabitants of Central Asian cities move, as we have already observed, from one city to the other. In the Caucasus city dwellers move slightly more than the rural people but, on the whole, both categories remain attached to their birthplace. This difference in behavior in comparison with the other peoples of the USSR is important on two levels; on the one hand because it reveals particular attitudes, and on the other because of the very dimensions of the phenomenon. Table 25 gives some idea of this.[24]

Can the rural population's attachment to the country in the southern borderlands be attributed to lagging urbanization that has not created outlets for rural migrations? Is the contrast between the two types of behavior linked to a contrast between a largely urbanized country and one where this process has hardly started? Here again a comparison of the data suggests that in dealing with the very special development of the southern peoples of the USSR, the classic explanations are of little help. To demonstrate this, it is necessary only to look at Chart IV,[25] which traces the history of urbanization in the Soviet Union from 1926 to 1975.

The Chart shows clearly that the urbanization process has had a very pronounced effect on Transcaucasia, while affecting Central Asia (except Kazakhstan) to a lesser degree. Nevertheless, urbanization in Central Asia has been a very steady and continuous process. In both regions the stability of the rural population is an obvious factor, contrasting with the greater population movements in places where urbanization has followed a comparable trend, for instance in Moldavia.

This regional or national differentiation in the structure of migratory flows was clearly noted by the Soviet authorities who, after

Table 25
**Comparative Migrations of Urban and Rural Dwellers
by Republics and Economic Regions**

Republics or economic regions	Number of migrants per 1,000 inhabitants		Frequency of rural dwellers' migrations compared to urban dwellers (urban dwellers = 100)
	Urban dwellers	Rural dwellers	
USSR	**51.8**	**64.7**	**124.9**
RSFSR	55.4	83.9	151.4
Northwest region	50.2	90.4	180.1
Central region	34.2	69.3	202.6
Volga-Vyatka region	47.9	77.2	161.2
Central Chernozen region	44.8	55.3	123.4
Volga region	48.3	72.9	150.9
North Caucasus region	58.9	62.3	105.8
Ural	65.9	102.8	150.0
Western Siberia	72.1	121.6	168.7
Eastern Siberia	86.7	128.5	148.2
Far East	101.1	147.1	145.5
Ukraine SSR	41.7	51.5	123.5
Baltic countries	41.7	63.2	151.6
Transcaucasus economic region	28.1	23.1	85.1
Central Asia economic region	46.7	25.1	53.7
Kazakhstan	75.5	85.5	113.2
Belorussian region	50.2	51.6	102.8
Moldavian SSR	48.2	42.4	88.0

1970, carried out many surveys aimed at analyzing all aspects of the phenomenon and its causes. These surveys supplemented general statistical data which emphasized regional peculiarities to the detriment of specifically national traits. The basic question which arises is whether in any given area, the entire population, including all the nationalities, is following the same behavior patterns, or whether the behavior patterns are peculiar to given nationalities. In other words, as regards the development of Central Asian cities, is this due to a movement of the whole local population toward the cities (which would contradict the data indicating low mobility of the native peasantry), or can it be ascribed to a natural growth of the population already residing in the cities? Or, lastly, is the urbanization there the result of the influx of migrants alien to Central Asia?

The ethnographic surveys carried out in the last few years provide

clear answers in this regard. In the first place, the behavior of nationalities originating in Central Asia is infinitely more sedentary or regional than that of the overall population residing in the region. The
1970 census brought out that, at the time they were queried, 5.7%
of the Soviet citizens had been living at their place of residence for
less than two years. This proportion fell to between 1.5% to 2% for
all the nationalities of Central Asiatic origin.[26] In a more general
way, it emerges from the census that all the nationalities having a recent migration rate of less than 2% belong to the Turko-Moslem
group, with the lowest figure being reached by the Azerbaidzhanis.

Surveys explain this situation. For instance, rural dwellers were
asked the question: "Are you planning to move to the city? If so,
when?". Some 16% of the Russian peasants in the Kaliningrad region answered affirmatively, and 11% indicated that they intended
to carry out this idea in the next two years. In Uzbekistan, on the
other hand, the adherents of such a change dropped to 5.5%, while
those planning to move in the near future fell to 2.9%.[27]

This weak attraction of the city for the rural Central Asian population has been confirmed by other surveys, such as the one in Turkmenia designed to determine the origin of new city dwellers. This
survey proved highly instructive since it showed that the new city
dwellers were not primarily former Turkmenian peasants, but were
immigrants who had come from other republics. The survey also revealed that, far from keeping pace with urbanization, the attraction
of the city has tended to diminish. In 1960, the Turkmenian
countryside furnished 68% of the new city dwellers, but in 1970, it
supplied only 27%.[28] These indices suggest that Central Asian farmers not only are not strongly attracted by the urban setting, but that
there is actual migration out of the cities back into the country. This
kind of movement, which statistics indicate is taking place throughout the USSR, generally involves older people. But in Central Asia
the movement away from the city concerns young men and women
who are unable to adjust to city living. This weak attraction of the
city is easy to understand in view of the socio-demographic conditions of Central Asia and the Moslem Caucasus.

Despite advances in urbanization in these regions, the rural population is quite largely predominant. This segment of the population
also accounts for the greatest gains in the demographic rise of these
non-Russian peoples. Everywhere else the shrinking and aging of
the rural population gives rural life its residual aspect and encour-

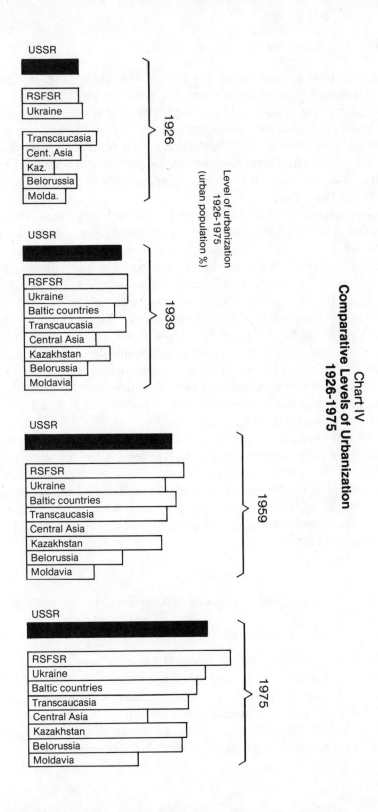

Chart IV
Comparative Levels of Urbanization
1926-1975

Level of urbanization
1926-1975
(urban population %)

1926

USSR

RSFSR
Ukraine

Transcaucasia
Cent. Asia
Kaz.
Belorussia
Molda.

1939

USSR

RSFSR
Ukraine
Baltic countries
Transcaucasia
Central Asia
Kazakhstan
Belorussia
Moldavia

1959

USSR

RSFSR
Ukraine
Baltic countries
Transcaucasia
Central Asia
Kazakhstan
Belorussia
Moldavia

1975

USSR

RSFSR
Ukraine
Baltic countries
Transcaucasia
Central Asia
Kazakhstan
Belorussia
Moldavia

ages the young, dynamic people to flee the countryside. In Central Asia, on the contrary, the countryside is the center of gravity for the indigenous nationalities. There the population is young, active, and little contaminated by outside influences. The immigrants are going into the cities, not to the countryside which represents a too homogenous setting for them. Conversely, the presence of Russians or Ukrainians in the cities breaks up the homogeneity of the local national society, altering the native culture.

Given these conditions, it is understandable that the nations of Central Asia or of the Caucasus regard the countryside as the preferred place for national life, and only venture into the cities with caution. Later on, we shall discuss this point, which is decisive for the future of the demographically strong regions. We must conclude, as Basile Kerblay[29] has done, that great migrations are a centuries-old characteristic of Russian history. But at the same time, when we examine this history, we find that it has two components: (1) the peoples who are spreading continuously, notably the Russians; and (2) the peoples anchored in their native setting, who seem to have lived through this past century untouched by great dispersals, principally the Moslem peoples as a whole and, to a lesser extent, the Christian peoples of the Caucasus.

Can this situation be maintained when the economic effects of demographic imbalances make themselves felt? What solutions can be found to the problems of employment and the allocation of resources in the face of such an uneven distribution of the active work force? Can migrations be organized in areas where they have never taken place, and can the Soviet population be redistributed in spite of acquired habits?

Redistribution of Population
or
Redistribution of Resources?

The USSR is presently facing a critical situation, one that affects the country as a whole. In this regard, three factors are crucial: (1) the scarcity of labor intensified by the distribution of the population; (2) the highly spontaneous, anarchic, and economic nature of migrations in recent times; and (3) the present economic situation in Central Asia which makes it ill-prepared to receive an increase in population.

The problem of the labor shortage needs no further discussion, but it is important to understand that the orientation of migratory flows, as they have developed in the post-Khrushchevian period with the relaxation of government pressure on the individual, has led to a situation that hardly lends itself to economic progress. The example of the Russian migrants, who are the more numerous, reveals the chaotic aspects of Soviet population movements.

Table 26 gives a very definite impression of organization. Each region of Russia has particular ties with certain republics. But the table also reveals startling weaknesses. First of all, there is out-migration from the Urals, Siberia, and the Far East—all regions short of labor—but no movement toward any of those places. The Russian dispersion, which in the past had made it possible to start the development of the most inhospitable regions, tends to turn toward the more attractive regions where the need for labor is not so great.

Table 26
Direction of Migratory Flows [30]

RSFSR Economic regions Country (regions moved from)	Federated Republics Cities (regions moved to)
Northwest	Estonia, Latvia, Belorussia
Center	Belorussia, Estonia, Latvia
Volga-Vyatka	Kazakhstan
Central Chernozen	Ukraine
Volga region	Uzbekistan, Turkmenia, Tadzhikistan
North Caucasus	Azerbaidzhan, Turkmenia, Armenia
Ural	Uzbekistan, Tadzhikistan, Kazakhstan
Western Siberia	Kirghizia, Kazakhstan
Eastern Siberia	Lithuania, Kirghizia
Far East	Georgia, Kirghizia

The flow pushing the peasants of the Northwest toward the Baltic republics illuminates this. The countryside of the Russian Northwest has reached a critical stage of depopulation, particularly in the Novgorod and Pskov regions, and the kolkhozes (collective farms) and sovkhozes (state farms) there are suffering from a labor shortage which affects their productive capacity. Nevertheless, the peasants of these regions flock to the Baltic cities where the new arrivals must compete for jobs with peasants who are natives there.[31] As these republics greatly attract Russian peasants, this migratory trend presents the twofold drawback of further depopulating Russian agricultural regions already suffering from labor scarcity, and creating national tensions in the newcomers' place of arrival, especially as the urban labor force tends to be too heavily concentrated in the Baltic republics.

Likewise, in Central Asia we observe the negative effects of Russian migrations. The migrants who leave Siberia or the Urals are going to create deficiencies in regions already very short of labor, exactly where the government is trying desperately to retain the work force on a permanent basis. On the other hand, they hold urban jobs in regions where the rising population and the determination of the government to break the homogeneity of national village life should lead to intense internal rural-urban migration. But the massive arrival of Russians is presently leaving little room for the increased urbanization of the indigenous population. Moreover, the arrival of the Russians is following a rather peculiar course in this region. The immigrants often stop off in the villages, notably in the region of Kirghizia, before proceeding on the second leg of their journey to the city.

Similarly, North Caucasus, which on the whole has a surplus of labor, maintains a favorable migratory balance despite a movement of rural people toward other republics, because the climate attracts many immigrants. These examples demonstrate the difficulties Soviet authorities face in their quest for a rational organization of the labor force, in a society where, with a lessening of constraints, individuals organize their lives as they see fit.

Perhaps the major cause for the Soviet government's anxieties over the future is to be found in Central Asia itself. The problem here is the economic capacity of Central Asia to confront its own demographic development. The primary consequence of the demographic increase here is a certain overpopulation of the countryside, a situation which had already been recognized by Soviet experts at a time when the impact of this increase had not yet been fully felt.[32] The density of the agrarian population has risen sharply, far exceeding the national average. While in the RSFSR there are 0.4 persons per cultivated hectare, and 0.7 in the Ukraine, the proportion is roughly tripled in Central Asia, reaching 2.1 in Uzbekistan and 2.4 in Tadjikistan. In the Caucasus human pressure on the land is even higher, reaching a density of 3.3 in Georgia.[33]

This change has taken place in a short span of time, inasmuch as the 1959 census showed that the number of persons in the region living on cultivated soil varied only slightly from the prewar figure. This sudden overpopulation raises two distinct problems. To what extent is the mechanization of agriculture, the goal pursued by the government, going to aggravate the labor problem? On the other hand, can new lands be reclaimed in Central Asia for the benefit of the increasing numbers of inhabitants?

The first point calls for a negative answer. Central Asia is chiefly a cotton-growing region, and cotton has considerable importance for the USSR. The traditional farm methods are costly. Mechanization makes it possible to lower the costs and increase the yields. The efforts begun in Central Asia on this score hardly seem reversible, and in addition the government has no intention of abandoning its goals.[34] It is therefore clear that mechanization implies fewer jobs just when workers are becoming more plentiful.

Is it possible to extend the area under cultivation indefinitely? The answer to this question depends on the climate and the nature of the soil. The number of irrigation projects has multiplied in recent years but, actually, irrigation has led to the reclamation of only about 5 percent more territory between 1960 and 1970.[35] Even a sizable increase in irrigation—assuming the soil lent itself to this— would in no way make it possible to keep pace with population gains. In addition, the newly irrigated areas also benefit from the mechanization program intended to offset the large investments made for irrigation. Therefore, human labor would not represent more than a small share in this process. Mechanization further complicates the problem, inasmuch as it demands qualified workers trained in technical schools, while the indigenous population is still far from being able to supply these technicians. One of the reasons for this difficulty is that the technical schools are usually located in urban centers, and parents are reluctant to send their offspring to schools far from home, in an alien environment. For this reason, technical jobs in the countryside are usually held by immigrants, Russians or Ukrainians, who are thus competing with the natives in a tight job market.

Couldn't the surplus labor force in the countryside be steered toward the city and employed in local industry? The economic development of Central Asia is ill-suited to a drastic rerouting of the work force from the countryside to the city. Central Asia is chiefly a producer of raw materials and, as such, is less developed industrially than the rest of the USSR. The economic specialization against which its national cadres fought so hard in the 1930s is now taken for granted. The dangers inherent in that specialization can be measured today.

With the exception of Kazakhstan, the Central Asian republics are chiefly engaged in cotton-growing and livestock raising. Related industries, such as food processing and textile manufacturing, have sprung up around this basic production, but the proportion between this production and the related industries is still markedly in favor of agriculture.

The last five-year plan makes it difficult to foresee any dramatic upswing in heavy industry, which would require considerable investments and a system for transporting the necessary iron. Iron is plentiful in Kazakhstan, which is the Soviet Union's third-ranking producer of iron ore. As a source of raw materials for industry, the republic plays a major economic role, but since the First Five-Year Plan (1928–32), the great resources of the republic, iron and ore, have been earmarked for Russia's heavy industry.

The Kazakh resources have been instrumental in the development of the Ural factories and the new industrial regions of Siberia. Both of these regions also depend on Kazakhstan's farm produce. But any rerouting of these resources to Central Asia seems highly unlikely, for it would entail the weakened productive capacity of industries already at a very high level of development.

An important foreign policy factor must also be mentioned in this regard. Central Asia, next door to China, would represent—if it were to become highly industrialized—an added attraction for a China in search of rapid development. Given the state of Sino-Soviet relations, the USSR has every reason not to give decisive, attractive importance to this region whose population belongs more to the East than to Europe. The demands of the economy and the proximity of China explain why Central Asia's paths to development are so narrow. These two factors also explain why, confronted with the problem of surplus labor in the region, government planners seem hesitant about promoting large-scale solutions[36]—for the moment, at any rate.

Actually, there seems to be no clear-cut choice as yet; hence, any definitive decision is left to waver between two poles. On the one hand, there is strong pressure both in Moscow and the borderlands in favor of industrial development in Central Asia, a measure intended to solve labor-supply problems there. Since 1971, Gosplan (State Planning Committee) experts have been calling for the rapid construction of industrial complexes that demand a great deal of manpower—machine building, chemicals, and food processing.[37] This idea gained support in the Gosplan during the 1970s, and its partisans have been basing their arguments increasingly on the local population's low mobility, a factor that they take for granted.[38]

The keynote for the advocates of this theory is that economic decisions in coming years will have to be based on local situations, namely, the existing distribution of the labor force, which can only lead to important economic development in regions well-supplied with manpower. Having said this, the Gosplan experts do not advocate a complete overturn of the economy, but suggest introducing industries in Central Asia which would be appropriate to existing conditions and local resources. But they are thereby solving only one aspect of the problem, that of the surplus labor force, and offer no answer to the other problem, that stemming from the demography. Who would work in the regions of labor shortages—precisely where all the USSR's heavy industry is located?

Rather, the problem of the labor-deficit areas seems to justify the opposing stand of other experts who defend the notion of "rational distribution of labor resources." Here, the approach is different. It is based on the unorganized, spontaneous nature of migratory flows and the gap existing between the general interest and individual initiatives. In a collective study published in 1974, various authors observed that migratory flows did not coincide, or coincided only slightly, with needs. Hence, they concluded that migration had to be regulated within the framework of a clear economic plan.[39] This idea was taken up and formulated in specific terms by A. Topilin, an economist who inferred from the Plenum of the Party's Central Committee in December 1974 that the Party's fundamental choice regarding the economy was aimed at a rational allocation of labor resources, hence at their redistribution.[40]

Analyzing the various methods of redistributing labor, Topilin wrote: "In order to overcome the growing shortage of labor resources, we must put an end to the lack of coordination reigning in the diverse territorial means of distributing the work force. This coordination, which covers the extent and direction of organized recruitment, migrations and appeals for various projects, should be handled by the Soviet Union's Gosplan on the basis of unique plans for the redistribution of labor resources."[41]

In this context, it is interesting to see how organized recruitment and social appeals are being related to migration. Organized recruiting (*Orgnabor*) held an honored place during the years of intensive industrialization as a method of transferring the work force from the country to the city. This method aims at regional redistribution of labor and its allocation to the most deficient sectors. According to experts, this method assures the hiring of workers suited to the needs of a given place and enterprise. In addition, the system should make it possible to supply labor to the areas which are most disadvantaged and at the same time vital to the economy—Siberia, the Far East, and the Far North.

The drawback is that the workers recruited for these regions are attracted by high salaries for only a limited period, which makes the investment in training unprofitable. "To retain the cadres recruited by *Orgnabor*, we would have to do everything possible to encourage family migration, which in 1969–1970 accounted for only 6% of the workers sent by Orgnabor."[42]

Up to now, family migration has been applied chiefly to the agricultural sector. Technical cadres—tractor operators, mechanics, etc. are sent to state farms in backward regions with a view to promoting progress there. Thus, for the period 1961–1970, nearly 20,000 mechanics came to bolster farm personnel in the southern districts of the Far East. To facilitate this type of migration, one of the more specific proposals calls for sending to the same village several families from one village, to mitigate the problems of initial isolation and adaptation in an alien setting.

The third kind of organized migration involves social appeals. It is a question here of meeting, in a very short span of time, the manpower needs in regions where natural conditions or isolation scarcely promote voluntary migration, or even organized social migration. Most of those answering the appeals are not workers but mostly Komsomol-led youths and young demobilized soldiers, mainly peasants, for whom this experience in remote areas represents an almost compulsory transition from military life to normal integration in the working world.

Nevertheless, this kind of migration has its drawbacks. Based on the zeal of the young recruits, migration of this type is characterized by the migrants' own restlessness. Shortly after reaching the remote assignment where they are needed, they request transfers to other enterprises or even leave the region. In fact, the problem is reminiscent of the one that usually arises over the fulfillment of plans. Each Communist organization—Komsomol most of all—must demonstrate its enthusiasm for great, far-off projects by having a certain contingent of volunteers ready to participate in it. Beyond this, however, the guidelines for the utilization of this work force remain vague. "The Central Committee of the Komsomol, in conjunction with the Gosplan, decides on the number of young people who are to answer this social appeal, and their approximate distribution in the various regions where they are being sent. After receiving their orders, these young people are still free to change jobs and even leave the region to which they have been assigned. Nobody assumes responsibility . . . it's deplorable."[43]

How can this situation be remedied? Two avenues have been suggested: first, a detailed plan for the temporary utilization of these young people; and secondly, strict control of their activities during the period in which they work as volunteers. Furthermore, this recruiting program should not be limited to a male labor force, but should aim at a balance of the sexes, to help keep volunteers from wanting to return to sunnier climes.

The experience of the Baikal-Amur Mainline illustrates these recruitment problems remarkably well. Working conditions in the Baikal-Amur region are so hard that female workers, despite all efforts to recruit them, are used for very different jobs and in other places, notably in the administration of the Trans-Siberian Railway. Meanwhile, the isolation and restlessness of the male labor force are major factors in its instability, hindering work on the railroad.

All the solutions proposed run in the same direction, i.e., they see the labor force as a mobile asset and move it to economic centers, rather than trying to gear economic choices to labor distribution. To implement this solution, several conditions must be met: (1) very stringent planning of labor policy, which must take into consideration problems related to the Union as a whole, not just to regions; (2) tighter controls than those now existing over individual movements and decisions; (3) a will to offset the relatively authoritarian or controlled nature of the policy proposed by relying largely on sentimental or material incentives. The moving of whole families to break the isolation of the worker recruited by organized placement, the grouping of several families in a single place so as not to break ties with the original community, the attempt to balance the number of men and women in the case of temporary migrations of young people are all steps intended to humanize displacements.

Migrations and Material Incentives

At the heart of this program lie material incentives. Salaries, housing, schools—every means must be used to induce migrants to leave their native homesteads and to settle permanently, or at least for a relatively long time, in labor-deficient areas. Th's theory of labor redistribution has an obvious advantage over the theory of adapting the economy to the existing work force. It makes it possible to meet the Soviet Union's economic needs, partially at least if not totally. This theory alone enables the more economically advanced regions to avoid stagnation and hence a recession in the Soviet economy. For relying only on the regions rich in manpower would create serious problems in all the great economic regions.

This being the case, perhaps two solutions should be considered: first, the local utilization of the existing labor supply through huge investments; and secondly, the maintenance of economic capacity in old industrial regions and in regions presently being developed through the importation of foreign workers. There are many indications that Soviet planners have entertained the idea of using foreign labor. Certain extensive projects carried on jointly by the USSR and other socialist countries involve the use of workers from those countries.[44] An example of this is the Orenburg gas pipeline. Likewise, foreign labor is employed at Soviet work sites, in virtue of trade agreements, exchanging raw materials or consumer goods for manpower. This is the case for the Bulgarians and, in all probability, the rather large number of Koreans in the USSR. Finally, workers from non-Communist countries come there—chiefly from Finland,[45] and even from the Western European countries. It is difficult to make an exact estimate of the number of foreign workers in the USSR; figures ranging from 50,000 to 160,000[46] have been cited. Nevertheless, it is clear that these workers cannot make up for the USSR's lack of workers. At best, their coming may offset the limited but steady flow of voluntary emigrants—Jews, Germans, and Armenians—who have been leaving since the early 1970s.[47]

Since it is apparent that any policy which does not entail moving manpower to the labor-deficient areas would have very serious economic consequences, the question arises as to how the Soviet government can organize such migrations on a large scale? To succeed, the government must obtain the good will of the people concerned, which it is believed should result from the advantages offered and from personal needs. One example of the regime's use of material incentives to encourage migration is the decree issued in May 1973 by the USSR Council of Ministers on "the new advantages granted to citizens who settle on the collective and state farms." This decree concerned the *kolkhozes* and *sovkhozes* located in the Soviet area bordering China. It provided for granting many important advantages to the new settlers—bonuses, vacations, and the possibility of buying cars and motorcycles.[48]

To what extent can such incentives bring about a movement of Central Asia's surplus work force to the labor-deficient regions? To what degree do they meet the real needs of the population? It is very difficult to make an equitable judgment in this regard, since there is such contradictory information about the present material situation of the Central Asian peoples. The Soviet authorities constantly claim that the levels of development in the republics have converged almost to the point of equality, and that the standard of living among the people of the borderlands is often higher than that of people living in the Central region.[49] Foreign observers who have visited Central Asia generally confirm this point, stressing the disparity that exists between center and periphery, to the latter's advantage.

A Western study for the year 1970 showed that the incomes of *kolkhoz* households were higher in the five Central Asian republics than in the USSR in general, and the Slavic republics in particular.[50] The periphery's more favorable position has, in all likelihood, been strengthened by the price differences existing in the various regions. In this regard, a survey carried out by Soviet researchers has furnished valuable information on the standard of living in the Moslem republics. In this survey the cost of groceries to feed a family of four, calculated at 100 in the central areas, went down to 97.7 in Kazakhstan and to 90.3 in this region's four other republics.[51] These figures indicate life is easy enough in Central Asia to offer no incentive to the inhabitants to go elsewhere for higher wages.

But this data does not entirely reflect the true situation, which is complicated by several variables, the most important being the difference in family size. If we go from family income to income per person living in a household, it becomes clear that the number of children—hence, demography—can alter comparisons hitherto favorable to Central Asia. The income of the *kolkhozniks* in the various republics of the Soviet Union can be ranked as shown in Table 27.

This table[52] shows that by taking family size into account, the rank of republics by income is completely altered. In terms of family income, Central Asia and the Caucasus stand above the national average and among the frontrunners, whereas the Slavic republics and also Moldavia stand at the very bottom of the ladder and below the average.

But when it comes to income per person, the breakdown is entirely different. Three compact, clearly differentiated groups appear: (1) the rich, namely, the farmers in the three Baltic republics; (2) the Slavs, Georgians and Moldavians, ranking just above and below the national average; and (3) the poor, i.e., the peasants of all the Moslem republics, plus Armenia, who all rank very much below the national average and whose income is sometimes less than half the average Balt income. This situation can be extended in a general way to the USSR's overall rural population, including the *sovkhozniks*.[53] If we add to this that the income of the rural population has been estimated at 87.4%[54] of the industrial workers' income, and

Table 27
Incomes of Soviet Kolkhozniks
(National Average = Index 100)

Republic	Annual income per family	Republic	Annual income per family member
Turkmenia	140	Estonia	182
Lithuania	136	Latvia	151
Estonia	127	Lithuania	143
Georgia	127	Ukraine	109
Armenia	122	RSFSR	108
Uzbekistan	120	Belorussia	107
Kazakhstan	119	Georgia	106
Latvia	119	Moldavia	98
Kirghizia	107	Turkmenia	78
Azerbaidzhan	106	Kazakhstan	77
Tadzhikistan	105	Armenia	77
RSFSR	99	Kirghizia	71
Belorussia	98	Uzbekistan	68
Moldavia	97	Azerbaidzhan	65
Ukraine	91	Tadzhikistan	58

that the indigenous population of Central Asia and the Caucasus is more heavily engaged in agriculture than industry, we can conclude that the income per capita for the majority of the population in these non-Russian areas is lower than the national average.

The migratory flows that have taken place until now barely correspond with Table 27, at least with its lower part. It stands to reason that the populations of the Baltic republics, which enjoy full employment and high incomes, do not want to move. It also stands to reason—and this is borne out by the facts—that high incomes and available jobs siphon the inhabitants of the central regions to these republics. On the other hand, based solely on the statistical data, it is inexplicable why Central Asian workers do not move towards areas offering employment opportunities and higher incomes.

The stability of the borderland populations demonstrates one of two things: either that there is no absolute necessity for them to emigrate, or that their attachment to their native region is a stronger factor than the difficulties of everyday existence. This second hypothesis leads one to doubt the effectiveness of material incentives in promoting migratory flows toward the center.

While there are clearly problems of employment and income in the borderlands, problems that can be expected to grow worse, the statistical data concerning income must be weighed against other factors, particularly the material and emotional conditions of the environment. On the whole, Central Asia and the Caucasus enjoy favorable climate conditions that make it difficult for those born there to adapt to the rigorous weather of the Center, and especially of Siberia. The climate has an impact on the lifestyle and eating habits that help make everyday life easier for the population. Thus, fruits and vegetables, which are gradually increasing in the diet of Soviet citizens, are a luxury that weighs heavily on incomes in Russia and most of the labor-deficit regions, while in the southern borderlands these foods are grown by the farmers for their own consumption and therefore represent an increment to their income.

Likewise, the traditional lifestyles prevailing in the borderlands—housing shared by several generations, children cared for by their mother or by a close relative, little or no consumption of alcoholic beverages in the Moslem regions[55]—reduce a number of expenses that burden family budgets elsewhere. Also, a self-sufficient economy generally is significant wherever family agriculture prevails. In this respect, it is worth noting that in Lithuania and Latvia, where farm income is very high, this self-sufficiency is also very high. A single Central Asian republic, Kazakhstan, escapes this rule, owing to the number of state farms in that region. But we should bear in mind that Kazakhstan also represents the only republic where the official population is in the minority.[56]

The conclusion that can be reached from these contradictory facts regarding the everyday situation of the people of Central Asia—where the major problems of the future will be, namely, those of labor and employment—is that these republics present an image of prosperity, even if the average inhabitant of Central Asia has a lower income, compared to his counterpart in the western republics. This image of prosperity cannot be totally false. It stems from an environment, habits, and behavior patterns peculiar to this region, all of which explain why it is so hard to uproot the people born there. Nevertheless, this apparent prosperity cannot conceal the real problems, immediate or impending, that lurk in the background.

How are these problems to be resolved? In terms of a change of attitudes? In terms of a break—even a physical one—with the established life of the milieu? Or, on the contrary, will they be seen in terms of demands on the Soviet authorities for a better distribution of resources and potentials throughout the entire area under their administration? This question holds true not only for the inhabitants of Central Asia, but for all the great national groups of the USSR, which now face a double challenge in determining their relations to one another and to the overall family of states to which they belong. There is the challenge of a central government that affirms the growing unity of the people in the standardization of economic conditions and of cultural development, and there is the challenge of an economy that is confronted with problems arising from divergent demographic choices or behavior.

CHAPTER IV

The Forces of Integration: Political and Military Power

S oviet society can be seen and described in two diametrically opposite ways: first, as a multi-ethnic society in which differences have suddenly grown deeper as a result of demographic divergences; or secondly, as a new society in which the integrating forces outweigh the differences and operate steadily to foster unity. The latter concept prevails in the 1977 Soviet Constitution.[1] In both hypotheses the role of the central government is decisive. Whether acting as an integrating force or as a tool for controlling diversity, the central authority can have a determinant influence on the future of Soviet society. It is therefore important to see how the Soviet government deals with the problem of nationalities and what future trend can be discerned in its functioning and options.

The Future in Question: Soviet Federation

Khrushchev bequeathed to his successors the keynote of "fusion of the nations" as an objective within reach. In spite of the distrust and actual hostility that met every plan he had supported, the theme of fusion was retained by the leadership team succeeding him. Until the Twenty-fifth Congress of the Communist Party of the Soviet Union in 1976—for twelve years—the group in power constantly affirmed its allegiance to this goal of unity. Very soon, however, it ran into the hostility of national elites on this very point.

By 1966 some controversies—on the surface, simple scientific discussions[2]—pitted the partisans of the unification thesis against intellectuals or national groups who passionately defended the cause of perpetuating national status. The position of those defending the nations was simple. The Soviet State had accomplished a remarkable historical task by providing for the flowering and equality of the nations. In so doing, it had demonstrated the importance and permanence of the national reality. Trying to weaken the nations, challenging their existence, meant challenging the regime's most notable success.

The Twenty-fifth Congress seemed to mark the victory of the nationality thesis. For the first time since 1961, all the speeches devoted to the success of the Soviet nationality policy[3] saluted the "flowering" and "friendship" of the nations, but omitted the passionately contested goal of "fusion."

To a certain degree the 1977 Constitution confirms this leaning, since it maintains the federal system (in Article 70) and its guarantee, the right of secession (Article 72). Nevertheless, this Constitution has certain ambiguities involving the future of Soviet federalism.[4] Presenting the new Constitution, Leonid Brezhnev[5] justified it by citing the economic progress made in forty years, the existence in the USSR of an "advanced socialist society" and, especially, the emergence of a new historic community, the "Soviet people." The Constitution's first obvious ambiguity can be seen in its affirmation that Soviet society is clearly moving toward the transcendence of national differences since the "Soviet people" exists, while at the same time maintaining federalism, which is the expression of national differences under the law. Which has more weight in the Constitution? The affirmation of unity, with the Soviet people? Or diversity, with the maintenance of federalism? Reading the Constitution prompts us to opt for the first hypothesis.

First of all, it presents the USSR as the embodiment of the Soviet people's unity as a state, the common instrument, the unifier of all the nations and nationalities for building Communism.[6] The definition of the Soviet Union which in 1936 stressed only federalism and freedom of choice for the nations that belonged to it, has now been amplified and modified by the emphasis placed on the goal of unity and on the already unified basis of this State.[7] Right from this opening Article, federalism appears as a survival of the past, compared to the unity that has now been developed. The right to secede has a strange ring in this series of provisions which refer constantly to the organs of state power in the USSR.

Actually, what does this mean? No one in the USSR has ever decided to exercise the right of secession, nor demanded that it be applied. The objection will be raised that no one has ever thought of doing so, or wanted to. On reading this new text, however, we find that, from the legal standpoint alone, the right to secession has become singularly complicated when compared to the text drafted in 1936. The Constitution of 1936 defined the State as a Federal State, amalgamating the various nations that had joined of their own free will (Article 13). Consequently, secession was the concern of the State but, legally at least, the State could offer no objections to it, as long as it came clearly within the framework of the Constitution.

In 1977 the very nature of the Soviet state was changed. "The State of the whole people" is an inherently ambiguous state. It is dominated by the Communist Party, which is henceforth—constitutionally—its leading force, the nucleus of the political system (Article 6). In addition, the organization and action of this State must conform to the principle of "democratic centralism" (Article 3), a principle developed by Lenin early in the century for the use of his revolutionary Party. Since 1918 the Party has almost constantly—but not always—dominated the State, or merged with it in the USSR. Since 1918 democratic centralism has been applied to the organization of the State. Nevertheless, the State and the Party remained legally separate, each one assuming a particular task and mission of its own.

By merging State and Party, by affirming that the Party is the force guiding the State, that democratic centralism is the fundamental principle of the State, the framers of the 1977 Soviet Constitution dealt a severe blow—legally at any rate—to federalism. The Party's mission is one of unity. National diversity enters neither in its program nor in its tasks.

This being the case, how could the right to separation be exercised in a State merged with the Party, the incarnation of the principle of unification? The Party would betray itself by accepting separatist aspirations, and would also betray the Soviet people—whose existence is established in the Constitution—by helping to break it up. Obviously, this is an entirely theoretical discussion. Nevertheless, it should be pointed out that, for the first time in the institutional history of the USSR, the meaning of federalism—keystone of the system—had been weakened.

Furthermore, the practical provisions of the Constitution also shed light on the retrogression of federalism. The place allotted to it now is much less important than under Stalin. It is not included in the section on the political system, but is relegated to a section following the description of the Soviet system, the principles of foreign policy, and the rights and duties of citizens, in the part devoted to the organization and operation of the system.

This subordinate position assigned to federalism, separate from the fundamental basis of the USSR, is further aggravated by the concrete provisions concerning the relations between the federal system and its federated components. The 1936 Constitution described painstakingly the powers of each republic, delineating their respective domains. The current text, on the contrary, only outlines the federation's powers, which cover just about everything. It is up to the republics to find out what powers they have and, lacking any reference to them in the text, the republics cannot even be sure of holding on to the prerogatives that have come to be theirs. For, to the long list of federal powers, the Constitution adds an article whose vague formulation can hardly be reassuring for the republics. The article leaves to the federation "the solution of other problems of federal importance" (paragraph 12, Article 73).

Only a humorist could call this situation one propitious to federalism. Taking into account that Stalin's Constitution, while highly favorable to federalism, very democratic, very respectful of every right, nevertheless served a centralizing, totalitarian design, elevating illegality to the rank of principle, is it possible to hope that the new Constitution's restrictions on national rights will have exactly the opposite effect? Perhaps a Constitution which gradually eliminates federalism will serve to strengthen it in the end? This kind of reasoning may be tempting, but mental gymnastics should not obscure the reality. The Constitution is a program for the immediate future. It is also a course of action for reducing heightened nationalist ambitions.

The 1977 Constitution represents primarily an answer to the debate opened by Khrushchev in 1961 on the future of the USSR. His inflexible will for unity, so often criticized in the borderlands, is the very fabric of this Constitution. Federalism certainly has been retained. But could the Soviets purely and simply have eliminated it without touching off a wave of protest in the republics?

The situation in the borderlands points up the fact that the central authorities must come to terms with the non-Russians, some of whom are most vehement. Could the center get into an open test of strength with the periphery? Could it provoke a wave of self-immolations? Bombing attempts? Or even a broad popular uprising? Scattered incidents in the last few years show that demonstrations of protest have become possible in the USSR—not easy, nor without risks, but possible. And they are hard to repress without the outside world immediately hearing about it.

The non-Russian attachment to the federal system is too pronounced for it to have been tackled head-on. The Constitution clearly means that federalism has been given a reprieve; but at the same time it has also taken away its guarantees and its institutional means of acting. Furthermore, Leonid Brezhnev, in summarizing the immense popular debate held in the summer of 1977 on the Constitution, pointed out that there had been "grass roots" proposals for the suppression of federalism.[8]

He went on to say that these proposals were not accepted because they were inopportune and premature. But he hadn't disagreed with the principle behind them. The warning here is clear: not only are the Soviets going through a transition period, but there is no real consensus on the issue of federalism. Khrushchev's successors have almost completely abandoned his utopian dream for the transformation of the USSR, and have made every effort to find out what was happening at the grass roots. Nevertheless, they have retained the idea that the unity of Soviet society implies the unity of the State.[9] (see Chart V, on p. 126.)

The Reality of Federalism

Turning from the future prospects implicit in the Constitution and taking up the political system, it must be emphasized that the State is—and remains—the domain in which the nations participate equally. This statement holds true on two levels: first, at the center; and secondly, in the federated and autonomous republics. The question is, how does this political equality work in practice?

At the center the Supreme Soviet of the USSR is, by law, the highest body of state power. The nations are more than equitably represented there.[10] In 1970 the non-Slavic nations, accounting for 26.1% of the population held 40.3% of the seats there. Yet, as soon as we turn to the authorities in which State power really resides—the Presidium of the Supreme Soviet, the Council of Ministers, and the

Chart V
Nations and Nationalities of the USSR
(Political Organization)

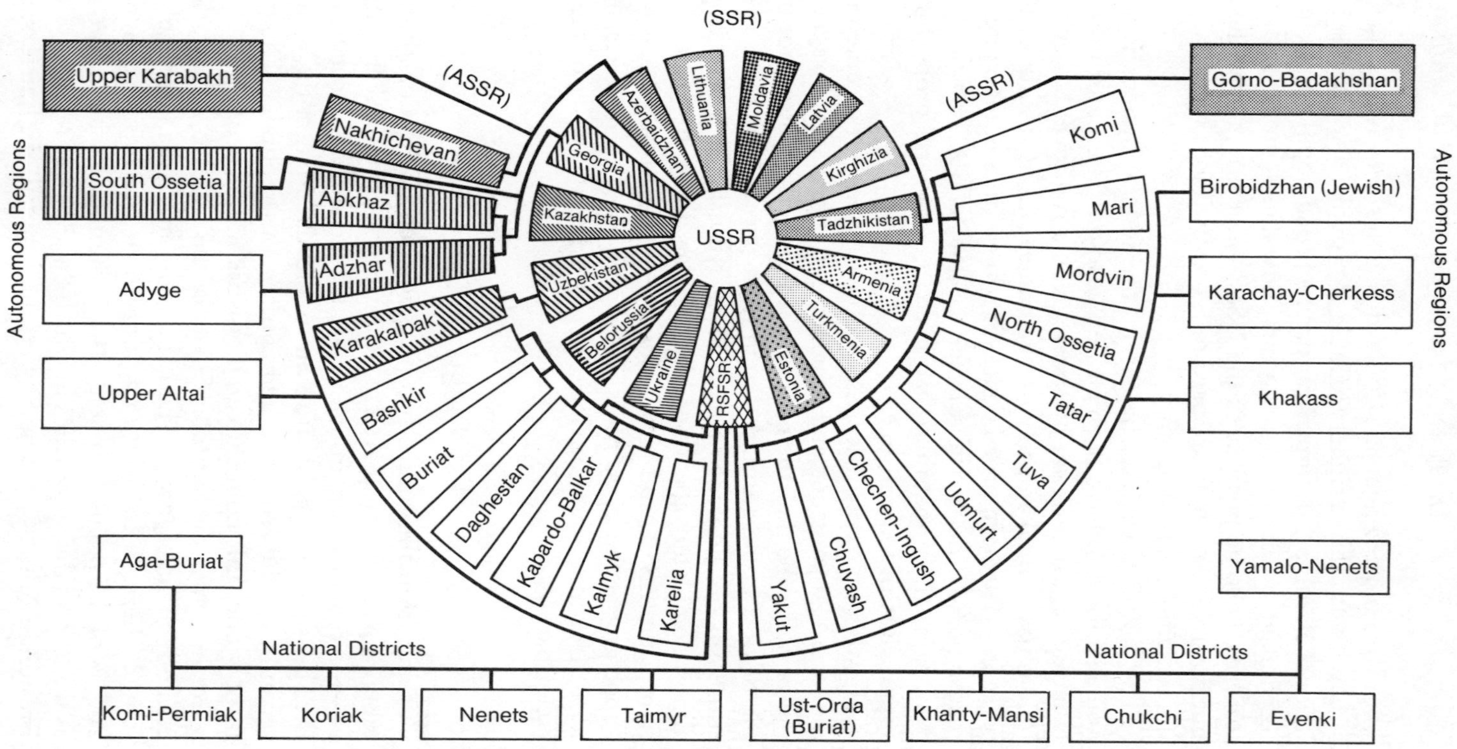

State Committees—the situation begins to change. The Presidium of the Supreme Soviet, the permanent organ of a very temporary assembly,[11] has always been chaired by Slavs, except in the case of Mikoyan (1964–1965).

The proportion of Russians—and, more generally, of Slavs—in the Council of Ministers of the USSR is overwhelming, since they hold 90% of the posts and have always chaired it (except for Stalin who, nevertheless, can hardly be called a representative of the nationalities any more than Mikoyan). The same holds true for most of the State Committees who have power both at the center and in the republics (Gosplan, State Security, etc.). This lack of national political leaders at the center prevents the nations from participating on an equal footing in the decision-making process.

On the other hand, are the powers of the republican states totally in the hands of the nationalities concerned? Here, too, theory and practice do not coincide. The assemblies and the governments of the national states do in fact, reflect the ethnic make-up of the populations. When the diverse organs of republican power are considered—supreme soviets and governments—it is apparent everywhere that the representatives of the official nation of a particular republic hold every post. The number of Russians there is small, often nonexistent. Furthermore, while under Stalin certain key posts, like Internal Affairs and Security, were apparently reserved for Russians,[12] now the prevailing rule seems to be to assign these posts to national cadres.

In the Ukraine in 1977 the Minister of the Interior was Ivan Golovtchenko, and the president of the KGB was Vitali Fedortchuk—both thoroughly Ukrainian names. In Latvia, Internal Affairs were assigned to Jannis Brolich, and the KGB (Commission of State Security) to Login Avdiukevitch. Numerous examples can be cited of this undeniable transfer of responsibility from Russians to their counterparts in the nations. Yet it would be dangerous to draw any hasty conclusions about the degree of autonomy of the republican powers. Several facts point out the limitations in that autonomy.

In the first place, the supreme soviets in the republics, patterned after the Supreme Soviet of the USSR, are—by law—granted all state power. Indeed, their deputies are local nationals who, in turn, elect a presidium also made up of national elements. But political practice shows that the republican soviets are lesser assemblies, inferior to the Supreme Soviet of the USSR. This is demonstrated most effectively by the moment chosen to convene these supreme soviets. They *always* hold their sessions after those of the Supreme Soviet of the USSR, suggesting that their discussions and decisions are merely repetitions of the ones which have already taken place in Moscow. If, on the contrary, the Supreme Soviet of the USSR wanted to expand the borderland debates—or even take them into account—the order of the meetings would be reversed.

This subordinate position of the republican soviets is also reflected in the publicity given to the proceedings in the press. They receive infinitely less coverage than the sessions of the Supreme Soviet of the USSR. As a result of this difference in the coverage given to the assemblies, far less—and far more incomplete—information is available on the activities of the republican soviets than on the sessions of the Supreme Soviet of the USSR. Thus, everything combines to underscore the fact that important decisions are made at the center and that the republican assemblies do little more than disseminate them.

The second feature of national powers concerns the distribution of ministerial powers between the center and the periphery. Looking at the make-up of the republican governments, we are struck by the disproportion existing between the scope of federal jurisdiction and that of the republics. The federation exercises its powers all over the Soviet Union through the intermediary of federal-republican ministries and State Committees subject to the double authority of the pertinent central organ and of the republic's Council of Ministers. Whatever the republic, so far as the ministries are concerned, the breakdown will almost always be the same. There will be about twenty federal-republican ministries for five or six republican ministries. Coupled with this preponderance of ministries having dual authority is the startling disproportion of their functions.

The federal-republican ministries cover all the important spheres. Taking, for example, the government of Belorussia in 1977, the federal-republican ministries are: agriculture, communications, industrial equipment, culture, education, finance, food industry, foreign affairs, forestry, health, specialized secondary and higher education, industrial construction, building, justice, soil and water resources, light industry, meat and dairy products, food reserves, rural construction, timber and wood processing, commerce.

The sphere of strictly republican ministries, on the other hand, is limited to questions of entirely local interest: construction and use of roads, consumer services, housing and communal services, local industries, motor vehicle transportation, peat industry, social security.

Basically speaking, all the republics use this organizational scheme. In Estonia the number of federal-republican agencies drops to nineteen—there are none for rural construction, water resources, or forestry—while the number of purely republican agencies dips to five. In Latvia there are twenty federal-republican agencies. In the Ukraine in 1975 there was an inflated number of ministries: twenty-eight federal-republican agencies for six republican ones.

Variations from one republic to the other stem generally from special economic factors. For example, in the Ukraine special importance is assigned to the problem of state farms, water development, and ferrous metals; and in Central Asia, to the problems of irrigation. In these particular cases it has been necessary to set up specialized ministries not found in other republics.

On the other hand, the scope of republican jurisdiction is very clear and residual: local roads, social security, local transportation, consumer services, municipal services. Here, the variations are of minimum importance.

The influence of the center on the borderland republics is further accentuated by the role of the numerous State Committees. In Belorussia there were fifteen State Committees or specialized administrative offices in 1977, twelve of which came under the dual authority of the center and the Council of Republican Ministers, and only three under purely Belorussian government control. Under this dual authority, Belorussia has: the *Gosplan*; construction; state control; cinema; publishing, printing, and distribution; radio and television; prices; labor; vocational and technical education; state security (KGB); agricultural technology and equipment; statistics. Under purely republican control in Belorussia are: environmental protection, material and technical supply, gas supply.

As can be seen, the State Committees are divided along the same lines as the ministries. The problems left to the exclusive jurisdiction of the republics are few and limited in scope. Here, too, the situation hardly varies from one republic to another.

Several remarks are called for in this regard. While neither the 1936 Constitution nor the present one specifically defined the respective areas of jurisdiction for the federation and the republics, there is nevertheless a clear trend toward the broadening of federal powers. This becomes evident when the two Articles added in

1944[13] are taken into consideration. These two amendments seemed to enhance the sovereignty of the national states, by granting their right to have national military formations, and an independent foreign policy.

However, the clause concerning national armies was never applied since it conflicted with military laws; furthermore, it was to be deleted in the 1977 Constitution. With regard to foreign policy, certain republics have tried to have one. The Ukraine and Belorussia each hold seats at the United Nations and in various international organizations.

All the socialist states of Eastern Europe (including Yugoslavia, but excluding Albania) have general consulates in Kiev, while Cuba, India, and Egypt have consulates in Odessa. Actually, the consulates were set up in Kiev by virtue of agreements concluded with the Soviet government, not with the Republic of the Ukraine. The Ukranian Minister of Commerce signed several trade agreements with Poland, Rumania, and Hungary in the early 1970s.[14] But these agreements are few in number and especially limited in scope. On the whole, the Ukraine either delegates or has to delegate its international powers to the USSR. At times the republic serves Moscow directly. In Canada, for instance, the existence of a large Ukrainian colony is probably the reason why the Soviet embassy there has so many diplomats of Ukrainian origin.

Alone among the other republics, Estonia enjoys somewhat preferential status internationally, inasmuch as she can maintain relatively easy relations with neighboring Finland, to which she is bound by common cultural ties.

Obviously, these meager bonds with the countries outside the USSR do not represent individual foreign policies; on the contrary, they only go to prove how little autonomy the national states have.

Note should also be made regarding recent tendencies toward broadening the functions of federal agencies through administrative procedures, which have appeared despite much insistence at the Twenty-fifth Congress on the need to transfer federal powers to republican authorities. A good example of this practice is furnished by the conversion of the State Committee of Labor and Salaries. Until August 1976, the date of its conversion,[15] this State Committee found itself in a rather peculiar position. Like all the others, it was represented in the republics by agencies under the dual authority of the local government and the center; and yet, while the Committee had republican agencies, many of the Soviet republics had committees of exclusively republican jurisdiction devoted to the problems of labor-supply utilization. This division of tasks—centralization of general labor problems and decentralization of employment problems—coupled with the fact that social security was still the special province of the republics, helped to leave them a sphere of their own, namely labor problems where republican authority could be exercised with some continuity and effect.

Reforming the State Committee on Labor and Salaries did not officially compromise this distribution of powers. Implicitly, however, it brought into question the usefulness of republican authorities. In fact, the State Committee now became the "Committee on Labor and Social Questions," something that gave it much broader jurisdiction than it had before, since in addition to salaries under the heading of social questions came the problems of employment, manpower distribution, and even social security.

The need for such reform is understandable. As long as manpower was abundant in the USSR and full employment assured, it seemed possible that all the issues could be settled locally. However, as a result of demographic disparities, the problems of employment and the geographic distribution of the work force now call for overall solutions, whether the Soviets opt for a redistribution of investments or a policy of labor migration. No republic can solve this type of problem by itself. The justification of this centralization of labor problems is obvious.[16] But so is the consequence of this reform. The purely republican ministries or administrations have become superfluous.

Thus, the private domain of the republics is being whittled down a little more. In the case in point, it is a question of increases in centralization which are dictated by immediate needs. It is undeniable, however, that this added centralization has not been offset by any shift of power into some other, less complex domain. In any event, this centralization falls under the heading of the eventual fading away of national state structures.

From this quick dip into the Soviet State's organization at the center and the periphery, two conclusions can be drawn. In the first place, there is a great difference between the Stalinist period and recent years with regard to the part played by the nationalities in the political life of the State. Indeed, this part is not the same at the center and the periphery. In the federal institutions the nations are perfectly represented in the Supreme Soviet, but scarcely present in the organs of State power and administration. In the republics, on the other hand, national cadres are to be found everywhere—even to the exclusion of others. Russians are no longer pushed into governmental posts the way they were in the past; in particular, there are no more "reserved posts," the ones that had importance as a means of controlling non-Russian populations. All government offices can be and are, as a rule, assigned to local nationals.

The second conclusion conflicts with the first. The preponderant share of Russians in the central government, along with the imbalance—one that is actually growing in the periphery—between the federal and republican spheres of jurisdiction,[17] means that policy-making is essentially centralized and consequently is out of reach for non-Russians. Soviet political and economic life is therefore subject to a cleavage wherein decisions are the concern of the central power, in which non-Russians are barely represented, while in their own localities the nationals have a quasi-monopoly on management or the implementation of decisions which they did not make.

This gap between centralized decision-making and local implementation explains the growing importance of the State ministries and committees subordinate to an analogous organization in Moscow. This subordination actually serves to keep watch on local cadres, which since Stalin's time shows up clearly in the area of control. Under Stalin, control was handled by individuals. The Russian cadres placed in key posts exercised direct control over the national state apparatus. For this direct, open control Stalin's successors preferred to substitute a more administrative control through the subordination of the state apparatus. There are no serious drawbacks to entrusting the responsibility of key sectors to local national cadres, insofar as they are responsible not only to their local government but also to the central administration in Moscow, to which, in the final analysis, they are subordinate. The proof of this is that in case of conflict between federal and republican jurisdiction, there is no arbitration procedure—only the recognized primacy of the federal.

In all likelihood, this situation does have some drawbacks. Will the republican cadres always be willing to limit themselves to carrying out policies formulated at a higher level? Are the republican elites always prepared to admit that their government has only secondary responsibility, and is subject to vertical control which limits the juridical sovereignty of the republics? In this regard, there are obvious reasons for tensions, even conflicts. If these tensions and conflicts remain latent or scattered it is because, coupled with the center's administrative control, there is the more direct, more effective control exercised by the Party.

The Party: Party of the Whole Soviet People?

More than the State machinery, the Communist Party of the USSR occupies an ambiguous position in the country's national equilibrium. Lenin had always conceived of his Party as the privileged organ of one class, the proletariat, therefore impervious to national interests and differences. Prior to 1917 he had rejected the idea of an organization of the working class embracing the national interests of Russian society.[18] Nevertheless, after the Revolution, the creation of the Federal State was accompanied by a parallel reconstruction of the Party. Within each federated republic, a republican Communist Party was established.[19] This is where the confusion starts.

Actually, these republican parties are an integral part of the Communist Party of the USSR and have no rights of their own superior to those of regional organizations. The members of these parties are officially members of the CPSU, so that the republican title applied to the organization is an appellation devoid of all specific meaning. The function of these parties is to bear witness to Soviet federalism by the sole fact of their existence. But the parties confer no autonomy, either *de jure* or *de facto*—on the local Communists. This is easy to understand; by vocation, the Communist Party is a structure of unity and integration, not of diversity.

Does the will to balance the diverse ethnic components within the federal system warrant the existence of the republican parties? Can their existence also be justified by the number of local nationals and by their participation in decision-making? Does the CPSU promote national equality through its republican and central organizations, or does it favor centralism? A first reply stems from our consideration of the CPSU's membership and the relative weight of the diverse national groups inside that organization. In this connection, the history of the USSR is marked primarily by the disparity in the representation of various national groups in the Party. As of January 1, 1976, the CPSU's membership stood at 15,638,891, and more than one hundred national groups were represented in it.[20]

Table 28[21] enables us to see both the Party's current national make-up and how it has evolved in the post-Stalinist years.

This table gives rise to several observations. In the first place, the

Table 28
National Composition of the Party

Nationality	Percentage of CPSU members			Nationality share in the total population	Ratio of Party to population	Number of Communists per 1,000 inhabitants
	1961	1967	1976	1970	1976/1970	1976/1970
Russians	63.54	61.86	60.63	53.37	1.14	74
Ukrainians	14.67	15.63	16.02	16.86	0.95	62
Belorussians	2.98	3.35	3.60	3.75	0.96	62
Uzbeks	1.48	1.73	2.06	3.80	0.54	35
Kazakhs	1.55	1.57	1.81	2.19	0.83	53
Georgians	1.77	1.65	1.66	1.34	1.24	80
Azeris	1.10	1.28	1.48	1.81	0.82	53
Lithuanians	0.44	0.56	0.68	1.10	0.62	40
Moldavians	0.28	0.37	0.43	1.12	0.38	25
Latvians	0.35	0.39	0.42	0.59	0.71	46
Kirghiz	0.28	0.31	0.32	0.60	0.66	34
Tadzhiks	0.34	0.37	0.41	0.88	0.47	30
Armenians	1.67	1.58	1.50	1.47	1.02	66
Turkmenians	0.28	0.28	0.31	0.63	0.49	32
Estonians	0.25	0.30	0.32	0.42	0.76	49
Others	9	8.78	8.35	10.07	0.83	54

weight of certain nationalities in the Party greatly exceeds their proportion of the total population. This is true of the Georgians, who are the most strongly over-represented, followed by the Russians and the Armenians. At the other extreme the Baltic peoples and most of the Moslem peoples, except the Kazakhs and Azeris, are strongly under-represented. Nevertheless, if the current situation is compared to the one prevailing in the early 1960s, we find a reduction of national disparities in the Party. While the weight of Georgians, Russians, and Armenians tends to decrease, others—chiefly, the Belorussians, Ukrainians, and Azeris—find their proportion improving slightly.

Unquestionably, this trend stems from a systematic policy tending to reduce national disparities in the Party's composition. In certain cases, the trend results from advances in urbanization or demography, or a combination of both factors. To what extent does this represent continuous progress toward equality? To what extent does it apply to the whole country? It is hard to make judgments about the CPSU's national composition over a long period, because the data is lacking. Since the early 1960s the Party has been supplying statistics on national representation, but this was not the case during the Stalinist period. All that was known then was the make-up of national delegations at congresses, from which it was possible to deduce the proportion each nationality represented in the Party. As it stood, this comparison bore out general tendencies identified for the subsequent period (see Table 29).

Although this table does not give an accurate picture of the Party's national composition, it can be deduced that in the war years and up to the end of the Stalinist period, Stalin assigned preponderant weight to the Russians, while considerably reducing the representation of Ukrainians and Belorussians who, up to then, had been much better represented. On the other hand, the Moslem peoples, who had been terribly under-represented in the Party before the war, began a slow upward trend at the end of the war.

Certainly, the post-Stalinist period, having broken with the excesses of Stalinism, is tending toward a somewhat better balanced situation, although not truly reflecting the national composition of the USSR. Actually, the present situation reflects certain historical tendencies. There is a large Georgian and Armenian membership in the Party, because before the Revolution these peoples had played an important role in social democracy. The Party had a long-standing foothold in the Caucasus, and the memory of pre-Revolutionary organizations and local national leaders had given the republican organizations a power of attraction that was lacking, for instance, in the parties of Central Asia, where before the Revolution Communism had been essentially Russian—and hence, "colonial." After 1917 the national parties in Central Asia had either been dominated by Russians or by political cadres who, issuing from national movements, transferred their national struggles to the Communist Party, which in turn led to constant purges of these organizations. It is no wonder therefore that the Communist parties remain weak in Central Asia, where they were so late in coming and are scarcely rooted in the local life.

The national make-up of the CPSU should also be considered at a lower level, namely, the nations not organized as sovereign states. No comprehensive presentation is possible, because the CPSU statistics are incomplete; but once more, the great variety of situations must be noted. An interesting case is that of the Jews, who nearly always have been over-represented in the CPSU. In the 1920s[23] they

Table 29
Republican CP Delegations to the CPSU Congresses [22]

Republics	Percentage of the Soviet Population		Percentage of Congress delegates		
	1939	1959	18th Congress 1939	19th Congress 1952	22nd Congress 1961
RSFSR	63.9	55.9	65.8	65	63.1
Ukraine	18.2	20	18	12.8	16.3
Belorussia	3.3	4.1	2.9	2.2	2.9
Georgia	2.1	1.9	2.5	2.7	2.1
Azerbaidzhan	1.9	1.8	2.5	1.9	1.6
Armenia	0.8	0.8	1	1.1	0.8
Uzbekistan	3.7	3.9	1.5	2.1	2.5
Turkmenia	0.7	0.7	0.4	0.7	0.6
Kirghizia	0.9	1	0.3	0.7	0.7
Tadzhikistan	0.9	0.9	0.3	0.5	0.6
Kazakhstan	3.6	4.5	2.5	3.5	3.9
Karelia-Finland [1]	—	—	—	0.3	—
Estonia [2]	—	0.6	—	0.5	0.5
Latvia [2]	—	1	—	0.8	0.9
Lithuania [2]	—	1.3	—	0.6	0.7
Moldavia [3]	—	1.4	—	0.6	0.7

1. Set up as a republic only between 1940 and 1955.
2. Incorporated into the USSR in 1940.
3. Became a federated republic in 1940.

represented 1.8% of the Soviet population (1926 census), but 5.2% of the Party in 1922 and 4.3% in 1926. In spite of the restrictions placed on their cultural rights, Jews represented 5% of the Party membership in 1940. Subsequently their representation clearly dropped, but 2% of the Party was still Jewish in 1976, when they accounted for only 1% of the total Soviet population.

Among the peoples who have suffered or are still suffering discrimination are the Tatars and the peoples deported for collaboration with the enemy during the Second World War. All of these peoples have constantly been under-represented in the Party. The Tatars, who with 5 million inhabitants make up 2.5% of the Soviet population, comprise only 1.9% of Party membership. In an even more serious situation are the peoples deported during the war; their party representation is continuously below their real weight in the population, as shown in Table 30.[24]

Obviously, without data on the other deported peoples, Germans

Table 30
Peoples Under-represented in the Party

Nationality	Party - 1976 25th Congress		Population (1970 Census)		Party/ Population Ratio
	Number	%	Number	%	
Balkars	3,893	0.02	60,000	0.02	1.00
Ingush	2,763	0.02	158,000	0.07	0.29
Kalmyks	6,411	0.04	137,000	0.06	0.67
Karachays	5,191	0.03	113,000	0.05	0.60
Chechens	12,959	0.10	613,000	0.25	0.40

and Crimean Tatars, no definite conclusions can be drawn concerning the position of the peoples listed in this table. Yet, everything seems to suggest that the regime continues to mistrust those who suffered so terribly in the postwar years, and prefers to keep them away from the decision-making centers.

Thus from the general table of Party composition contradictory situations are emerging, our understanding of which is however aided by history. Though removed from positions of leadership and deprived of their national rights, Soviet Jews have a high degree of education and an almost exclusively urban distribution, which guarantee them—even now—an important place in the Party's base. Then there are the peoples suppressed by Stalin—legally—and afterwards rehabilitated (except for the Crimean Tatars), but whose dispersal and national destruction favored neither their existence nor development after 1956. Whether they keep to themselves out of bitterness or, what is more likely, because the regime wants to keep them secluded, the results hardly vary from one people to another, and their political standing remains very limited.

At times, peoples who traditionally share similar levels of development and ways of life diverge to an astonishing degree in terms of the membership assigned them in the Party. Taking the Party-to-population ratio for a yardstick, there is a strikingly high degree of participation by the Karelians (1.67%), the Komis (1.54%), and the Kumyks (1.25%), as opposed to the very low degree of participation by the Maris (0.40%), the Tuvins and Khakasses (0.67% each), and the Udmurts (0.69%). Why is there such a large number of Communists among the first group and not among the second? Neither history nor sociological factors seem to offer an explanation. The concern to reduce disparities between the large nations does not seem to apply to the small nationalities.

On the whole the CPSU appears to indicate a growing participation of non-Russians in political life, and at the same time an equalization of the political role played by the various nations. Nevertheless, this impression is contradicted by a number of facts of a different kind. First of all, a glance at the national composition of certain republican organizations shows that the share of local nationals in the Party is often far from corresponding to their weight in the republic. For instance in Latvia and Moldavia, where the official nationalities respectively represent 56.8% and 64.6% of the total population, their share in the Party does not reach 50%. In Lithuania the gap between Lithuanians in the population (88%) and in the Party (66%) is even more salient. With 34% of the membership made up of Ukrainians, Poles and Russians, the CP of Lithuania has an international coloring only remotely reflecting the national composition of the republic's population.

Even more disturbing is the disparity between republican parties and national Communists within the CPSU. Latvia furnishes an example of these hard-to-explain eccentricities. At a conference of Latvian Party leaders held in Riga on February 1, 1977[25] to discuss Party organization problems, First Secretary August Voss stressed difficulties in recruitment. In fact, Voss's statements give us an insight into the discrepancy existing between the CP in Latvia, whose membership is growing very slowly, and the Latvians in the CPSU whose numbers are increasing more rapidly.

An identical situation emerges from the statements made at the last congress of the Azerbaidzhan CP by the chairman of the Vote Committee, I. Askerov. He emphasized that, in the period separating the last two congresses of the CP, 1971–1976, the ACP had admitted 29,274 members to its ranks, but for the same period he also cited 47,502 new Azerbaidzhan Communists in the ranks of the CPSU.[26] Even without data permitting us to extend these facts to other republics,[27] this puzzling situation may perhaps be explained by the fact that temporary residents in the republics (soldiers, technicians, etc.), although included in local population statistics, can belong directly to the CPSU without going through the republican organization, despite the territorial nature of the Party's activities. This hypothesis serves to reveal the artificial nature of the Party's republican echelon, which is in fact a mere branch of the CPSU that is often neglected by Communists without roots in the republic.

From this glance at Communist membership, we can already make one contradictory inference. Despite some imbalances, the CPSU tends to appear as the reflection of Soviet multi-national society. At the same time the weaknesses of the republican organizations underscore the CPSU's centralizing role. It is the one Party of all the nationalities and not a grouping of all the local national parties.

In order to determine whether better-balanced recruiting is synonymous with relatively equal participation in political decision-making, it is necessary to consider the Party's organs of power, both at the center and locally. Turning to the central organs where decisions are made, namely the Central Committee, the Politburo, and the Secretariat, the situation is suddenly upset by a weakening in the representation of nationalities.

Even in the Central Committee, 82% of the delegates belong to the Slavic group, which represents only 73% of the population.[28] This disparity becomes even more pronounced in the two higher organs. Among the members of the Politburo, there are only two nationals out of sixteen, and three out of six among the candidates. And the Secretariat has no representative of the nationalities. Secretary General Leonid Brezhnev and the ten secretaries are all of Slavic origin, all Russian or denationalized—as in the case of Brezhnev—and all spokesmen for a policy of centralization.

For this reason it is important to examine the make-up of the present local nationals in the Politburo. What is the explanation for their exceptional position in the CPSU? Are they there as representatives of the local national cadres or as the representatives of central policy in the periphery? Their biographies shed light on their positions. Among the members of the Politburo are a Kazakh, Kunayev, and a Ukrainian, Shcherbitsky.

Kunayev, First Secretary of the Kazakhstan Communist Party since 1964, is an authentic representative of the Stalin-trained Kazakh political class. Having joined the Party in 1939 at the age of twenty-seven, Kunayev was on the technical cadres committee, then on the national policies committee which appeared just after the purges that destroyed the whole national elite of the postrevolutionary period. In Stalin's time, Kunayev was a career official in the State apparatus and did not rise to an equivalent post in the Party until the early 1960s. He reached a privileged position as a member of the Politburo in 1971.

The case of Vladimir Chtcherbitski is quite different. Fifty-eight

years of age at the time of the Twenty-fifth Congress, Chtcherbitski
has been an apparatus man ever since, his career being closely linked
with that of Leonid Brezhnev. As a young man, he held posts in the
Komsomol before handling leadership functions at every level of the
Ukrainian Party. In the 1960s he was also chairman of the Ukraine's
Council of Ministers. This double career gives him perfect mastery
of all the organs of local power, where he appears primarily to be a
Brezhnev representative, responsible for the success of the latter's
policies in the Ukraine. If Chtcherbitski seems much less representative of national interests than his Kazakh colleague, what can one say
about the Azerbaidzhanian Geidar Ali Reza Ogly Aliev, who was
named a Politburo candidate-member at the Twenty-fifth Congress?

Aliev's promotion gave the Caucasus the Politburo representation
it had lost with the fall of the Georgian, Mzhavanadze, in 1972. As
First Secretary of the Azerbaidzhan CP, Aliev is primarily a security
department man. In 1941, at the age of eighteen, he joined the
NKVD (Soviet secret police) and served as an official in the organs of security, sometimes in the center but mainly in Azerbaidzhan, where he was chairman of the local KGB (Committee for
State Security) between 1967 and 1969. In the latter year Aliev became First Secretary of the Azerbaidzhan CP.

Aside from this newcomer, two other borderland representatives
are to be found among the Politburo's candidates: the Belorussian,
Masherov, and the Uzbek, Rashidov. Both are members of long
standing. Masherov served in the Komsomol apparatus (starting in
1944), then in the Belorussian CP, and joined the Politburo at the
Twenty-third Congress in 1966. Rashidov, First Secretary of the Uzbekistan CP, has had a long career in the apparatus of the Party and
of the Uzbek State since he joined the Party in 1939 at the age of
twenty-two. Elected to the Politburo at the Twenty-second Congress
in 1961, Rashidov is now the dean of the candidate-members and
one of the senior members of this organ after Brezhnev, Kosygin,
and Suslov.

This glimpse of the national makeup of the Party's real organs of
power prompts several observations. In the first place, at this level it
is no longer a question of looking for a reflection of the national
structure of the USSR, or even of the Party. Russian pre-eminence,
followed by that of the Slavs, is complete. The makeup of the Secretariat proves this.

Secondly, some nationalities seem better represented than others
in the Politburo—the Ukraine and Belorussia, as compared to Cen-

tral Asia or, more generally, the Moslem republics. On the other hand, note should be made of the total absence of Georgians and Armenians (although they are over-represented in the Party), and the Balts. This gives evidence of the ambiguity of the criterion, "representation of national groups in the Party," as a means of evaluating a national group's access to the sphere of decision-making.

Thirdly, it is noteworthy that the demographic movements of the early 1970s have had absolutely no impact on the makeup of the leadership organs, which are scarcely being restaffed. The Politburo's newcomers are Russians, so far as the official members are concerned—Romanov, First Secretary of the Leningrad Regional Committee, and Marshal Ustinov, Defense Minister. Of the Politburo's candidate-members, the only newcomer, Aliev, replaced a national leader removed from office, Mzhavandze.

A final remark concerns the access of local nationals to an essential area of political life called "nomenclature."* Under this heading fell the posts appearing on a list drawn up by the Central Committee of the CPSU. There are 30,000 to 40,000 of these posts, the assignment of which comes under the exclusive jurisdiction of the Party organizations.[29] Although this list of appointments lies within the jurisdiction of the Central Committee, it is clear that small organs in charge of cadre problems decide on the person assigned to any given post listed. One section of the Central Committee is responsible for cadre problems. The absence of local national leaders from the Central Committee's Secretariat, the Party's real executive body, suggests that at this level the nationalities are excluded from the basic decisions regarding the selections for the most responsible posts in the USSR. Nevertheless, the question arises: how much influence can the nationalities exert on this problem at the other end of the political system, i.e., in the secretariats of the republics' parties? This prompts us to analyze the makeup of the leadership machinery in the republics and to determine the extent to which national Communists control their own destinies in their own localities.[30]

In the republics—as in Moscow, the Party's highest authority *de jure* is the Central Committee, but the Secretariat is the supreme authority *de facto*. A permanent organ, the Secretariat is characterized in the borderlands by the decisive roles of its two first secretaries

---

* TRANSLATOR'S NOTE: *Nomenklatura* (jurisdiction). These are lists of Party appointments to be filled and the names of the particular officials who are to decide on the appointments listed.

and by the division of duties between them. Does the selection of these secretaries (undoubtedly, the result of central decisions) provide the key to the nomenclature policy? What criteria govern the choice of the two main figures in the republics' parties? Precisely what are the functions that warrant their having such privileged positions? Let us discuss these tasks in an effort to understand the policy that leads to the selection of the men in question.

The First Secretary of a republic's CP has a specific function. Officially, he is the highest-ranking person in the Party. On behalf of the Central Committee, he directs, controls, coordinates. The Second Secretary is a more complex figure. Although in recent years the practice of putting forward a Second Secretary bearing this title has prevailed, there have been instances where the person discharging the duties of Second Secretary is officially called the Secretary, or switches back and forth from one title to the other.[31] Another difficulty stems from the rather vague nature of the duties assigned to him. Since the end of the 1950s the Second Secretary has had complete jurisdiction over leadership appointments and organization. In certain cases, however, he is responsible for economic matters, while the First Secretary handles cadres.[32]

Since Khrushchev's fall, the trend has been toward a strict specialization in the functions of the secretaries. Corresponding to the official managerial functions of the number one man are the Second Secretary's decision-making functions involving the selection of cadres. In the republics the Second Secretary is actually responsible for the nomenclature. He thus becomes the central regime's true representative in the republics. It is no accident that a leading specialist on Party problems, Jerry Hough, used the term "prefect" in this connection.[33] Looking at how the system has operated for the past fifteen years or so, one can note the growing importance of the Second Secretary, an importance warranted by the part he plays in cadre selection at the republican level. It is also evident that a delicate balance has been established between the first and second secretaries. The first enjoys considerable prestige which marks him for promotion to membership in the Party's central organs.

The representatives of the nationalities in the CPSU's Politburo are the first secretaries, not the second ones. Does this imply preeminence and greater power in the first secretaries? In practice it appears that this is not at all the case. Far from being subordinate to the First Secretary, the Second Secretary actually serves to balance and control him. An insight into their respective positions is provided by considering the holders of these appointments for each republic— except the RSFSR, which has no Communist organization of its own—in the recent past and in early 1978, when the new Constitution came into effect.

For the past, an Australian expert on the CPSU[34] attempted to describe every possible case for the makeup of the secretariats in the federated republics, and also in the autonomous republics, covering the period 1954 to 1976. There was one flaw in his method; it is hard to compare autonomous republics with federated republics, owing to their different status, an environment that makes them more readily assimilable and generally a difference in population size. But despite this defect, the Australian's analysis deserves to be cited here because it reveals certain guidelines and underscores the individual character of the large republics.

Using 259 first and second secretaries in thirty-four republics (fourteen federated, twenty autonomous), the author cites six typical cases, based on the nationality of the secretaries. It should be pointed out that when the Australian scholar refers to Ukrainians who play an important role alongside Russians in the non-Slavic republics, he considers them Ukrainians when they are in their own republic, but equates them with Russians when they are outside the Ukraine. By grouping the careers of these 259 leaders over a period of twenty-two years (1954–1976), the local national breakdown is as shown in Table 31.

Table 31
National Composition of the Secretariats [35]
1954-1976

Posts	Russians		Nationals		Total
	Absolute figure	%	Absolute figure	%	Absolute figure
*SSR - 1st Secretary	6	4.8	38	28.4	44
SSR - 2nd Secretary	48	38.4	25	18.6	73
**ASSR - 1st Secretary	28	22.4	38	28.4	66
ASSR - 2nd Secretary	43	34.4	33	24.6	76
Total	125	100.0	134	100.0	259

*(SSR: Federated Republic)
**(ASSR: Autonomous Republic)

This table reveals that the classic idea about the First Secretary always being national and the Second Secretary always Russian isn't entirely true. Without doubt the number of Russians and of nationals is not far from being even: 134 to 125. In addition, the table reveals that a fairly substantial proportion of nationals has held the post of Second Secretary both in the republics and in the autonomous formations.

Yet, an analysis shows that, in this apparent variety of situations, guidelines have gradually been established reducing the diversity that seems to stem from the figures cited.

First case: Both the First and Second secretaries are nationals—during most of this period. This situation prevailed from 1954 to the early 1970s in three federated republics: the Ukraine, Belorussia, Armenia; and in two autonomous republics included in the Georgian SSR: Adzharia and Abkhazia.[36]

Second case: Both secretaries are nationals—during the early days of de-Stalinization. In four republics—Latvia, Lithuania, Georgia and Azerbaidzhan, both secretaries were nationals in the 1950s, but the end of the decade brought the replacement of the national Second Secretary by a Russian. In this way, the following were eliminated: in Latvia, Kruminsch, who was dismissed first in 1956, then returned briefly only to be ousted permanently in 1960; in Lithuania, Sumanskas (Second Secretary from 1954 to 1956); in Georgia, Georgadze (Second Secretary from 1954 to 1956); and in Azerbaidzhan, Samedov (1952–1955). Since then, in these four republics, the Second Secretary has always been a Russian.

Third case: The First Secretary is a national; the Second Secretary is a Russian. This has been applied consistently in only four federated republics, all located in Central Asia, Uzbekistan, Kirghizia, Tadzhikistan, and Turkmenia, and in four autonomous republics, three in the Caucasus—Nakhichevan, North Ossetia, and Daghestan—and the Karakalpak ASSR in Central Asia.

Fourth case: Both secretaries are Russians. These are temporary situations that existed immediately after Stalin's death in only two republics: Kazakhstan between 1954 and 1957; and Moldavia from 1954 to 1959. In both republics this Russification of the posts was at first replaced by an identical division of duties but in an unusual order—a Russian first secretary and a national second secretary. By 1961 the order was reversed and the third type became the rule.

Fifth case (temporary): Russian First Secretary; national Second Secretary. This case appeared temporarily in Kazakhstan (1957–1960) and Moldavia (1959–1961)—as noted above. Significantly, it has reappeared nowhere else since 1961. This also characterized the situation in several autonomous republics: Karelia (1950-1958), Bashkiria (1953-1957), Tataria (1957-1960), Kalmyk (1957-1961). But in the ASSRs the early 1960s marked a shift to the third model.

Sixth case (permanent): First Secretary Russian, Second Secretary national. This model applies permanently to some of the autonomous republics: the three Finnish-speaking republics of the middle Volga—Maris, Udmurts, and Mordvins—and the Chechen-Ingush ASSR in the Caucasus.

This breakdown of local national groups into "political situations" gives the impression that every combination is possible. Yet, on closer examination, it is found that while every combination has been or is applicable in the autonomous republics, the federated republics fall into the first four cases only. In addition, in the federated republics there has been a development which has led to uniformity in the regimes under which they live.

Before moving to the current situation, an attempt might be made to explain the different statuses held by the republics in the past. Among the most favored regimes, highest status was granted to the two Slavic republics, the three republics of the Caucasus, and the three Baltic republics. The most unfavorable situation has been that of Kazakhstan and, for a short period, Moldavia. The situation closest to the present guidelines is that of the four Central Asian republics. Why these differences?

In the first group of most favored republics which retained national cadres for a long time, the privileged status of the Ukraine and Belorussia is easy to understand. Slavic solidarity, cultural proximity, and the partnership of Ukrainians and Belorussians with the Russian regimes in the other borderland republics, all have long dissipated the strength of national feeling in the Slavic peoples, putting them in the position of "second eldest brother."[37]

The Armenians have shown great loyalty toward the USSR, inasmuch as the 1916 massacres showed them that their nation's survival depended on Russian protection. Moreover, the size of the Armenian diaspora in Soviet territory brought Moscow the help of denationalized cadres who played a significant role in the central organs. In addition, Armenia enjoyed privileged cultural status even during the Stalinist era, as did Georgia. While all the Soviet peoples were stripped of their alphabets, the Armenians and the Georgians kept the integrity of their languages. After 1954, Moscow's tolerant attitude toward the Patriarch of Echmiadzin restored Armenia's character as a national homeland for the whole diaspora. Obviously, Stalin's successors could not jeopardize peremptorily the rather extraordinary status of the Caucasus. Decisions and guidelines had to be modified for this region.

In the Baltic republics, particularly Estonia, it is plausible that the national cadres, who for a while conferred privileged status on these republics, were much less representative of their nationality than appeared from their names. The example of the Estonian CP's Second Secretary between 1953 and 1964, Lentsman, illustrates this statement. Lentsman was the son of Estonian Communists who had taken refuge in the Soviet Union at the time of their country's independence. In fact, Lentsman was born in the Crimea, was educated there, and did not enter Estonia until just after the war. We find countless cases of this type among the Baltic national leaders of the 1950s, men who were denationalized by their education received on Soviet territory, and were used afterwards as representatives of the national elite in a country they scarcely knew.

By the early 1960s, however, this diversity became organized around a rule which would be hallowed by time. The post of Second Secretary became decisive. This man represents centralization, while the First Secretary embodies federal diversity. One model became standard, the First Secretary would be national in all localities. He would be representative within the republics and representative of the republics in the CPSU. On the other hand, the Second Secretary was to become the incarnation of the center in the republics, the one who would relay central decisions and submit important nominations to the center.

In a few years all the republics would have a diarchic regime, i.e., a national First Secretary and a Russian Second Secretary. The situation became completely standarized by the beginning of 1978. A close examination of this should be made because this pattern illuminates the Soviet concept of the Party's role, to which the 1977 Constitution assigns a decisive importance in Soviet political life. Tables 32 and 33, which show the current breakdown of the diarchy in the Secretariat, reveal the recent trend.

A number of observations can be made by juxtaposing these two tables. First of all, there is a clear-cut contrast between the stability in the corps of first secretaries and the quick turnover of second secretaries. In only four republics out of fourteen—Armenia, Georgia, Lithuania, and the Ukraine—did the first secretaries take office in the early 1970s. On this score, the case of Lithuania is exceptional, inasmuch as the change of secretary was due to death of the previous officeholder, Antanas Snieckus. In the three other cases, the removal of the office-holders was the outcome of political crises.

In Georgia, Mzhavandze, who had assumed the office of First Secretary during the bitter struggle over Stalin's succession, was removed from this post in 1972 after holding the office for nineteen years. The reason for this ouster was the widespread corruption which Mzhavandze and his associates had encouraged in the republic.[38] Undeniably, Mzhavandze's era was marked by scandalous practices at all levels, and nowhere more than in Georgia did the corruption infect the very heart of the regime. But his removal led to a violent reaction from the population, who regarded Moscow's delayed indignation as an anti-Georgian operation—not an attempt to stop notoriously long-standing corruption. The new First Secretary's personality only confirmed this interpretation. Succeeding Mzhavandze in September 1972, the forty-four-year-old Chevarnadze had a long career as an *apparatchik*. After entering the Party at the age of twenty, he had almost never stopped working in the machinery of the Komsomol and the Party. From 1964 to 1972 his career turned toward the security organs. Without doubt, both in the Party and at the head of the Ministry of the Interior, Chevarnadze has always worked in Georgia. Yet insofar as the struggle against corruption results from decisions made in Moscow,[39] where his shortcomings are constantly criticized in the Party's central apparatus,[40] Chevarnadze is seen by his compatriots as a tool of Moscow and not the embodiment of local national policy.

In Armenia, also, corruption served as the pretext for a series of purges which, from 1971 to 1974, altered the leadership of the republic and put Karen Demirchyan in the post of First Secretary.[41] But unlike his Georgian counterpart, Demirchyan is not exclusively a man of the apparatus but also an engineer who had devoted a good portion of his life to his profession. The rise of a technocrat in the Party's apparatus was a response to certain anxieties in the republic over the region's industrial development.

In the Ukraine, the ouster of Pierre Chelest coincided with a gen-

Table 32
First Secretaries of Republic CPs in 1977

Republic	Name	Year of birth	Nationality	Position in CPSU	Date of taking office	Previous office
Armenia	Demirchian (Karen)	1932	Armenian	CC member	Nov. 1974	2nd secretary of the gorkom of Erivan in 1972. Secretary of the CC of the CP of Armenia in 1974.
Azerbaidzhan	Aliev (Geidar Ali Rza Ogly)	1923	Azeri	CC member; Politburo Candidate	July 1969	President of the KGB of Azerbaidzhan
Belorussia	Masherov (Petr)	1918	Belorussian	CC member; Politburo Candidate	March 1965	2nd secretary of the CP of Bielorussia
Estonia	Kebin (I.G.)	1905	Estonian	CC member	April 1950	1948-1950: secretary of the CC of Estonian CP.
Georgia	Chevarnadze (Edouard)	1928	Georgian	CC member	Sept. 1972	1st secretary of the gorkom of Tbilisi
Kazakhstan	Kunaev (Dinmukhamed Akhmedovich)	1912	Kazakh	CC member; Politburo member	1960-1962: then 1964	President of the Council of Ministers of Kazakhstan

148

Table 32
First Secretaries of Republic CPs in 1977

Republic	Name	Year of birth	Nationality	Position in CPSU	Date of taking office	Previous office
Kirghizia	Usubaliev (Turdakun)	1919	Kirghiz	CC member	May 1961	1st secretary of the gorkum of Frunze
Latvia	Voss (A.E.)	1916	Latvian	CC member	April 1966	Secretary of the CC of the CP of Latvia
Lithuania	Grishkiavichius (P.P.)	1924	Lithuanian	CC member	Feb. 1974	1st secretary of the gorkom of Vilna
Moldavia	Bodiul (Ivan)	1918	Moldavian	CC member	1961	2nd secretary of the CP of Moldavia
Tadzhikistan	Rasulov (D.R.)	1913	Tadzhik	CC member	1961	USSR Ambassador Extraordinary to Togo
Turkmenia	Gapurov (Mukhamed-nazar)	1922	Turkmenian	CC member	1962	Party apparatus of Turkmenia
Ukraine	Shcherbitski (Vladimir)	1918	Ukrainian	CC member; member of the Politburo	May 1962	President of the Council of Ministers of the Ukraine
Uzbekistan	Rashidov (Sh.)	1917	Uzbek	CC member; Politburo Candidate	March 1959	President of the Presidium of the Supreme Soviet of Uzbekistan

149

Table 33
Second Secretaries of Republic CPs in 1977

Republic	Name	Year of birth	Nationality	Position in CPSU	Date of taking office	Previous office
Armenia	Anisimov (P.P.)	1928	Russian	CC Candidate	March 1973	Assistant Head of the Organization department of the CC of the CPSU
Azerbaidzhan	Pugatchev (Yu.N.)	1926	Russian	CC Candidate	April 1977	2nd secretary of the Kirghiz CP
Belorussia	Aksenov (A.N.)	1924	Belorussian	CC member	July 1971	2nd secretary of the obkom of Vitebsk
Estonia	Lebedev (C.)	1918	Russian	CC Candidate	Feb. 1971	Section head of the Organization department of the CC of the CPSU
Georgia	Kolbin (G.V.)	1927	Russian	CC Candidate	April 1975	2nd secretary of the obkom of Sverdlovsk
Kazakhstan	Korkin (A.G.)	?	Russian	none	August 1976	Secretariat of the Kazakh CP in 1976 - formerly in heavy industry.
Kirghizia	Fomichenko (K.E.)	?	Russian	none	July 1977	

Table 33
Second Secretaries of Republic CPs in 1977

Republic	Name	Year of birth	Nationality	Position in CPSU	Date of taking office	Previous office
Latvia	Belukha (N.A.)	1920	Ukrainian	CC Candidate	March 1963	Assistant Head of the department of the Party organs of the CC of the CPSU
Lithuania	Kharazov (V.I.)	1918	Russian	CC Candidate	April 1967	Inspector of the CC of the CPSU
Moldavia	Merenichtchev (N.V.)	1919	Russian	CC Candidate	Dec. 1973	2nd secretary of the Party Committee of Leningrad
Tadzhikistan	Polukarov (Iu. I.)	1920	Russian (apparently)	CC Candidate	May 1975	Section Head of the Organization department of the CC of the CPSU
Turkmenia	Pereudin (V.N.)	1923	Russian (apparently)	CC Candidate	April 1975	From 1963 to 1965 in the "Bureau of Central Asia" of the CC of the CPSU. Then president of the Committee of State Control of Turkmenia
Ukraine	Sokolov (I.Z.)	1928	Russian	CC member	Feb. 1976	1st secretary of the obkom of Kharkov
Uzbekistan	Grekov (L.I.)	1928	Russian	CC member	July 1976	2nd secretary of the gorkom of Moscow

eral onslaught against Ukrainian nationalism, which gave the internal crisis a particularly serious dimension.

Aside from these four cases, where various crises brought younger men into power, the first secretaries of the republics seem to hold office longer. Compared to them, the quick turnover of second secretaries is striking. In only two cases—Latvia and Lithuania—did the present second secretaries assume office prior to 1970. More than half of them were appointed after 1975. Yet when we compare the careers of the republican secretaries over a 22-year period, we find greater stability of tenure at this level. Table 34 reflects this trend.

Table 34
Stability of Republican Secretaries

Number of years in office:	1955	1960	1965	1970	1975
First secretaries	4.8	5.2	7.5	8.3	9.9
Second secretaries	1.9	3.2	3.6	5	6.6

This table clearly shows that, in spite of purges and the fairly general changes of second secretaries, the trend has been toward stabilizing the leading cadres. This stabilization has not prevented the gradual rejuvenation of the national secretariats. More mobile, the second secretaries are on the whole younger than their first secretary colleagues. Actually, a new political generation can be seen emerging in the second secretary posts, composed of fifty-year-old men who, having reached adulthood during the last years of Stalinism, by and large were not involved in the Stalinist brutality. But this does not necessarily mean that they are very different from their predecessors, for under Stalin they experienced war and unity of action in the struggle. They are accordingly more inclined to go along with the system than to oppose it.

Another fundamental difference between the two groups lies in the patterns of their respective careers. The first secretaries spend their lives chiefly in their own republics. If they do leave, it is only for brief employment in the apparatus of other borderland republics, but rarely at the secretarial level. In some cases they are assigned to posts in the RSFSR. This holds true especially for Slavs who have received special cultural preparation for such transfers, and for Balts who emigrated to Russia when their countries were independent.

In the other national groups we find two notable exceptions: Mzhavandze, the ex-First Secretary of Georgia whose military career had at first taken him away from his native republic; and the Armenian First Secretary, Demirchyan, who worked for a while in Leningrad before starting a continuous local career in 1966. Entirely different is the case of the Russians, who have generally moved from one republic to another.

In the majority of cases the second secretaries come from the RSFSR; but some seem to "tour" the various republics. Such is the case of V. Kharazov, who was posted in Kazakhstan (1954–1961) before being appointed to Lithuania in 1967. This is even more true for Yu. Pugatchev, who was successively Second Secretary of the Kirghiz CP and then that of Azerbaidzhan. This practice was quite common until the end of the 1950s,[42] but then the central regime seems less inclined to have certain of its cadres specialize in "Russian posts." Certainly, Russians who reach the key post of republican second secretary have a great deal of experience in the apparatus. At the present time, more than half the secretaries have served in the Party's central apparatus—that is to say, they have worked in the various departments of the Central Committee. The others are almost evenly divided between those who have served in regional organizations in Russia and those who have served in non-Russian regions. In all cases it seems clear that practically all the Russians, whatever their previous training, are not novices in national problems.

This fact emerges from analyzing the previous functions of the secretaries rather than the geographical framework of their operations. Here also the difference between the first and second secretaries can best be seen by comparing their respective careers. In general, the first secretaries have been appointed to the post after holding a similar post at the regional level, or a lower post in their own republic's central apparatus. Another avenue of approach to the secretariat is chairmanship of the Council of Ministers, where many candidates to the Party's highest posts are to be found. This very close relationship between the chairmanship of the Council of Ministers and the Party's secretariat confirms what has been underscored many times, namely that the post of chairman of the Council of Ministers (but not the post of minister) belongs to the Party hierarchy. A chairman of the Council of Ministers can move easily to the head of the Party and vice versa. This does not hold true for ministers, with the exception of the head of the Committee for State Security (KGB), who also has a very special place in the governmental chain of command.

In the case of second secretaries, an absolute prerequisite for promotion appears to be a period of service in the apparatus of the CPSU Central Committee. Within the central machinery two tracks lead to the republican secretariats, judging from actual case histories. On the one hand, a number of secretaries have assumed the duties of "inspector" or "section head" or even "assistant department head" in the Organization Department of the Central Committee of the CPSU. In this department the problem of cadre appointments is clearly of prime concern. In addition, there are regional subdivisions within the organs of the Central Committee.[43] Certain executives in the central apparatus appear at the republican CP congresses as representatives of the Central Committee, indicating regional responsibilities as well.

In some cases we find shifts from one geographically specialized post in the central apparatus to a republican second secretariat. This was the case for Pereudin, who worked from 1963 to 1965 in the Central Asian office of the Central Committee, and at the present time is Second Secretary of the Turkmen CP. The same holds true for Lebedev,[44] who moved from the Belorussia and Baltic republics sector in the Central Committee to the secretariat of Estonia. Likewise, Polukarov was moved to Tadzhikistan. It is not certain that second secretaries have always been trained in the central apparatus of the republic to which they would later be assigned. Nevertheless, many of them have regional experience acquired in the Central Committee or experience in cadre selection problems, which are the main responsibility of second secretaries.

In general it appears that first secretaries often have experience in the affairs of state and in administration, while second secretaries are Party apparatus men. The differences in career, experience, and origin serve to assure the effective subordination of the first secretaries to the second ones. This subordination actually goes hand in hand with the first secretaries' outwardly greater prestige. They have the honor of embodying the national parties, of speaking on their behalf, of representing them.

Their subordination and what they represent may explain one final difference between first and second secretaries—the great vulnerability of the first ones. The fact that first secretaries are more stable in their posts than second ones in no way implies they are better protected. Quite to the contrary, in a penetrating study of national cadres Y. Bilinsky notes the high rate of "political losses" among national first secretaries.[45] He does not deny that first secretaries enjoy undeniable political longevity, but he attempts to show that this longevity often leads to spectacular falls. In purges first secretaries are the ones exposed to public censure. A first secretary's career often ends in sudden expulsion. Second secretaries, on the other hand, generally vanish discreetly if they have fallen into disgrace, or are promoted to other posts.

These observations show that the secretariat of the national parties is delicately balanced between "real power" and "centralized control" as against the "representation of power" and "apparent sovereignty." Control of men and institutions operates through a key authority in the Party's apparatus—the post of Second Secretary. Recent history demonstrates that, after a long period of pragmatic and sporadic policy, the central government has worked out a clear and coherent strategy that makes it possible to control the selection of political, administrative and technical cadres at all levels in the non-Russian republics. Standardization of control procedures and greater cohesion in the political system seem to be characteristic of the current national policy of integration.

The Army: A Tool For Integration?

Soviet authors today who analyze the stages of the country's development strongly emphasize the decisive role played by the army in creating this historic new community. Actually, this role is too often overlooked in the West, where the army is always seen as an instrument of the USSR's international might, turned toward the external world. This results in a partial misunderstanding of the Soviet army, its problems and ambiguities. Is it really the monolith which the West sees developing at its frontiers? Is it solely power and external threat? To regard it only that way is to overlook the fact that the Soviet army, like the USSR as a whole, is multinational, and that one of its functions is to aid in the integration of the nations. To understand this function and its consequences, it becomes necessary to look into the past.

The czarist Empire sought to build a cohesive army and therefore barred many of its subjects from joining. These were called "allogenic" peoples, comprising forty-five national groups. In the forefront were the Moslems. For the first time, war and revolution were to raise the problem of national armies.[46] In the ferment of national movements that shook Russian territory in 1917–1918, local military formations appeared. The newly formed national states strove to found independence on hastily assembled armies which, they hoped, would be capable of maintaining their recently acquired status. Meanwhile, the government that emerged from the October Revolution was striving to mobilize nationalist energies for its own purposes. Wherever Bolshevik control was established, Lenin and Trotsky had to soften it by integrating the local armed forces into the incipient Red Army.

From the first hour of the Revolution, this task had seemed imperative to Lenin and Trotsky; but until 1920 they ran into almost insurmountable difficulties. Civil war and foreign intervention dictated the utmost prudence. Weak and isolated, the Bolsheviks could not run the risk of having the border nations join their adversaries. For these nations independence mattered much more than the Revolution. To gain their support, the Soviet leaders had to settle their differences with them and tolerate the presence of armies which only heightened their desire for independence. Very soon, the drawbacks of such a compromise appeared. National armies were being raised in the Caucasus and the Ukraine. Even the Moslems, so consistently removed from military life, made great efforts to form an army and, a most disturbing fact, even used Soviet institutions for this purpose.

Within the Commissariat of Nationalities led by Stalin, one Moslem commissariat had been set up early in 1918. The chairman of this body, a Tatar, Mulla Nur Vakhitov, was to authorize the creation of a Central Moslem Military College to set up a Red Moslem army. In principle, all this was subordinate to the Commissariat of War, hence, Trotsky. In practice, the two men leading this operation, the Tatars Vakhitov and Sultan-Galiev, were pursuing goals totally alien to those of the Bolsheviks. They believed that for the backward nations, which had no proletariat, leadership should be provided by an army—an idea which was to reappear later with Mao Tse-tung—a hierarchical, politicized army, embodying incipient national consciousness and serving as a breeding ground for national cadres. Thus, by 1920, the future role of the Third World armies was defined by Russia's Moslems, a fact too often ignored. While the effort to form a single Moslem army failed because whole sectors rallied to the Soviet side, some Moslem nationalist units did develop within each national group.[47]

By 1919 Lenin attempted to take the situation in hand, having astutely recognized the danger that it posed.[48] Repeated decisions of the Bolshevik Party affirmed that all military activity must be under the authority of the Red Army. The extension of the Soviet regime in 1920–1922, which led to creation of the federation, was the result of coordination between the Red Army and national armies, which meant the latter's total subordination to the former. This stranglehold of the Bolshevik regime on military units, which each national group considered a symbol of reconquered sovereignty, resulted in a crisis which in 1923 pitted Soviet authorities against the nationalities. While revealing itself in diverse ways, this crisis had identical repercussions from one end of the USSR to the other.

In Central Asia the crisis took the form of an armed rebellion which took years for the government to crush. Armed bands of guerrillas, the Basmachis, created a climate of insecurity in the region and embodied the spirit of resistance in their compatriots' eyes. The leaders of the Ukraine operating within the system denounced the violence used on them by the Red Army. Speaking from the rostrum of the Twelfth Party Congress, in April 1923, Nikolai Skrypnik, a Bolshevik with an unimpeachable past,[49] declared: "Today, the army remains a tool for the Russification of the Ukraine and for the whole non-Russian population."[50] Another Ukrainian took over after Skrypnik and leveled the same charge: "Let's not forget that the Red Army is not only a tool for educating the peasantry to the proletarian way of thinking, it is also an instrument of Russification. We send tens of thousands of Ukrainian peasants to Tula and force them to understand everything in Russian. Is this right? Of course not. Why does the proletariat need this? No one knows. This is purely the result of the inertia in the Great Russian chain of command. Our high command is predominantly Russian. Even so, Ukrainian peasants sent to Tula and placed under Russian command could receive political and cultural training in their own language. Here is a second issue, to train military cadres to speak the national languages."[51]

Here Skrypnik and his companion clearly stated the problems of the army. The Soviets were using the army to Russify the non-Russians and to control them. Entirely dominated by the Russians, the Red Army served no real educational function in the context of the equality of nations.

The Soviet leaders responded to this crisis with two solutions intended to appease the nationalities while avoiding the drawbacks inherent in local national armies. Lenin was then a sick man, no longer able to take an active part in affairs of the state, but it can be assumed that his colleagues' reaction were in conformity with his own anxieties on this score. Their response was to reject local national armies as such, but at the same time the regime offered all nationalist groups the chance to join and assume responsibilities in the Red Army. The rejection of local national armies followed the systematic dismantling of Moslem units and the sentencing in June 1923 of the Moslem Red Army's theoretician, Sultan-Galiev.[52]

At a dramatic conference of the Communist Party held in Moscow from June 9–12, 1923, Stalin formulated the main lines and limits of national policy in the course of his attack on Sultan-Galiev. Militarily, this policy was to be based on the promotion of native cadres capable of leading national units within a Red Army representing the whole Soviet Union, and under unified command.[53] This policy entered into the framework of a military five-year plan begun in 1924. Replacing Trotsky in the People's Commissariat of War, Mikhail Frunze formulated the plan as follows: "We are building our army in such a way that no nationality will feel left out or victimized. At the same time, the army must be a single, strong body."[54]

By the end of the 1920s those efforts led to a profound change in relations between the population and the army. Military service was then extended to almost the entire male population, which was more readily drafted by local national leadership. But the massive promotion of officers of non-Russian origin and the raising of ethnically homogeneous formations failed to give the army's command a new coloring. The Soviet Army's high command remained very Russian, and national differences applied only to the lower and middle echelons. As it stood, such a concession was soon viewed as obsolete.

On March 7, 1938, new laws radically changed the army's physiognomy and put an end to the national "liberalism" that had been a principal factor in its organization since 1924.[55] All Soviet male citizens regardless of nationality or cultural background now faced compulsory military service. The army was unified. National units from the localities were disbanded and replaced by ethnically mixed units. The regulations specified that military service was to be performed in a multinational environment. The military schools and the training of cadres both escaped the national principle. Aside from the dispersal of individuals of the same national group, this meant that the army's language became the one language common to the Soviet peoples, namely Russian.

Since 1938 these principles of military organization have only been dropped once. During the Second World War, the concern for efficiency prompted Stalin to go back momentarily to national units set up hastily and supplied by the republics which they represented. But the era of Kazakh or Azeri divisions did not last in spite of the fact that on February 1, 1944 the Supreme Soviet adopted a law calling for the creation of republican armed forces and the transfer of defense commissariats from the federal level to the republican-federal level.[56] The Constitution was to reflect this change until 1977. Actually, the Soviets were doing this to give the country a new image for international reasons. Basically, the theoretical right to maintain armed forces demonstrated the sovereignty of the federated republics. Using this argument, the USSR obtained two extra seats in the postwar international organizations, seats that would be allotted to the Ukraine and Belorussia.

In practice, the postwar period, which seemed to establish the military autonomy of the republics, actually established a return to the 1938 concepts. Once the war ended, the national units disappeared. The army was something far too serious to be entrusted to the nationalities. On October 12, 1967 a military law stipulated clearly that compulsory military service had only one end—to fuse recruits into mixed units and serve as a cultural melting pot by the constant use of the Russian language. Thus, after hesitations and changes in policy, the Soviet Army became the preferred instrument for national integration.[57] Depending on the branch selected, recruits from the various localities now find themselves uprooted from their geographic and cultural origins for a period of up to three years. They are plunged into a different environment, one theoretically multi-ethnic but predominantly Russian. The constant use of the Russian language, along with political education, is intended to alter national awareness and the perception of the world of young conscripts. This specific mission of the Soviet Army has often been underscored by the country's leaders. Speaking at the fiftieth anniversary of the federation in 1972, Brezhnev said: "Our army is a special one. It is a school for internationalism, instilling sentiments of fraternity, solidarity and mutual respect for all the nations and nationalities of the Soviet Union. Our armed forces form a single family, the living embodiment of socialist internationalism."[58] This exceptional role assigned to the army explains why the new Soviet Constitution introduces the obligation of universal military service in the fundamental laws of the Soviet system (Article 31), and not, as one might expect, in the administrative organization and functioning of its institutions.

The integrating function assigned the army is seen clearly in the texts setting forth its organizational structure and in the statements of Soviet leaders. However, two key questions arise as to the relationship between Soviet intentions and the reality. Is the army really this united, cohesive family, patterned after a multi-ethnic society and thereby contributing to the integration of the various components of this society? Does the army have a measurable influence on the consciousness of those who join its ranks?

Does the army really reflect the nation? The Soviet specialists reply that it does, because each branch of the armed forces accepts representatives from all the nationalities. Basically, as far as the recruits are concerned, the universality of military service suggests that the army, considered as a whole, is a reflection of Soviet society. Can it be deduced from this that all the branches of military service accept recruits from all the localities on an equal basis? Soviet military documents are very positive in this regard.[59] However, logic and the observations at our disposal suggest a more subtly shaded situation. Highly sophisticated armies require a certain degree of education and a good knowledge of the army's language, Russian. Accordingly we find that Central Asian recruits are more readily assigned to construction battalions than to certain modern units.[60] Knowledge of Russian and the kind of education associated with urbanization undoubtedly leads to a process of selection. While this does not give the various army corps a precise ethnic mix, it does reflect in part the demographic gap between the more advanced western republics and the agrarian, more monolingual eastern republics.

The national problem shows up most vividly in the selection of military leaders. No precise data exist regarding the ethno-cultural composition of the officer corps and the high command, but scattered information helps to give a plausible picture of the military cadres. A career in the armed forces is based on various factors: first, personal choice linked with the individual's perception of the intellectual and material advantages that this type of career offers; and secondly, the aptitude corresponding to such a choice that is based on a suitable level of education and a complete mastery of the Russian language.

In certain national groups these prerequisites are easily met. They are found primarily in peoples of Slavic origin and certain non-Slavic groups enclaved in the Russian republics. The latter groups, which include Tatars, Chuvash, Mordvins and others, have traditionally supplied the army with leaders. The only available information on ethnic origin goes back to the Second World War. At that time both the troops and the officer corps were predominantly Slavic. The USSR's one hundred artillery divisions were 90% Slavic, of which 51.18% were Russians, 33.93% Ukrainians, and 2.04% Belorussians.[61] The officer corps therefore reflected this predominantly Slavic representation, although disproportionately favoring the Russians, who then accounted for nearly 90% of the officers, followed by the Ukrainians and the Belorussians.[62] In Table 35, a breakdown of air force and artillery leadership during the war years reveals other strange gaps in addition to this "Slavization" of the army.

Two points are particularly noteworthy. First of all, the author of this data indicates that the Russians represented the bulk of the leadership. Next, the fact that all the great Moslem nations are missing from these statistics suggests that the number of officers from those

Table 35
**Nationalities of Air Force and Artillery Officers
in the Second World War**

	Low and middle rank air force officers in 1943	High rank artillery officers at the end of the war
Ukrainians	28,000	6,000
Belorussians	5,305	1,246
Armenians	1,079	240
Tatars	1,041	173
Georgians	800	129
Chuvash	405	-
Mordvins	383	99
Ossetians	251	-

nations was lower than the lowest figures appearing in this table. No data of this kind have been published for the current period, but surveys of the socio-geographic origins of officers confirm what we know of the situation prevailing during the War.

The Red Star,[63] the official organ of the Soviet army, published the results of a survey based on 1,000 junior and middle-grade officers, according to which 82.5% came from worker families while only 17.5% were from peasant families. The sampling undoubtedly included men from all the nationalities, but the worker origins suggest that we are dealing primarily with more industrialized nationalities. The Soviet high command is always portrayed as emanating from a unified Soviet nation, and in this regard local national origins are never mentioned. A Western writer compiled a number of lists of general officers and, based on the names, came to the following conclusion: "Among the generals appointed between 1940 and 1970, 91% are Slavs (20% Ukrainians, 4% Belorussians, 7% of undeterminate origin, with 2% probably Polish)."

With regard to general officers who have membership in the Supreme Soviet of the USSR, 95% are Slavs (80% Russian, 15% Ukrainian). In a list of 42 general officers mentioned by the press in 1975–1976, 40 are Slavs, one an Armenian, and one of German origin. Among the members of the CPSU Central Committee, the general officers elected between 1952 and 1976 numbered 101 (including Brezhnev by virtue of his recently acquired military title). 97 general officers are of Slavic origin, including 78 Russians (35 members of the Central Committee, 36 candidates and 7 members of the Central Commission of Control). Among the four non-Russians, aside from Brezhnev, the four members of the Central Committee all appear to be Ukrainians; the ten candidates may be broken down into eight Ukrainians and two Poles. The four non-Russians are Marshal Bagramian (Armenian) and three others whose patronymics suggest either Jewish (in two cases) or German origin. In certain respects this ethnic makeup appears to express differences in levels of education, which would explain why there are no high-ranking officers of Moslem origin in the army. However, this explanation cannot justify the absence of Balts or Georgians, who stand at the top of the Soviet educational pyramid. Likewise, the very small number of Jews is hardly compatible with the fact that this community ranks first in the USSR in terms of education, just ahead of the Georgians.

Thus, the Soviet army does not reflect the society but rather the regime and the degree of assimilation or cooperation of national groups. The Ukrainian group plays an important part in the armed forces, even if this part is not in exact proportion to its size. In this respect, just as in the area of political power, the Ukrainian group appears as a "partner" of the Russian people. This partnership has another side to it implying the Russification of Ukrainian military leadership and therefore the existence of a profoundly Russified national milieu.[64]

Does the army have an influence on the thinking of men who have joined its ranks? Is it an efficient tool for socialization? Does it instill the Russian language and Soviet social values in its recruits by removing them from their national environment? T. Rakowska-Harmstone, who studied this problem, emphasizes that the situation varies with the level at which it is found. Those who choose to remain in the army after compulsory service have implicitly chosen to conform to the attitudes and convictions required by the army. Choosing the army not only means accepting Soviet values but also Russification.[65] The case of recruits leaving the army at the end of their compulsory service is quite different. To what extent have these men been marked by this exceptional period in their lives, during which they have been isolated in an alien environment? For Ivan Dziuba, the army is a remarkable tool for denationalization, which he describes in the following way: "Millions of young Ukrainians come home after their years of military service disoriented nationally and demoralized linguistically. In turn, they become a Russifying influence on other young people and on the population as a whole. Not to mention the very large number of them that never go back to the Ukraine. It's not very hard to imagine how damaging this is to national development."[66]

Do Dziuba's remarks apply to the other national groups in the USSR? Surveys are necessary to answer this. In one survey devoted to bilingualism in the USSR, the question of a second language (clearly Russian) in the army was raised. Curiously enough, the scholarly work in which the survey appeared mentions various ways of spreading the Russian language but does not discuss the army's contribution in this respect.[67] Without exact information, we have only hypotheses and the data furnished by the 1970 census. According to that census, some peoples become Russified slowly and others can hardly be Russified at all. The former are more mobile and the latter never leave their own territory. The Ukrainians are found in the first category along with the Belorussians. While subject to conscription like all the others, the Moslem peoples, the Caucasian peoples, and the Balts show no sign of denationalization.

One conclusion can be drawn from these contradictory situations: the peoples most vulnerable to Russification, Slavs or smaller nationalities, are undoubtedly those whom the military service helps to sever from their national setting. On the other hand, those who come from a barely Russified background do not seem to emerge from military service any more Russified. Perhaps, on the contrary, by living in a purely Russian background they become more aware of the forces of integration at work, of the distance between theory (a supra-national army) and reality (a Russian army), and draw from this one more argument for their deep attachment to national values.

Reading the Soviet press makes us wonder whether the young people in the federated republics aren't tempted more than the others to avoid military service, and whether the local authorities don't sometimes lend a helping hand. Without doubt this is a common practice in every society, but significantly it is the Armenians and also the Ukrainians who are denounced for a lack of good citizenship on this score.[68]

State, Party, Army—these are the three tools of integration working together to reach a goal clearly defined in 1917: the transition from diversity to unity. Are these the tools of social integration? Or are they primarily tools for control? It may be true that the apparatus of these three formations has incorporated the elites of the formerly subject borderland peoples. But this incorporation entails two conditions: that these elites must adhere unconditionally to the regime's plan which implies the transformation of the societies from which the elites were drawn; and that these elites must themselves be the vanguard of this transformation, rather than the representatives of their original culture. Centralization around the RSFSR employing the Russian language as a vehicle is the essential function of the three organs to assure Soviet authority from one end of the country to the other. This interpretation of integration is clear; it is founded primarily on the center's control over the periphery. But it would be simplistic to reduce the Soviet concept of integration to control pure and simple. Nor should we overlook the fact that together with this control comes the promotion of national elites trained in the work of unification.

CHAPTER V

Languages in the USSR: Tools for Integration? Or for the Consolidation of Nations?

I n the twentieth century no government has devoted more attention to the problem of the languages spoken by its citizens than the Soviet system. Political linguistics are unquestionably the most original aspect of Moscow's handling of the nationalities, and represent Moscow's most successful accomplishment. Even if this accomplishment is not without ambiguities, the meaning of this policy must be considered to determine where it is taking Soviet society, and what effect it is having on national integration.

The Equality of Nations through Equal Development of Languages

If the Soviets from the start have given such great attention to languages it is because they had discussed the question long before their leaders rose to power, and especially because under the Empire the problem of training national elites and the problem of cultural change in the different societies had been passionately debated. By 1917 the Bolsheviks were aware that the choice of a political language and of educational languages was a key issue in a multi-ethnic society. The political pattern and the nature of inter-ethnic relations depended on that choice. In the very beginning, the Soviet authorities had to take several problems into account. First of all, there were national susceptibilities to be considered. What better way of reassuring nations that had just left the "prison of the peoples" than giving them back the most tangible sign of their existence—their languages?[1] Then the strictly political problem of different nations living together had to be faced by a regime which professed to be an egalitarian emancipator of nations. To avoid being a disguised version of the Empire, the new government had to bring together all the national groups on an equal footing of power and progress. In the name of equality, the Soviets chose to unite them while allowing them to keep their special characteristics, hence their languages. Finally, there was the problem of rapid education of all societies throughout the USSR. The easiest way of accomplishing this mass education was via the languages that the people knew. In 1917–1918, everything—political realism as well as generosity—seemed to dictate the promotion of the national languages.[2] It has already been noted how this policy was carried out through the development of languages and alphabets, followed by the standardization of alphabets. By the end of the 1950s, when practically all of society was covered by the educational system, this situation was remarkable for the great number of languages which had been formalized and used in the school systems of the respective groups.

In principle, all these languages are equal since the Soviet Constitution stipulates that all citizens have "the possibility of using their mother tongue and the tongues of other peoples of the USSR,"[3] and makes no reference to a single language for all.

Nevertheless, over the years a *de facto* hierarchy has been set up, comprising four language groups:[4] (1) Russian, the language of international relations for the peoples of the USSR; (2) the national literary languages of the federated republics: Ukrainian, Belorussian, Uzbek, Kazakh, Kirghiz, Turkmen, Tadzhik, Armenian, Azerbaidzhan, Georgian, Moldavian, Latvian, Lithuanian, Estonian; (3) literary languages of the autonomous republics and regions: Tatar, Bashkir, Udmurt, Avar, Adygei, Ossetian, Khakass, Chechen, etc. (in all about forty languages); and (4) written languages that serve very limited social functions in the national districts of a few peoples in the north and elsewhere: Koryak, Nenets, Kurd, etc. (in all, scarcely more than ten languages).

This description gives a very accurate account of the present situation, one that is more rational than the situation prevailing in the early 1930s. Of the 130 languages existing at that time, the local dialects set up quite artificially as languages for tiny communities have died out by themselves, simply because those who spoke them preferred assimilation to a common language that would enable them to take their places in national life, rather than continue to use a language incomprehensible to the rest of the country.[5] For the smaller nations of the North, Russian generally served as a common language. Even so, nearly seventy languages coexist in the USSR. Their continuance presupposes the existence of schools, publications, and all the facets of a written culture. It would be a mistake to equate this preserved linguistic wealth with mere folklore or some meaningless eccentricity of the Soviet system. By their very existence, these languages have enabled communities to preserve their identity in a system which, quite beyond linguistic differences, sought to achieve a deep unity of political culture. The national languages convey, or are supposed to convey, a common culture, i.e., socialism and modernity; the fact that it travels via different channels makes it all the more acceptable.

Nevertheless, linguistic egalitarianism is not an ultimate goal in Soviet planning. It is the first phase in a shift to the required bilingualism, the local national language coupled with the language of all the Soviet peoples, Russian.[6] Subsequently, in a later phase, the Soviets will move toward an increasingly broad but voluntary use of the common language. Gradually, the national languages are to become an accessory component in the transformed national personality, the Homo Sovieticus, when what is common to all will be gaining constantly over particularisms.

Basically, the development of national languages was to promote bilingualism as well. In the first place, the almost total Cyrillization of alphabets in the late 1930s—with the exception of the Baltic, Georgian and Armenian languages—eliminated a major obstacle in the way of linguistic contacts. A second factor favoring bilingualism was the use of technical words, borrowed from the Russian, in every language.[7] In the 1940s this process seemed able rapidly to transform even languages remote from Russian.

What is the present status of this egalitarian policy with its underlying plan for cultural integration? After sixty years, or two generations, who are the members of the various Soviet nations? What languages do they speak? What languages do they study? To what degree have they been integrated culturally?

Increasing Use of National Languages

It is easy to gauge the linguistic situation of the USSR because every census, including the one carried out under the Empire, has stressed language. Table 36 shows how the various groups identify with their languages.

What can be deduced from this table? First of all, there is a significant difference between the nations. On the one hand, we find those which have a republic within which language rights have been solidly preserved. In these places the national languages have been retained as primary languages by more than 90% of the inhabitants. The lower percentages (Ukrainians, Armenians) are obviously due

Table 36
**Percentage of Members of National Groups who Consider
Their Language as Their Mother Tongue** [8]

Nationalities	1926	1959	1970
Russians	99.7%	99.8%	99.8%
Ukrainians	87.1	87.7	85.7
Belorussians	71.8	84.2	80.6
Lithuanians		97.8	97.9
Latvians		95.1	95.2
Estonians		95.2	95.5
Moldavians	92.3	95.2	95
Georgians	96.5	98.6	98.4
Armenians	92.4	89.9	91.4
Azeris	93.8	97.6	98.2
Kazakhs	99.6	98.4	98
Uzbeks	99.1	98.4	98.6
Turkmenians	97.6	98.9	98.9
Tadzhiks	98.3	98.1	98.5
Kirghiz	99	98.7	98.8
Tatars	98.9	92	89.2
Chuvash	98.7	90.8	86.9
Bashkirs	53.8	61.9	66.2
Mordvins	94	78.1	77.8
Maris	99.3	95.1	91.2
Udmurts	98.9	89.1	82.6
Komis	96.5	88.7	83.7
Karelians	95.5	71.3	63
Kalmyks	99.3	91	91.7
Kabardians	99.3	97.9	98.1
Ossetians	97.9	89.1	88.6
Chechens	99.7	98.8	98.8
Daghestan peoples	99.3	96.2	96.5
Karakalpaks	87.5	95	96.6
Buriats	98.1	94.9	92.6
Yakuts	99.7	97.5	96.2
Jews	71.9	21.5	17.7
Germans	94.9	75	66.8
Poles	42.9	45.2	32.5

to important diasporas. On the other hand, the nationalities living in autonomous republics or regions are often less well protected linguistically. At the bottom of the scale we find two groups having no territory of their own, the Jews and the Poles. The Germans, on the contrary, in spite of losing their national territory, have retained their own language to a higher degree than the two preceding groups.

A second observation concerns the position of languages in the period between the two most recent censuses. In 1961, Khrushchev claimed that the use of national languages was decreasing. However, most nations demonstrate remarkable linguistic stability, even a growing attachment to their national languages. The groups most attached to their native tongues are those in the Moslem borderlands or the Caucasus. Among the smaller nationalities it is also among the Moslems or the Buddhists that one finds the highest degree of fidelity to local languages, and sometimes even an increase in their use.

When the general census data is analyzed, we find that the urban population has a somewhat weaker attachment to its national language; and the same holds true for the male population. But on this score, too, the overall data varies with the nations considered. The Moslem peoples and those of the Caucasus, even in cities, hardly ever give up the use of their native languages; likewise, there is very little—if any—difference between the spoken language behavior patterns of men and women. In other words, wherever the mother tongue retains a very strong position, neither urbanization nor sex have any real effect on the situation. On the other hand, nationalities who are slowly dropping the use of their language are more subject to outside influences.

In short, far from revealing the gradual obliteration of minority languages, the census shows that Soviet society in the 1970s, educated and subjected to frequent contact with Russian through the media, cherishes its mother tongues.

Has this stability, or even increased use of the national languages gone hand in hand with simultaneous progress for the Russian language? The 1970 census provides an answer to this question since the Soviets were canvassed about their ability to use another language of the USSR. On this score, it should be noted that, in 1959, of those who had dropped their own national language, 10,183,000 had exchanged it for Russian.[9]

In 1970 the number of people opting for Russian rose to

13,019,200, which represents a sizable gain in absolute figures, but no gain at all expressed as a percentage of non-Russians, who dropped from 9.5% to 8.6%. Two conclusions can be drawn from this. Linguistic assimilation, with all languages merging, has made little headway in the last eleven years. Proportionately, the share of the Russian language has hardly changed, either. The real problem is bilingualism, one which is of concern to the Soviet leaders and educators.[10]

To what extent have the non-Russian peoples, who cling to the use of their native tongues, acquired the use of Russian? In this connection, the census reveals highly divergent groups. A first group is made up of Jews, the majority of whom have opted for the Russian language, and for whom their mother tongue is now their second language.[11] In fact, 72.8% of Soviet Jews now consider Russian their mother tongue (82% in Birobidzhan) and 16.3% (15.7% in Birobidzhan) speak Russian as a second language. For all intents and purposes, the linguistic assimilation of the Jewish group can be considered complete.

The Germans and the Tatars seem to be headed the same way. More than 70% of the Germans speak Russian perfectly, even if they have retained a better knowledge of their own tongue than the Jews. As for the Tatars, who remain deeply attached to their mother tongue, they exemplify the progress made in bilingualism, for 62.5% of them have an excellent command of Russian as well as their own language.[12]

The reasons for the fairly rapid assimilation of these three nations are clear. Either they are totally deprived of territories of their own and accordingly have limited or nonexistent rights in the sphere of education; or, as in the case of the Tatars, they are very scattered and immersed in an alien environment which heavily favors the adoption of a language other than their own.

A second group emerges from our analysis, a group whose ethnogeographic situation is much less clear. Here, an already considerable proportion of the population, varying between 25% and 50%, is bilingual. At the same time, this group manifests a great affinity for its own language. Three elements are found in this group: (1) the Slavic peoples whose bilingualism can be explained by linguistic kinship; (2) the culturally advanced Baltic peoples; and (3) the culturally backward Moldavians. Among the Slavs, the Belorussians seem to be the ones most in the grip of rapid linguistic Russification.

The use of their language has declined markedly between the two censuses, to the benefit of Russian, which has been adopted by nearly 10% of all Belorussians living in their own republic, and nearly 57% of those living in other localities.

Coupled with this increasingly large proportion of assimilated Belorussians is the mass of those who speak Russian in spite of their attachment to their own language. This category represents 52% of all Belorussians in the republic itself and 35% of those living outside. This is an important phenomenon. More than 60% of the Belorussian population within the republic has a good command of Russian. Almost all the dispersed Belorussians—about 20% of the total with a tendency to still greater dispersion—have acquired a good knowledge of Russian, either with or without an accompanying loss of their own tongue. In this connection, the inexorable trend toward Russian seems all the more pronounced inasmuch as between the two censuses there was every indication of a drop in the use of the mother tongue, a wider use of Russian as a second language, and increased dispersion.

The situation for the Ukrainians appears to be headed exactly the same way, but at a slower pace. The decline in the use of Ukrainian, for both those living in the republic and those who have been dispersed (who represent a little less than 14%) is exactly matched by the adoption of Russian as a primary language by 8.6% of all Ukrainians at home and by half of the dispersed Ukrainians. While among the dispersed Ukrainians knowledge of Russian is widespread, less than a third of the Ukrainians living in their own republic have adopted Russian as a second language.

Two factors separate the Belorussians from the Ukrainians and, in certain respects, make the Ukrainian trend seem less alarming. First of all, the Russification of the Ukrainians is proceeding more slowly. This statement hold true both for switching from Ukrainian to Russian and for using Russian as a second language. In addition, unlike the Belorussians who are steadily leaving their republic, the Ukrainians now seem more concentrated in theirs than ever before.[13] Moreover, the Ukrainians seem more urbanized than the Belorussians. If one recognizes the fact that cities represent the most favorable setting for a swing to Russian, there is clearly developing in the Ukraine a resistance to this linguistic shift, despite urbanization, in an evident effort to preserve the national language.

The linguistic individuality of the Moldavians is also threatened.

In Moldavia the Russian language is making slow but sure headway, with a corresponding decline in the national language. Nearly 34% of the Moldavians residing in their own republic are bilingual; the same holds true for half of the 14.5% of Moldavians living outside the republic. Theoretically, two factors should have saved the Moldavians from rapid Russian penetration: first of all their language which, even though employing the Cyrillic alphabet, is not a Slavic language, but a modified form of Rumanian; and secondly, their low degree of urbanization. Despite these factors apparently favoring the development of the national language, the Moldavians are fairly high up on the scale of linguistic assimilation.

Outward appearances seem to militate in favor of classifying the Baltic peoples in the same group. While Russian is scarcely gaining ground there over the local national languages, it is quite widespread as a second language. Russian is spoken by 45% of the Latvians, 35% of the Lithuanians, 27% of the Estonians. But the fairly widespread knowledge of Russian reflects a high degree of cultural and urban development more than any relinquishment of national languages. The Balts are protected primarily by the impermeability of their languages to Russian. All three peoples belong to linguistic groups totally alien to the Slavic; they use a Latin alphabet. For the Baltic peoples, Russian is really a foreign language, not a related one. As is the case in all nationalities, the use of Russian develops faster among Balts outside their republic than within it. But the years separating the two censuses were marked by a heavier concentration of the Baltic populations within their own republics.

One last case, that of the Kazakh people, can be cited among the relatively bilingual group of peoples. The Kazakhs are unquestionably much more solidly attached to their language than, for instance, the Ukrainians. But they are also more adept at bilingualism—Russian is spoken by 41.8% of the Kazakhs, both those residing in the republic and those living outside. The Kazakhs are the only Central Asian people falling into the category of bilinguals who might be termed "advanced." They are also the only people whose bilingualism has developed both inside and outside the boundaries of the republic. But this immediately calls for an explanation. The Kazakhs constitute a minority within their own republic, since they comprise at the present time scarcely one third of the total population, despite some gains that have been made. The preservation of the local national language is always a difficult task when it involves a minority situation.

So it is evident that Russian can make headway in some very different situations, notably wherever its penetration is fostered by linguistic similarities or, at least, by a common alphabet, but also in places where the languages are totally dissimilar. It can progress not only in essentially urban societies but also where urbanization is developing slowly. Russian advances in step with intellectual development, but also in intellectually less-favored milieux.

Finally, the peoples for whom Russian remains a very remote language comprise a third group. All the larger peoples of the Caucasus and Central Asia fall into this category. The Armenians are again the ones who lend themselves most readily to Russian-language penetration, for they have a very large diaspora (45% of the total Armenian population). What is remarkable here isn't the degree of their linguistic Russification, but rather the degree of attachment to the Armenian language. Over the years separating the two censuses, Russian became the primary language of only a small number of Armenians more than before (19.6% instead of 17.1%). Even as a second language, Russian is spoken by only 23.3% of all Armenians living inside their republic, and by 41.2% of those outside it. What more obvious sign of a group's national vitality than that? More than half of this group is living in an alien environment, yet more than 90% of them have retained their native tongue and less than 40% have learned Russian. It is true that a good number of Armenians live in neighboring Georgia, where linguistic nationalism is openly demonstrated. Georgian is kept as a mother tongue by nearly all those who live in their own country. The language has lost ground to Russian outside Georgian boundaries (28.1% have chosen Russian); however, this is negligible in view of the fact that only 3.5% of all Georgians live outside their native land. Despite a very high cultural level, few Georgians use Russian as a second language (20%). On the other hand, they take pride in the fact that their language, though having a unique alphabet and no connection with any other linguistic family in the USSR, serves as the primary language for 100,000 people living in the republic and is spoken fluently by an additional 164,000 non-Georgians.[14]

Turning to the Moslem peoples, we find the knowledge of Russian becoming weaker and weaker. Only a trifling percentage use Russian as a primary language in the Central Asian republics and in Azerbaidzhan (less than 1% of the population living in the latter republic). When it comes to Russian as a second language, the most advanced are the Kirghizs (19% of whom know Russian), followed by the Tadzhiks (16%), the Azeris (14.9%), the Turkmenians (14.8%) and the Uzbeks (13%). Particularly noteworthy about these figures is the fact that the national language—far from declining over recent years—has consolidated and even improved its position in nearly all these areas. Also worthy of note is the fact that Russian is only moving ahead at a snail's pace.

In short, if the trends for these three large groups are compared, we find that the rise of the Russian language is geared less to a clear-cut sociological situation—i.e., the rise of urbanization[15] and the decline of the rural world—than to political status (absence or existence of a national state of their own) or geographic situation (the Caucasian and Central Asian borderlands seem much less vulnerable than the western part of the USSR). But one factor must be taken into consideration, namely, the authenticity of national cultures, or even languages. In its present form the Belorussian language was shaped by the Soviet authorities on the basis of different sub-dialects. It was imposed on the population in the name of the "Belorussization" policy prevailing in the 1920s.[16] It is actually an artificial creation, which was long in gaining acceptance, and in all likelihood is incapable of competing with Russian, so closely related and more authentic. To some extent, the case of Moldavian is similar. To give the Moldavians a personality of their own, to convince them that they were not Rumanians, Soviet authorities imposed the use of a regional dialect of Rumanian on them, modifying its written form by the adoption of the Cyrillic alphabet. So the Moldavian language appears as artificially manufactured as the Moldavian nation itself, and this is probably what prevents Moldavian from effectively resisting Russian.

In complete contrast, the languages of the Caucasus and Central Asia, which have served rich cultures and are identified with a long historical tradition, are symbols of national existence, which the members of each ethnic community defend all the more tenaciously because of their historical depth.

Nevertheless, for a language to live, it must be taught. Furthermore, the language has to be the very basis of instruction, since it serves as the medium for the transmission of all other knowledge. Do the nations and nationalities have the necessary educational means to keep their languages intact? To what extent do the respective positions of the national languages and of Russian reflect the Soviet educational system?

Education and National Integration

Are these two terms joined in a policy appropriate to the time and the place?

As we have already seen, each national group has the absolute right to develop its cultural resources—schools, universities, and publications—in its own language. Soviet doctrine has come a long way in this respect.[17] In the 1920s national education was imperative because it symbolized the Soviets' professed egalitarianism. Since the mid-1930s and with the advent of the Second World War, however, the acquisition of Russian has become a prerequisite for social advancement. Moreover, Khrushchev, who had a domineering attitude toward national evolution, tried to accelerate what he considered a decisive criterion of development: the changeover to the Russian language. It was toward this end that, in the educational reform which he promulgated in 1958, he inserted a clause granting the right of parents to choose the language in which their children would be educated.[18]

This seemingly innocent provision was of capital importance. In the first place, it implied that it was in the children's best interests to learn a language other than their own. Secondly, by replacing the general principle of an education in the national language with a choice, Khrushchev was placing non-Russian citizens in a very awkward position. Since 1958 the regime had been laying great stress on the role of the Russian language in drawing the nations together and on the necessity for universal bilingualism. Leaving parents a choice that would not lead to this bilingualism was making them run the risk of not seeming to be interested in the rapprochement of the nations. This was clearly a matter of moral pressure. But the element of choice was not the sole factor in the issue. There was another: do parents everywhere have the possibility of choosing between a national school program and a Russian one? On this score the variations from one region to the other and the factors that have to be taken into consideration are multiple.

First of all, the Soviet system comprises three types of schools: those where the teaching is in the national language; those where the teaching is in Russian; and those with a mixed program. Another variable has to do with the number of years spent in school. Some schools do not go beyond the elementary level; others, in spite of the complete ten-year program of education, cover only eight years.

A third variable concerns the rules for teaching Russian in non-Russian schools, which differ from one republic to another or within a single republic. It is very difficult to give a general picture of the education of the nationalities; for, in addition to these variables is a lack of information. The censuses, so replete with data on the general development of education within each national group, ignore the problem of the teaching of languages. To fill this important gap there is only incomplete and often conflicting information. To try to understand the situation of schools among the different nationalities, the larger nationalities having status as republics must be separated from those incorporated in a different framework as autonomous republics or regions.

As can be expected, the position of the Slavic nationalities is dominated by the linguistic kinship they have with each other and with the Russians, which is a factor tending to promote the spread of Russian. For the Ukraine, information dating back to the time of the latest census[19] brings to light the difficulties in Ukrainian education. Out of 27,500 regular schools in the republic, 22,000 teach in Ukrainian, 4,700 in Russian, and the rest in the various minority languages (Polish, Hungarian, Moldavian). To all appearances, the situation for Ukrainian seems good. In practice, however, it is much less so. First of all, within twenty years the number of schools teaching in Russian has almost doubled, while the number of Ukrainian schools has fallen from 28,000 to fewer than 23,000. Secondly, these figures lump together all schools, regardless of the length of the curriculum and the size of the school. An urban school offering a complete course of instruction can have ten times as many students as a four-year rural school, and partial information suggests that city schools tend to be Russian, while the ones in the country are more often Ukrainian. This being the case, we can only assume that the proportion of teaching in Ukrainian is considerably smaller than would appear at first sight. With regard to higher education in the Ukraine, everything suggests that the Russian language is pre-eminent there. The ethnically mixed character of the students, and of the teachers as well, favors this hypothesis.

In Belorussia the Russification of education is much more clearcut at every level. While there is no exact information about the Russian and Belorussian breakdown of the schools, two points seem certain: one, that Russian predominates in the city schools; and secondly, that Russian is taught in all Belorussian schools, just as Belorussian is taught in all the Russian schools.[20] The parallel seems to end there, however. In the Belorussian schools, Russian is compulsory from the second to eighth grade, for five hours weekly until the sixth grade, and afterwards dropping to two hours weekly in the eighth grade.

Thus, for seven out of ten years of compulsory education,[21] the students at Belorussian schools receive fairly intensive training in Russian. In the Russian schools, on the other hand, Belorussian is only studied from the third to eighth year, and, except for the first two years when the course loads are three and four hours respectively, from the fifth year on the instruction of Belorussian is limited to two hours. This easily explains why all university instruction, with the exception of a few courses, is given in Russian. The students are well prepared for it.

For two reasons the Moldavians should be safe from intense Russification: first, because they are for the most part rural; and secondly, because their educational level lags far behind the average for the USSR. In spite of this, Russian is dominant in the schools—at least in the cities[22]—especially because in Moldavia it is a question of weakening the Moldavian language to break down the linguistic ties linking the Moldavians with Rumania. As for the university, a knowledge of the Russian language is required.

In contrast to this low level of instruction in the national languages of the Slavs and Moldavians is the high status assigned to national languages in republics where the cultural level and degree of urbanization is very high—the Baltic countries and Christian nations in the Caucasus. In Estonia and Lithuania the schools teaching in these national languages are very solidly entrenched: 73% of all Estonian schools teach in Estonian; 84% of all Lithuanian children are taught in their mother tongue.[23] In Latvia the position of teaching in Russian seems slightly more favorable. To offset the weak attraction of Russian schools in the Baltic countries, the teaching of Russian becomes compulsory at an early age—in the first year of primary school in Lithuania, in the second year in Latvia and Estonia. However, higher education is given mainly in the national languages, and universities like Estonia's Tartu have a considerable reputation all over the USSR.

Georgia's position is very similar to that of the Baltic countries. Three-quarters of the schools teach in Georgian, and the number of Russian schools barely surpasses the number of Armenian schools in

Georgia (each has less than a tenth of all Georgian schools). Higher education, which is dispensed primarily in Georgian, is of high quality and supplies the country with a numerous elite. Proportionately, Georgians rank second behind the Jews as far as graduates of higher education are concerned, compared to the population as a whole. In fact, this situation gives rise to an underemployment problem for the Georgian elite. Brought up in Georgia and little inclined to emigrate, even though fluent in Russian, these educated elite do not always find openings within the framework of their own republic. The resulting discontent of these "unemployed intellectuals" is one of the components of Georgian nationalism.

The situation of the Armenians is very different. They are deeply attached to their own schools, whether in Armenia or in the diaspora. In Russia itself, they have Armenian schools with a complete curriculum of study, and in the Russian schools Armenian courses are offered throughout the ten-year program.[24] But this advantage is counter-balanced by the obligation to study Russian from the first year and on into higher education. Yet, these provisions have in no way hindered the development of an elite fully trained in its own language. Sixty-two percent of the Armenians who receive a higher education pursue their studies in Armenian at Erivan.[25] It is not surprising that the Armenians rank third (after the Jews and Georgians) in the proportion of their university-trained class compared to their total population. But unlike the Georgians, these elite readily leave their territory and use their abilities wherever possible.

In the Moslem republics, once more, a homogeneous situation prevails, with the exception of the Kazakhs. There is a definite cleavage in this group between the rural population studying in Kazakh schools and the urban population generally attending Russian schools. Being in the minority in their own republic, and not yet having enough educated people to meet their own needs, the Kazakhs adopt the Russian language of their own accord because it is their surest way to social advancement and access to important posts.

In the other Central Asian republics and in Azerbaidzhan a relatively homogeneous educational situation exists. The population of the official nationality of the republics, whether in a rural or urban setting, prefers its own schools. Soviet authorities try to offset this withdrawal toward national education by making Russian compulsory from the first grade on;[26] by developing an extended (ten-year) period of schooling in Russian, which contrasts with the situation in the national schools where an eight-year program prevails;[27] and especially by applying pressure on students to attend universities, either by imposing the knowledge of Russian as a prerequisite for higher education, or by showing favoritism in the selection of cadres to those who have completed university training in Russian.[28] Despite inducements to study Russian—and even pressure at the stage of higher education—the Moslems show the utmost reluctance to give up their schools for Russian ones. A limited fraction of their graduates may go on to Russian higher education; in Kirghizia, for example, the almost total absence of a strictly Kirghiz university program compels them to do so. But in general, the present educational trend among Moslems is characterized by two factors. The level of proficiency in Russian is so low that these peoples insist on the development of higher education in their national language, which will assure them access to all posts. They are clearly fighting for the training of national elites, not for social advancement through a knowledge of the Russian language. Add to this the fact that women leave school early and it is easy to understand why the national languages are so solidly entrenched. Between the demands of the Moslem peoples and the Georgians on the one hand, and the policy of bilingualism advocated by the Soviet regime on the other, an impasse has been reached, one that seems to have become entrenched during the period between the last two censuses.

Thus, with varying degrees of success, the communities recognized as nations are as a rule able to preserve their languages through an educational system that provides for the training of a national society "in form." But this rule, stemming from the status of the nations, hardly applies to less complete national entities set up as autonomous republics, much less the autonomous regions, or national districts. When one national group is enclaved geographically and attached politically to another state in the federation, its cultural rights are diminished in fact, if not in theory. The political organization of the USSR is such that most of the nonsovereign nations are enclaved in the Federated Republic of Russia.

In this connection, the cultural status of the peoples reveals a process of rapid Russification precisely by means of the schools. An American study[29] has attempted to describe this process. The position of the non-Russians in the RSFSR has several characteristic features. First of all, even where the national entities possess a complete system of secondary education (only two nations fall into this category—the Tatars and the Bashkirs[30])—Russian is *obligatory* in all schools from the first grade on. Thus, without exception, the study of Russian is mandatory from start to finish in the educational system. A second factor is that in all cases except for the Tatars and Bashkirs incomplete national education compels children to change over at some point from instruction in their own language to instruction in Russian. Thirdly, the general trend during the last twenty years has been away from national schools toward an ever earlier transfer into the Russian schools. Finally, the existence of national schools in no way implies that the whole group benefits from them. On the contrary, it can be assumed that parents, knowing their children are headed for a Russian school and then a Russian university, prefer to have them prepare right from the start for a Russian education, while preserving their own language as a means of communication within the family and the group around them. This trend in the direction of a gradual suppression of national education is clear from Table 37, which summarizes the situation for the autonomous republics.

Table 37
Number of Years of Education in the National Language [31]

Official nationality in the autonomous republics	1958	1972
Bashkirs	**1-10**	**1-10**
Buriats	1-7	1-6
Chechens	1-4	preschool education only
Churash	1-7	1-4
Ingush	1-4	preschool education only
Kabards	1-4	none
Balkars	1-4	—
Kalmyks	1-4	—
Karelians	unknown	unknown
Komis	1-7	1-3
Maris	1-7	0-3
Mordvins	1-7	0-3
North Ossetians	1-4	none
Daghestan peoples (Avars, Darghins, Kumyks, Lezghians, Laks, Nogais, Tabasarans	1-4	0-2 (with the exception of the Avars 0-1)
Tatars	**1-10**	**0-10**
Tuvinians	1-7	0-7
Udmurts	1-7	0-3
Yakuts	1-7	1-8

This table is very revealing. It shows that, aside from the Tatars and the Bashkirs, only the Yakuts seem headed toward a complete educational program of their own. For all the other peoples the national language tends to be relegated to early childhood and the period normally devoted to learning to read and write. Furthermore, even the rural population, which has only four-year elementary schools, must go to Russian schools. Thus, the cleavage found in the federated republics between a rural population studying in its own language and an urban population more apt to be Russified is obliterated in this type of territorial formation. The Russian school has penetrated everywhere.

The situation becomes still more unfavorable in the autonomous regions and national districts. Often, national elementary education existed there as late as 1958, but eleven years later, national education had disappeared except for the Altaic peoples, the Khakass and the Komi-Permiaks, who have only three years' elementary education in their own language. More serious still is that while in the autonomous republics and regions the national language is taught in the Russian schools throughout the program, in the national districts it is not taught beyond the third grade (again except for the Komi-Permiaks).[32]

Clearly, a probably irreversible movement is going on within the RSFSR to reduce the number of languages used in education among the non-Russian population. For the enclaved nations, it must be assumed that Khrushchev was right in thinking that a convergence followed by linguistic fusion could take place in the space of a generation. Neverthelesss, it is a question whether this trend toward the assimilation of smaller nations by those which surround them has always succeeded in Russifying them. In the RSFSR the reply can only be affirmative.

In Georgia and Uzbekistan—republics that encompass other national entities within their own boundaries—it is still difficult to say which language the group undergoing assimilation is leaning toward—Russian or toward the language of the republic. This question cannot be answered on the basis of the census, which sought to determine the level of proficiency in Russian for peoples tied to another language, but made no attempt to state *which* other languages had been used. The example of the Tatars living outside their republic does, however, prove that while they are easily assimilated by the Russians, especially in urban settings, they are also attracted by the language around them whenever this belongs to a linguistic group close to their own—Kazakh, Kirghiz, Uzbek, Turkmenian. The influence of the surrounding politico-linguistic setting is illustrated by the case of the Ossetians. Those who live in the RSFSR chose Russian when they were being assimilated. In Georgia, on the other hand, they opt for Georgian.[33] Noteworthy also is the case of the Gypsies. A people without territory and without rights, the Gypsies—unlike the Germans or the Jews—have shown a heightened degree of national linguistic consciousness in recent years. The percentage of those now recognizing Romany as their native tongue has risen from 59.3% to 70.8%.

Can we then conclude, as the American Brian Silver[34] suggests, that the erosion of national languages in the RSFSR might well serve as a pattern for similar trends in the national republics? In the present state of affairs, the answer is emphatically no. The contrast between the status of national languages in the republics and in the enclaved territories is striking. The consolidation of languages in the sovereign republics (except for the Slavs) is also an undeniable factor in the problem.

To the strong attachment of people to their own language, another element should be added, namely the de-Russification of the national languages. It has already been noted that the national languages have passed through a phase of transformation and weakening where the massive penetration of modern Russian terms seemed to be leading to a Russification of the languages themselves. [35] The last few years have been marked by a trend in just the opposite direction. All the great languages of the USSR have been purged of those borrowings and have coined their own words to describe technological advances of the twentieth century.[36] And this de-Russification of languages actually adds to their strength. Thus the gradual assimilation of small and medium-sized nations can be contrasted with the vitality of the larger nations. Nevertheless, Soviet leaders are not alone in predicting the obliteration of linguistic barriers. From republics apparently well protected against assimilation, voices are now being heard denouncing an insidious Russification. What meaning can be placed on these warning cries, which seem to contradict the facts?

Russification Accepted as the "Lesser Evil"

While the Soviet press rarely reports protests on the theme of linguistic Russification, it nevertheless gave ample coverage to the alarm voiced by writer Revaz Djaparidze at the Eighth Georgian Writers' Congress. It goes without saying that Djaparidze's speech was never published in any official organ; but from the attacks launched against it can be deduced his two main arguments,[37] and also the fact that there had been "a sympathetic attitude on the part of a portion of the public that happened to be there. Emotional as soon as it became a matter of defending their language, the immature, irrational mood of the public became apparent when they prevented one of the best language instructors from speaking. . . ."[38]

What was Djaparidze saying? That the massive introduction of Russian in the republic is a threat to the Georgian language; and that Russian is conveyed by pedagogy and the reform projects associated with it.[39] According to Djaparidze, there is a plan to change the program at the University of Tbilis in such a way that the different subjects would be taught in Russian, thereby altering the university's national character, and warranting the dispatch of Russian instructors to that university. The other innovation concerns secondary school education. It deals with generalizing an isolated experiment in one boarding school where a number of subjects are taught directly in Russian from the fifth grade on.[40] This would result in converting Georgian schools into *mixed* schools, or even reducing Georgian to the bare minimum, turning them squarely into Russian schools with some compulsory instruction in the Georgian language and literature. The use of boarding schools to promote Russian in the non-Russian republics is certainly an idea that has been making headway. At the same time, in Uzbekistan, the Minister of Education announced that the number of hours of instruction in Russian language and literature had been increased in all the Uzbek schools, and that 20,000 teachers specializing in Russian (undoubtedly Russians) had been assigned to this task. For its part, the Central Committee of the Uzbek Communist Party insisted on the need to expand the knowledge of Russian in the republic, and recommended the establishment of boarding schools geared to teaching in Russian. In 1976 there were 150 schools of this kind in Uzbekistan.[41]

To improve and expand the teaching of Russian in the federated republics seems to be the watchword issued recently by the Party. Throughout the press in the republics are found many exhortations of this type and many denunciations of inadequacies regarding the teaching of Russian.[42] In keeping with this, from October 21 to 23, 1975, a conference of teachers from all over the USSR was held in Tashkent to discuss ways of improving Russian teaching in the national schools.[43] This conference clearly demonstrates the mobilization of efforts to break the crust of indifference on the part of the larger nationalities regarding the Russian language.

The example of Tatar shows that, when it comes to enclaved nations, it is simpler to accelerate the development of Russian. At the start of this decade, either despite or because of increased Russification in Tatar territory, the people reacted vehemently against the fairly massive transfer of Tatar children to Russian schools. Even the authorities of the autonomous republic reacted. The result was that in 1970 the Minister of Education stressed the fact that parents could choose whichever school they preferred—Russian or Tatar.[44] He further urged parents not to transfer their children to Russian schools until they had acquired absolute mastery of their mother tongue.[45]

In 1973 the Kazan Pedagogical Institute set up a conference, attended by cadres from the various autonomous republics, to study ways of improving the teaching of Tatar and probably also of other languages in the region. A year later, a more official conference was set up under the authority of the republic's Minister of Education,[46] who insisted on the need to train many Tatar teachers—and train them better.[47] This is quite clearly the reaction of a national group trying to safeguard its own language. But two facts reduce the extent of this reaction, both linked to the geopolitical position of the group: its inability to influence the decision-making process which affects educational policy, and the group's migrations. The first point is illustrated by the textbook problem. The Tatars studying in their own schools are seriously hampered by the lack of textbooks in Tatar, a scarcity that the Ministry of Education's republican organ denounces constantly but to little avail.[48]

Yet the Tatar ASSR has considerable publishing facilities at its disposal, since in the year 1975, for school use alone, the Tatars printed 350 different books with a total press run of 11,616,000 copies.[49] If the Tatars are short of school textbooks, it can only mean that many works they publish are intended for other national groups. It is easy to see where the problem lies. In the general publishing program there is a certain amount of arbitration in favor of given groups or expenditures. However, neither the plan nor the arbitration fall within the jurisdiction of Tatar authorities; instead, they are handled at the republican level (the RSFSR). Another aspect of Tatar educational difficulties derives from migration within the republic. Attracted by the development of petrochemical plants, Tatar workers are moving to the industrialized regions, and in so doing they are shifting to areas where the schools are chiefly Russian. As a result, these migrants are exerting pressure for setting up Tatar schools.

There is no question that there is pressure from the Kremlin for a greater use and knowledge of Russian. To make this clear, it is only necessary to consider the statements made from November 30 to December 2, 1976 at the conference held in Tallin on nationality problems.[50] In his introductory report the vice-president of the USSR Academy of Sciences, P. Fedoseev, stressed that the drawing together of the nations had given rise to a pan-Soviet culture in which Russian was the *lingua franca*, the means of communication for everybody.

There is therefore, on the one hand, the regime's insistence on Russian; on the other, resistance which appears both among the Georgians, closed off by their particularism in their homogenous republic and the more dispersed Tatars. This leads one to wonder about the significance of central pressure and local protests. Are these pressure tactics really aimed at Russifying the schools? Or is the regime, aware of the difficulty of the problem and weary as Sisyphus going over the same road every day, trying to convince itself of the success of the policy? Conversely, how are we to interpret the alarmist statements of the writer Djaparidze when everything points to the Georgians' impermeability to Russification? There is some truth on both sides. The Russification of the schools certainly won't come overnight. But by denouncing the non-Russians for their lack of proficiency in Russian, the Soviets are paving the way for another kind of pressure, which is far from being a hypothetical one for the future. What Moscow is really underscoring is that there just aren't enough local nationals fluent in Russian to fill responsible posts.

In a state where the Soviet people has become a reality, the knowledge of Russian, the common language, can be required and is increasingly required for admission to all leadership appointments, even rather low-level ones. The Balts are already complaining of the fact that a great many technical posts are in the hands of non-Balts (chiefly Russians), who not only hold the best jobs but actually chart the course to be followed in the republics.[51] This gradual takeover of posts has come about because the training of the Baltic elites was not considered on a high enough level to meet the demands of technical progress. The Balts are quick to add that even truck drivers must be fluent in Russian! By proposing educational reforms in Georgia, the regime is paving the way for the coming of teachers—

Russian specialists. In fact, a man like Djaparidze isn't so much denouncing compulsory Russification as an insidious choice between either voluntarily agreeing to fluency in Russian, or continuing to neglect the language and paying for this linguistic nationalism with an influx of Russian cadres to make up for the republic's lack of bilinguals. Apparently, the choice is between gradual linguistic Russification—true bilingualism being seldom attained—and Russification of jobs. But here again one can only wonder about the viability of such a project. At a time when the supply of labor is dwindling in the USSR, how can it be dispersed to the borders? And while the Russians are very inclined to move into the Baltic republics, are they equally willing to settle in such homogenous societies as those in the Caucasian or Central Asian periphery?

Any discussion of the linguistic problem in the USSR generally winds up where it started, by acknowledging that the flowering of languages and the training of elites in every Soviet language represent Moscow's crowning success. But this raises a number of questions. Is there a general linguistic dynamic leading from the flowering of languages to a community in which Russification and bilingualism would diminish the role of national languages? Have the rights granted for the languages served to integrate the nations of the USSR? Finally, to what extent should loyalty to the mother tongue be systematically identified with national feeling?

Considering Soviet linguistic complexity today, we can only conclude that there are no evolutionary laws applying to all the languages. Clearly, ethnic groups placed in a peripheral position, living in relatively homogenous states, and having a political framework that strengthens cultural rights, have greater capacity to defend their languages than groups that are enclaved or dispersed and, hence, weaker politically. On the whole, the position of people enjoying federated republican status is better than that of the others; and the groups with a large population are also better suited to defend themselves than the small groups. Nevertheless, there are many exceptions to outweigh the rule. The relatively large Belorussian group, living in a federated republic, even possessing international privileges, manifests notable linguistic weakness. Conversely, the Tatars, numerically large but three-quarters dispersed, tenaciously resist Russification.

Moving down the numerical ladder, how can one explain the deep attachment of the Maris to their language? In 1970 they numbered 599,000, with 91.2% of them retaining their mother tongue and more than two-thirds of the population (68.6%) speaking Russian fluently. Here, neither the small population, nor the environment (there are in the Mari ASSR 46.9% Russians for 43.7% Maris), nor the knowledge of Russian, nor advanced bilingualism (71% Maris), nor even the decline of teaching in the national language has been able to shake the fidelity of the Maris to their native tongue.

Why, on the other hand, does a group like the Mordvins—only slightly larger than the Maris—show greater vulnerability to the Russian language? Only 77.8% of the Mordvins speak their own language, while 87.8% are totally bilingual. Does the fact that the Mordvins represent only 35.4% of the population in their ASSR, as opposed to 38.9% for the Russians, explain the gradual shift to Russian? But then what is the explanation for the fact that the Tatars, who have been dispersed and subjected to a continuous process of linguistic and cultural Russification for the last four centuries,[52] are so deeply attached to the Tatar language?

*
* *

The dividing line is neither political nor numerical, nor even sociological. Urbanization isn't automatically the cause of linguistic assimilation. The cities of Belorussia most certainly are centers of Russian life and, hence, of Russification. But one need only stroll through Tashkent, which is actually less "traditional" than other cities in Central Asia—to see that even in this city where there are many Russians and tourists, the Uzbek population speaks Uzbek. The same holds true for Tbilis. These conflicting examples show that linguistic assimilation is governed less by external factors—environment, status, urbanization—than by one fundamental fact, the historical and cultural richness of ethnic groups.

The Belorussian nation, as it exists today, has been shaped by Moscow. Its language is an artificial creation. There is no doubt that a Belorussian culture has sprung up in a half century, but it lacks the weight of history, of native traditions. The Tatars and the Georgians possess old languages that have been the vehicle for old cultures. Even if these languages were to die out, both groups would be able to recapture the monuments of their culture—in Russian or English translations—and in history books the great events of a past that belongs only to them.

The Mari people have another type of culture, an unwritten culture shaped from pagan traditions, linking them to their most remote past and isolating them from others. On the other hand, the

Mordvins, long-standing converts to Orthodoxy, cannot be linked to a socio-religious tradition of their own—for want of a written culture. Their religious integration paved the way for linguistic assimilation. The difference in the linguistic behavior of the Soviet nations bears witness to the highly contradictory results of the policy adopted in this sphere. Without doubt this policy has led to "accepted" assimilation for a number of groups who, not having been "forced" into Russification, come to it of their own accord, for the sake of convenience, but mostly because these groups have no historical cultural heritage to defend—and to defend *them*.

For other peoples, on the contrary, instead of being a tool for integration, the linguistic policy has opened an astonishing Pandora's box by liberating national yearnings. Linguistic nationalism is now being reinforced by the frustrations of the Balts threatened with ethnic extinction and of the Georgians exasperated by the underemployment of their elites, as much as by the satisfaction of the Moslem peoples on seeing the new strength that they derive from their growing populations, their cohesiveness, and their intellectual progress.

When seen close-up, linguistic policy sometimes acts to promote the integration of nations, but much more often to heighten national differences. On this basis, can it be assumed that temporary differences are involved, ones destined to fade away and not to be deepened? Some authors feel that rising bilingualism is all-important.

When languages are competing or coexisting, the shifts from one to the other require a very long time and an intermediate phase of bilingualism.[53] Seen in this light, the Soviet trend would seem rather positive. It would suffice for fluency in Russian to become general and consolidated, to enable the Soviet nationalities to move to the next stage, that is, to change to the Russian language. Of course it is impossible to predict the future. The USSR has only existed for the space of two generations, a short period of time where processes of linguistic change are involved.

But regardless of the future linguistic evolution of the Soviet peoples, one question remains: Is language the decisive criterion of national affiliation? It is difficult to answer this in the affirmative, considering recent history in which many peoples have used the language of other powers—like English in India—and where this loss of linguistic identity failed to stop them from making their national existence known. Undoubtedly, language helps a nation to assert itself. That language symbolizes the nation's existence is not at all certain.

CHAPTER VI

Crisis in Integration[1]

T he year 1967 marked the fiftieth anniversary of the Revolution; 1972, the fiftieth anniversary of the Federation; 1977,
a new Constitution for a new society. So many opportunities
for Moscow to affirm the country's national cohesiveness and the
success of integration.[2] Nevertheless, it was precisely during these
ten years that demonstrations of open disagreement were to snow-
ball in the nationality sphere, suggesting that integration is not as
complete as it appears. Under Stalin also, the world of the Soviet nationalities went through crises. But the integration policy was then
in its early stages and created deep divisions between Moscow and
the non-Russians under its administration. Moreover, Stalin was on
the watch for the slightest divergence and in successive waves decimated all elites, all groups or individuals who might rally compatriots battered by his inflexible will for uniformity.

Khrushchev's policy of appeasement and concessions enabled the
nations to rebuild elites capable of representing them, but at the
same time elites that, nearly half a century after the revolution,
would attest to the success of integration. The Soviet people, in
which the regime takes such pride, is primarily made up of the elites
that embody it, and of the most intellectually advanced societies.

The noteworthy feature of the crises that have erupted in the
sphere of nationalities in recent years is the often decisive role
played by the elites. In addition, these crises primarily affect the
most highly educated national groups, and frequently those with the
highest standard of living. While in 1967 they might have been dis-

missed as sporadic outbursts of discontent, with the passing years these growing manifestations of disagreement in certain nationalist groups rule out any possibility of being considered "negligible incidents." When republics or regions are the scene of repeated incidents so serious that heavy penalties are imposed by the government, the weaknesses of Soviet integration are thereby revealed. An analysis of the local troubles raises questions about their significance and extent. Are the crises in the local national groups due to particular situations or circumstances, and therefore easy to overcome? Or do they show that integration is far from being attained?

The "Stateless Citizens" of the USSR

Every Soviet citizen has his nationality stamped in his passport. And the equality of all the nations—the equality of their cultural and political rights—is a fundamental concept of the Soviet system. Nevertheless, certain national groups, even if they are legally recognized, are not like the others. Their first motherland—the one to which they lay claim, according to their passports—is refused them. These "stateless citizens," long reduced to silence, have been in recent years among the most dissident members of Soviet society, so intolerable have become their feelings of being wronged. They comprise the Tatars, the Germans, and the Jews, separated historically and culturally, but united by the aspiration to become "national," with a real country of their own. Their bitterness is evidenced in different ways. The Tatars want to go back home to the Crimea. The Germans and the Jews no longer feel at home in the USSR and want to leave. What lies behind this disaffection so deeply rooted that it is expressed by these people in total disregard for their own physical safety and freedom?

Consider the Tatars first of all. The Western world has hardly heard about them. They are known to us mainly from fuzzy photographs and stories taken out of context. We have heard that Tatars were demonstrating in Tashkent, without really understanding why; and also that General Grigorenko, a respected hero of the Second World War, wound up in Soviet courts and psychiatric institutions for defending them.[3] But these remote, sporadic events have scarcely helped to acquaint us with this people whose features are blurred by the Soviet statistics themselves. The term "Tatar" is applied indiscriminately to the Kazan Tatars and the Crimean Tatars. The former group has an autonomous republic located to the east of Moscow. Outside the USSR, no one can understand why the Tatars in Tashkent complain about having no country of their own. Soviet censuses add to the confusion because they have a single appellation—Tatar[4]—under which they lump both groups. Grouped in this way, the Tatars represent a sizable mass of nearly six million people in 1970, making them the fifth-ranking ethnic group in the Soviet Union.

But in reality the Crimean Tatars are a distinct group, separated from the Kazan Tatars by language and culture. It is impossible to calculate their population accurately. They claim to number half a million, but in all probability this figure should be in the neighborhood of 300,000.[5] In 1921 Moscow recognized the centuries-old presence of the Tatars in the Crimea,[6] their national identity, and Russia's former domination over them. The Soviets set them up as an autonomous republic, the Crimean Republic, incorporated in the RSFSR where, despite their minority position,[7] the Tatars for a number of years did enjoy all the rights granted to the nations: an official language, schools, their own culture.[8] After these years in which the Tatars enjoyed the same status—privileges and purges—as the USSR's other nationalities, the Second World War was to tear them away from the country's common destiny and mark them for a special, exceptionally harsh fate.

Living in a region occupied by the Germans until April 1944, the Tatars were placed on the list of "collaborator nations"[9] as soon as the occupying troops withdrew. Set up quite arbitrarily by Stalin, this list gave collective responsibility to whole nations. On May 18, 1944, barely six days after the Crimea had been liberated, the entire Tatar population—children and the elderly included—were deported in a few hours to Central Asia, the Urals and Siberia. More than 200,000 persons, the bulk of whom were resettled in Uzbekistan, met this fate. The Tatar deportation, though brutal, was not made official until long afterwards. On June 25, 1946, a decree announced that, owing to the population's collaboration with the Germans, the Crimean Republic (along with the Chechen-Ingush ASSR) had been eliminated and its inhabitants "settled in other regions of the USSR where they would receive land and governmental aid."[10]

While the Tatars lived under permanent surveillance in their places of exile, Moscow set out to destroy all trace of them in the Crimea. The mass arrival of Russian or Ukrainian colonists, the suppression of all Tatar place-names, the systematic destruction of their houses—everything was done to make an eventual return impossible for them. Until 1956 the Tatars shared this tragic destiny with the six other nations Stalin had accused of treason. After 1956 only the Tatars were excluded from the measures of reparation enacted by Khrushchev. At the Twentieth Congress, Khruschev included the 1944 deportations in the long list of Stalin's crimes, but he omitted any mention of the Tatars in his list of deported peoples. Here, the fate of the Tatars took a very special turn. All the other deported peoples were rehabilitated, regaining their territory and national status in January 1957. The Tatars, on the other hand, enjoyed only limited clemency which received almost no publicity.

After Stalin's death in 1954, conditions of exile for Tatar veterans and partisans were eased. A decree of April 28, 1956 granted normal status to all Tatars in their place of residence. However, this decree was never made public. Furthermore, it stipulated that the Tatars could not recover possessions that had been confiscated from them, nor return to the Crimea. In addition, their native land was ceded by the RSFSR to the Ukraine in 1954.[11] Thus, the Tatars had to remain where they were (the right to settle anywhere in the USSR except the Crimea in no way fulfilled their yearnings) and had to go on living there as an isolated minority having only minor cultural rights.[12] A Tatar newspaper has been published in Tashkent since 1957;[13] the works of Tatar writers are published in their own language, but only for a small, scattered audience. A theater group has also been authorized to give performances.

The Tatar problem really arose during the euphoria surrounding de-Stalinization and the rehabilitation, when the Tatar people felt completely forgotten and excluded from the changes that were taking place. The limited, unofficial character of the provisions enacted regarding the Tatars brands them a guilty people. Beyond their moral status as a nation, the issue concerns their ability to survive as a national group. Stripped of their territory and their cultural rights, the Tatar people are doomed to melt gradually into their ethnic and cultural surroundings. This explains the ferocious battle this small group is waging against the regime. What they want is political rehabilitation and the right to return to the Crimea—a Crimea restored to the Tatars, set up again as their national homeland, where a community can enjoy all the rights inherent in its status.

Legally, the Tatars' struggle for existence began in 1957,[14] as soon as it became clear that nothing they held to be essential would be restored spontaneously. All of the Soviet Union then believed in the power of petitions and court appeals. Had not the Party's watchword after the Twentieth Congress been the return to legality? This would explain why the Tatar demands were not visible at first. Concerned with conforming to Moscow's professed principle of legality, the Tatars appealed to the government. Between July 1957 and October 1961, six petitions bearing anywhere from 6,000 to 25,000 signatures were sent to the Party and to various State authorities.[15] All these petitions involved a single demand: equal treatment with the other deported Peoples, leading to the return of Tatar political and national rights. The absence of governmental reactions to these collective demands and the repression of more militant Tatars accused of stirring up "racial hatred," soon prompted the group to seek new, but still legal, courses of action.[16]

Convinced that they would have to come closer to make themselves heard, the Tatars decided to set up a kind of permanent delegation in the capital in 1964. Cities and villages inhabited by Tatars began electing representatives who, bearing a regular mandate, were sent to Moscow at the group's expense. They were to serve as an official lobby on behalf of their electorate, to hand over the petitions signed by their constituency and lastly, to reach the media. This was a startling procedure in the Soviet Union where the channels of expression are those controlled by Moscow. But it was also a procedure in keeping with the Tatar position. Deprived of their political rights, they had thereby been stripped of national representatives. No one was empowered to represent them as a national group. It was also a procedure in keeping with the thinking of that period. In announcing the creation of the "State of all the People" in 1961, Khrushchev had called for his fellow-citizens' initiative and participation. At the time, the means of bringing Soviet citizens into political life were under discussion. Committees of all kinds were springing up. By taking this initiative, the Tatars could legitimately believe that they were in tune with the change then in progress.[17]

For a time the Tatars were encouraged by an apparent thaw. In 1965 and 1966 the Supreme Soviet of the USSR, as guardian of socialist legality but also representative of the Soviet population, at last seemed to take an interest in them. The Tatar representatives, bearing their mandates and petitions, were received in August 1965 by Mikoyan, then Chairman of the Presidium of the Supreme Soviet, and in March 1966, by the Secretary of the Presidium, Georgadze. The representatives of a wronged nation had been heard by leaders who themselves came from non-Russian nations. Wasn't this a sign of change? But the apparent miracle soon proved delusive.

The fact that Tatars had been received by Caucasians was to change nothing in the course of events. Yet, at the time, the extent of the Tatar movement was impressive. In early 1966, when Moscow was preparing to receive the delegates of the Twenty-third Congress of the CPSU, the Tatar "delegation" numbered 125 persons. More than 15,000 signed letters and telegrams were sent to everyone in a position of authority. Finally, a petition was drawn up to be placed on the rostrum of the Congress. It bore 120,000 signatures, practically the whole adult Tatar population had signed. In the USSR of the 1960s, where many documents still went unsigned, the fact that a national group agreed to commit itself in this way was exceptional, and yet the petition was there. Perhaps this explains why Georgadze chose to be reassuring and promised an immediate review of the Tatar dossier. And then proceeded to do—nothing! Disappointed but undaunted, the Tatars gathered 115,000 signatures in three months (March–June 1966) for a new petition. They also sent over 20,000 messages and telegrams, and bolstered the strength of their Moscow delegation with new representatives. Up to then, the regime had tried to ignore the movement and avoid confrontation. Perhaps the speed with which the Tatars mobilized and the numbers answering the call prompted the authorities to act. The Moscow hotels were asked to refuse accommodations for the Tatar delegation. On June 26th a large group of Tatars, having come to leave a petition at the Central Committee of the CPSU, was arrested and immediately expelled from the city.

In Uzbekistan a speedily informed constituency grew angry. Demonstrations took place. On every street corner, in public buildings, Tatars sought to rally the population to their cause. After all, both the Uzbeks and the Tatars are Moslem peoples. But Moscow chose to take a hard line, and the government persisted all the more because the outlook was alarming. October 18th would mark the forty-fifth anniversary of the Crimean Republic's founding. The Tatars made no secret about commemorating the past, they would expand the number of demonstrations aimed at attracting attention.

At that time, in 1966, no one in the USSR was yet aware that they had to go outside their own borders to force Moscow to yield. It is true that writers were beginning to seek an audience and protection abroad. But what a nationalist group needs is to be heard in Moscow and to be heard and understood by its compatriots. It was this domestic campaign that the regime wanted to stop. In haste, Moscow had two articles inserted in the criminal code of the Uzbekistan SSR, one aimed at stopping the circulation of information and documents concerning the fate of the Tatars, the other banning participation at meetings. With the enactment of this legislation, even activities entirely in keeping with the law became illegal and opened the way for repression.[18]

Despite these repressive measures and the obstacles they had met on their stay in Moscow, the Tatars were by then too deeply committed to break off the fight. Because legality was coming to have an increasingly restrictive meaning, the Tatars tended to bypass it, opting for more spectacular methods—even illegal ones. Although denied the right to stay in the hotels, more and more Tatars came to Moscow. In the summer of 1967, 400 of them were there, announcing that they meant to hold a meeting in Red Square in order to be heard at last. The time had been well chosen. Moscow was at the height of its tourist season.

For the first time the Tatars were bringing the outside world into their movement by staging a demonstration which foreigners could witness. It was an intelligent plan. The government, concerned with staying in control of the situation, decided to come to terms. On July 21, 1967, a meeting took place in the Kremlin. On the one hand, those responsible for public order were present: Andropov, head of the KGB; Rudenko, Procurator-General of the USSR; Shchelokov, Minister of Internal Security; and Georgadze, who had probably become the government's specialist on the problem. Facing them at the meeting were the Tatars, representing their constituencies, with their mandates that the Soviet State found unacceptable but, at the same time, had accepted.

During the meeting Andropov promised political rehabilitation for the Tatar nation and amnesty for those Moscow had repressed, but he indicated the greatest reservations as far as any Tatar return to the Crimea was concerned. The issue of restoring the republic was not taken up. Andropov promised that steps would be taken without delay. But a month and a half went by and nothing happened. The Tatars were wondering if the 1967 meeting had, like the two previous ones, been designed to pacify them for a while and leave them exposed to new reprisals. For this reason, the last few days of August saw Tashkent on the brink of riot. The police had to disperse many demonstrations and arrest those who could be accused of disturbing the peace.

On September 5th the Tatars learned that they had won. A decree was issued that read as follows: "After the liberation of the Crimea, the whole Crimean Tatar population was unjustly accused of collaboration for which only certain individuals had actually been to blame. In view of the fact that a new generation has now taken its place in professional and political life, the accusations leveled indiscriminately against all citizens of Tatar nationality residing in the Crimea are to be dropped. . . ."[19]

"The Tatars who formerly resided in the Crimea are settled in the Uzbek republic and in other republics . . . " This decree gave back to the Tatars all the privileges of citizenship, i.e., freedom of residence and cultural rights. On one point, they doubtless obtained what they wanted. Exonerated of the crime of treason, the Tatars became a people like the others once more. But very soon it became clear that they would have to be content with this; they were not quite equal to the other Soviet peoples. To be sure they were now rehabilitated, but this fact had scarcely been revealed. Only newspapers in republics where Tatars lived published the decree. Elsewhere, it remained a secret for a long time.

More serious still was the fact that the 1967 decree failed to give back to the Tatar nation its collective rights. Without doubt, the members of the group could go anywhere they wished ("within the limitations of the provisions concerning employment and passports"), and they were also entitled to certain cultural rights. But they actually had had freedom of movement since 1956, as well as the cultural rights related to the 1967 decree. On the other hand, the term "Tatar nation" had been omitted from the text, which also failed to mention a possible restoration of their republic. By referring to them as "Tatars having resided in the Crimea," the decree had eliminated the permanent bond between ethnic identity and soil, which constitutes one of the four criteria determining a nation's existence. By equating their past in the Crimea with their present in Central Asia, the decree suggests that they came from both Central Asia and the Crimea. For the Kremlin, it seemed clear that these reservations, offset by rehabilitation, were to close the Tatar issue. Meetings were set up in various public places—official meetings under governmental and Party sponsorship—to obtain expressions of satisfaction from the people concerned.[20] This unique procedure proved worthwhile (the idea hadn't occurred to Moscow in 1957 for the other nationalities), and also reveals the embarrassment of the authorities and their awareness of problems left unsettled.

More than ten years have elapsed since then, years in which the Tatars have tried ceaselessly to win their case on a point that now appears essential to them: their return to the Crimea. To accomplish this, the Tatar movement follows three lines: (1) legal, which consists of harassing the Soviet authorities with mass petitions, especially during commemorations when Moscow may celebrate the success of its nationality policy; (2) a course bordering on legality, which links Tatar demands with those of the democratic movement in the USSR; the Moscow dissidents scarcely bother about nationalist movements, but since 1970 have paid attention to the Tatars, including their demands in the general program for the defense of human rights;[21] (3) the last avenue ignores legality and is now the royal road of the Tatar movement. Forbidden to live on their native soil, the Tatars make a point of going there in defiance of the ban. Only a few families have actually managed to get around the myriad regulations on residence permits. Most of these clandestine expeditions have resulted in forced repatriation in Central Asia of Tatars willing to risk losing everything in their places of exile, on the slim chance of being admitted into the Crimea.[22]

After winning the battle for rehabilitation, the Tatars have clearly lost the one for the reconstruction of a normal national life. They remain foreigners in Central Asia, not because the surrounding peoples refuse to accept them—on the contrary, there was everything to bring them together—but because they themselves will not renounce the dream of their lost motherland. They were exiled nearly thirty-five years ago. A new generation has grown up and stands in the forefront of the struggle for a return to the Crimea.

Like other peoples in other places, the Tatars have chosen to remain stateless rebels just so long as they are forbidden to put down new roots in their native land. The Soviets are trying to ignore this challenge by denying the reality of the bond which links the Tatars with the Crimea. The official thesis concerning this people is that the Crimea was peopled by inhabitants of varied ethnic origins, the Tatars among them. According to *The Great Soviet Encyclopedia*, what marks this territory as multi-ethnic is the fact that, contrary to the general rules for naming national republics, the Crimean ASSR—when it existed—bore a geographical name instead of one denoting a nation. There could be no clearer denial of the Tatars' historic right to live in the Crimea and hence of their national existence.

Why such severity against this small people? Actually, it is not the 300,000 Tatars that the USSR is uneasy about, but the Moslem nationalist movement. It should be noted that Tatar nationalism made a considerable contribution to the Moslem world of Russia in the pre- and post-Revolutionary past. The Tatars generated the main ideas that would stir Russian Moslems to revolution.[23] In 1944 Stalin succeeded in reducing the space occupied by the Tatars and threw them out of the Crimea. His successors have no intention of broadening their world again. At the same time, they are struggling against Moslem nationalism, which would also stand to regain lost territory through the restoration of the Crimean Republic. Under existing conditions in the USSR, doing justice to 300,000 Tatars deprived of their homeland would mean adding one more stone to the building of the triumphant and isolationist structure that is Turko-Moslem nationalism.

The case is quite different for the Germans in the USSR. In 1970[24] they represented a compact group of 1,800,000 people, a small portion of which has been in the Soviet Union only since the Second World War. However, they are chiefly the descendants of settlers living in Russia since the eighteenth century. From 1924 to 1941 the Germans had an autonomous republic located on the Volga, from which they were deported in accordance with a decree of August 24, 1941. At the time Moscow said that it was not a case of deporting collaborators but, as a safety measure, "transferring" a people who might otherwise have been tempted to collaborate. While less harmful than the treatment meted out to the Tatars, the fate of the Volga Germans was no less dramatic. In practice, Soviet "transfers" and "deportations" bear a singular resemblance. One month later, their republic was eliminated.[25] In the postwar years an external factor did more to shape their future than the intentions of the Soviet leaders themselves—USSR relations with West Germany. Coming to Moscow in September 1955, Chancellor Adenauer registered his concern over the fate of his compatriots. On December 13, 1955, a Soviet decree gave them back their civil rights, and their political and cultural rights were soon expanded.[26]

In 1964, while trying to improve Soviet relations with West Germany, Khrushchev issued a decree rehabilitating the Volga Germans.[27] As in the case of the Tatars, rehabilitation came without restoration of the national homeland. To make sure that the issue did not become a bone of contention, Moscow pointed to economic imperatives—not to the non-existence of a German nation[28]—and endeavored to give the Germans the political and cultural advantages of a nation like the others, despite the absence of territorial status.[29] Actually, the Germans showed less obstinacy in defending the restoration of their republic; they themselves were not unanimous on the question.[30] Yet dispersal had a serious drawback, which the advocates of a return to the Volga perceived clearly, namely, that in spite of cultural rights, there remained the threat of gradual assimilation.

The Germans are settled in two dense groups in Kazakhstan (858,077 persons, or 46% of the total) and in border territories within the RSFSR (761,888 persons, or 41%). Two smaller groups should be added, comprising 89,834 persons in Kirghizia and 31,712 in Tadzhikistan. Only a small number of Germans (6%) have really been scattered across the USSR. Yet, despite their grouping and the cultural advantages that they enjoy, the census reveals rapid progress toward assimilation. In 1926 less than 5% of the Volga Germans listed Russian as their mother tongue. In 1959, 24% defined themselves as Russian-speaking, while in 1970 their proportion reached 32.7%.[31]

In the eleven years separating the last two censuses, few national groups registered such an increase (8.7%) for the Russian language.[32] On the contrary, as previously noted, the general tendency has been toward a consolidation of national languages in their status as mother tongues.[33] Among a number of reasons for this particular trend are: the fact that a great number of the Germans settled in Kazakhstan, in a rural setting, where their children are often unable to study in predominantly German schools; and emigration involving the departure of the least assimilated members of the community. The latter is indeed the characteristic feature of the German community and the problem that it raises for Moscow.

In the course of Soviet-German relations, Bonn's leaders have constantly sought to obtain the right of return solely for Germans who have been in the USSR since 1940 (owing to the war and boundary changes).[34] In 1958, the USSR and West Germany signed a consular agreement which provided that the principle of "family reunion" could be applied to the Germans who had not been Soviet citizens prior to 1940 and to their descendants.[35] Perturbations in the relations between the two countries delayed the implementation of the accord; but Chancellor Brandt's *Ostpolitik*, along with the final Helsinki agreement, gave the principle new strength. In 1970 German emigration—limited to family reunion—began, and until 1977 the Soviet attitude seemed to tend toward increasing tolerance, as indicated in Table 38.

Table 38
Emigration of the Germans from the USSR
1970-1976

Year	Number
1970	340
1971	1,100
1972	3,100
1973	4,400
1974	6,300
1975	5,800
1976	9,600

It therefore appears that in six years over 30,000 Germans have left the USSR. In the early 1970s the German Red Cross estimated that there were 40,000 Germans who wanted to emigrate and who could avail themselves of family ties in Germany. Taking into account the people who have left, it might seem safe to assume that soon all who wish will be able to return to their own country, and before long there will be no German problem in the USSR, but only a community that has lived there for almost two centuries, a community apparently headed for cultural assimilation. This is probably what the Soviets thought when they agreed to open the borders to Germans who were not rooted historically in the USSR. However, the opening of the borders triggered a reflex of national identification on the part of the German community, although they had lived on Russian soil for two centuries. Emigration requests were submitted by groups of Germans, not for the sake of reuniting families, but on the basis of "ethnic solidarity" with the German people.

Soviet subjects, descendants of settlers who had regarded Russia as their native land for generations and no longer had ties with Germany discovered that they were rooted in that distant country by ties of remote history, culture, and language. This demand, expressed publicly in the form of demonstrations,[36] involves an unknown number of Germans, estimated in German newspapers to reach 300,000.[37]

This confronts the Soviet authorities with an extremely difficult situation. For Moscow to admit that ethnic groups feel foreign in the USSR—when they had been a part of the czarist empire[38]—amounts to admitting the total failure of the Soviet nationalities policy, recognizing the permanence of ethnic bonds to the detriment of bonds created by a life in common, and thus implicitly acknowledging that any ethnic group which does not identify with the USSR has the right to leave. This is what the German demands mean for the Soviet regime. Already Armenians are turning toward the American or Middle Eastern diasporas, asking to join them on grounds of family ties or ethnic solidarity. The right of emigration, which Moscow thought could be limited to the very special case of the Germans and the Jews, might be generally asserted.

To deal with the possibility of such a landslide, the Soviet leaders are now trying to curb German emigration requests. The applicants are being discouraged by administrative hazing[39] and intensive propaganda aimed at convincing them right from the start that they will be unable to adapt to life in West Germany.[40] But at the same time, Moscow cannot clash too openly with German aspirations. The group's numerical size and concentration warrant Soviet caution, and international considerations make this prudence even more necessary.

The Federal German Republic—West Germany—is a precious economic partner for the Soviet Union.[41] Politically, too, West Germany has considerable influence on the USSR's strategy.[42] In addition, it is sometimes to the Kremlin's advantage to treat West Germany with consideration. In line with this, Chancellor Schmidt, anxious to give as many Germans as possible a chance to emigrate, realized that discreet negotiations bore more fruit than noisily framed demands.[43] He therefore remained silent after President Carter's vehement statements on human rights and the right of emigration, and maintained this attitude at the Belgrade Conference.

The dilemma in which the Soviets are placed by the German demands becomes apparent. Yielding, even to a very limited degree, helps to solve burning issues of foreign policy. But by yielding the regime is admitting its weakness in the national domain and is paving the way for bigger demands, or even a contagion involving the dreaded idea of national identity on a purely ethno-cultural basis. A trend in this direction would weaken solidarity within the USSR. Nor would restoring a German republic seem any better able to solve the problem. In the present situation, to restore the republic might risk bolstering the nationalism of those Germans who do not wish to be assimilated; it would also run counter to assimilation, which is on the rise in another segment of the German population. Restoring national states at a time when the USSR is said to be at the stage of a new historic formation, i.e., the Soviet people, would weaken this formation and deny that integration was progressing.

Unlike the Tatars and the Germans, the Jews have a national territory in the USSR—theoretically, at least. Nevertheless, even more than the others, the Jews are considered citizens of a special kind. The Soviet State gave them a land of their own in the 1920s, the Jewish Autonomous Oblast (Region) of Birobidzhan, situated in the Far East not far from the Chinese border. The Soviets also granted the Jews—quite logically—a nationality of their own, which appears in their passport. However, while granting them national status, the Soviet government has always denied that the Jewish community was a nation.[44]

This negative approach was further complicated by the creation of the State of Israel, marking the victory of the Zionist ideal. In a recent book, a specialist in anti-Zionist propaganda constantly stresses the differences between: (1) Jew (*evrei* in Russian) in the sense of Hebrew, i.e., an ethnic category; (2) Jew (*judei*) as a religious category; and (3) *Zionist*, a political category.[45] For the author, Judaism cherishes the idea of an international Jewish community, a global Jewish nation. But doesn't the Soviet Jewish community, on which national status was conferred, represent on a small scale the very model and confusion condemned by our expert? This community is composed of many groups totally different from one another, inhibited by their very pasts and cultures from gathering together as a single nation, unless this were based precisely on the rejected criteria—affiliation with Judaism. The whole issue becomes difficult when we consider the fate of Soviet Jews.

The number of Jews in the USSR ranges from 2 to 3.5 million, depending on whether we refer to the census or other sources.[46] The important fact is that the number of Soviet citizens who consider themselves Jewish dropped 5% from one census to the other, while during the same period the overall Soviet population registered a gain of 16%. One cannot deduce from this that the number of Jews (taking emigrants into account) has remained perfectly stable, but simply that the number of Jews listing themselves as such in the census is declining. Should one conclude from this that Jewish national consciousness has diminished? The linguistic criterion indicates a positive answer to this question.

In the 1897 census 96.9% of Russia's Jews considered Yiddish their mother tongue. In 1926 this category still accounted for 70.4% of Soviet Russian Jews. By 1959 the situation changed radically: 17.9% of the Jews used Yiddish as a primary language and, if we add those who speak another language peculiar to some Jewish communities,[47] only 21.5% of the Jews were speaking their own language.[48] In 1970 this figure fell to 17.7%, representing a drop of 3.8%. However, to this 17% should be added the nearly 9% comprising Russian-speaking Jews who indicated that they had a good knowledge of Yiddish or of another Jewish language. This means that 26.4% of all Soviet Jews retain linguistic ties with their native culture. But the impact of these figures must be gauged in the light of expanded use of the Russian language.

The number of Jews considering Russian their mother tongue rose to 78.2%, while 16.3% of those not giving Russian as their primary language nevertheless spoke Russian well. In other words, 94.5% of the Jews know Russian well and 28.8% are fluent in one or more other Soviet languages.[49] In the USSR knowledge of the national language is an undeniable index of the degree of national consciousness. The geographic distribution of Jews who speak Russian and those who remain loyal to their own language sheds light on the causes of this trend. The highest degree of linguistic Russification is found among the Jews of the RSFSR and the Ukraine. On the other hand, the use of Yiddish, or another language spoken by the Jews, remains widespread in the Baltic communities, particularly in Lithuania where 62% of the Jews speak Yiddish, and in the communities of the Caucasus—in Daghestan, for example, 87% of them speak the Tat language. In the RSFSR only 21.3% of the Jews are capable of speaking Yiddish (as a first or second language); this index drops to a mere 20.3% in the Ukraine.

Observance of religious customs and holidays by Soviet Jews represents another index of national identification, even if Moscow does not acknowledge the index as such. But does it parallel linguistic trends or, on the contrary, does it compensate for them?

In an article written in the late 1960s,[50] Zvi Gitelman, who ranks as an authority on the situation of Soviet Jews, noted pessimistically: "The Jewish religion is declining in the USSR—perhaps faster than the other religions." This judgment is based primarily on concrete data: (1) only sixty synagogues are open; (2) there is no central religious organization capable of publishing a bulletin, prayer books, or the Bible; (3) no facilities exist for training rabbis; and (4) no facilities are available for obtaining the special food required by their religion. It must be said, however, that more recent information[51] tends to brighten this dismal picture somewhat.

Information brought into the West by émigrés suggests that there are about ninety synagogues open,[52] sixty-two of which have actually been identified. In any case, these figures are ridiculously low for a community of nearly three million people. Using this yardstick, the experts arrive at highly pessimistic estimates about the number of Jews actually practicing their religion.[53] Based on the criteria of a Jewish community undergoing rapid linguistic Russification and losing its faith or, at least, not practicing it, we may conclude that the Soviet Jewish people are well on the way to assimilation. Moreover, the indices reveal the reasons for such a situation.

The Jews are an essentially urban population,[54] hence, they live in an environment that does everything to facilitate assimilation. Under Soviet policy prevailing in the 1930s, shifting Jews from their traditional areas of residence to the large cities which had formerly been closed to them, urbanizing them, giving them access to an occupational sphere from which they had been barred until then—i.e. the apparatus of the State and the Party, the administrative machinery, the army, etc.—calling upon them to steep themselves in Russian culture in order to prepare for this change of professions: in all this the government was subjecting them to a process which Annie Kriegel, an expert on the Jewish problem, aptly terms "Russianization," signifying access to modernity.[55]

Despite the limitations of this Russianization, one of its results was the settlement of Jews in a geographic and social milieu which did not foster the revival of closed societies. It is significant that Jews become most easily linguistically Russified in their new environments, but remain more attached to their own language in their old places of residence. In short, the cultural policy adopted toward them does little to preserve their linguistic identity. In spite of their national status, the Jews no longer have any schools of their own like the other national groups, and there are no Yiddish courses offered in the

Soviet schools attended by Jewish children. In Birobidzhan, the regime uses the fact that only a small number of Jews live in the region[56] as a pretext for not setting up a Jewish national educational system; elsewhere, Moscow claims that there are too few requests. As the Jews are the most highly educated group in the Soviet Union,[57] it can be assumed that this exceptional degree of education also implies a high degree of linguistic Russification.

The two notable factors, declining use of the Jewish languages and a low level of religious observance, led one Western reporter to conclude in 1962[58] that "All hope of seeing the emergence of a viable Jewish community must be founded more on conviction than on current realities." Yet, in today's USSR, no observer of the national scene can fail to see that the Jewish problem is growing, not waning. Linguistic Russification and declining religion go hand in hand with the rise of a Jewish movement characterized chiefly by the quest for national identity. This Jewish renascence is manifested in several areas: (1) authorized culture; (2) Hebrew (which is unauthorized); (3) religion; and (4) the desire for emigration.

In the official sphere of culture, more and more action is being taken to give back to the Jews their long-forgotten linguistic and cultural heritage. To accomplish this, the Soviet Jewish community plays with the interpretation of the laws. Moscow says that nothing prevents the Jews from studying Yiddish if they so desire. Soviet Jews are showing the government that they want just that. Tired of waiting for concessions in this area, they are availing themselves of the few cultural organs that they can call their own.[59]

The magazine *Sovetish Heimland* has been partially converted into a Yiddish-language teaching aid by reprinting the Yiddish alphabet and lessons from a textbook.[60] This magazine serves as a regular clearing-house for Jewish culture. It publishes the material most representative of contemporary Soviet Jewish culture; it promotes and encourages Jewish writing, in addition to publicizing and even co-ordinating Jewish artistic activities, including the Moscow Yiddish theater, various actors' troupes (some of which are amateurs), musical groups, and art exhibitions.

The bounds of legality are frequently overstepped, particularly in teaching Hebrew, because of the highly ambiguous position of this language, which is not recognized as a language of Soviet Jews. Hebrew is of course taught in the USSR, but at an advanced level within the framework of Eastern languages, not in a national school program. Because of the bonds between Hebrew and the Jewish religion, there seems to be an attempt to set up a network for the teaching of Hebrew, which is illegal.[61] From the materials for a symposium on Jewish culture which the Jews tried vainly to hold in Moscow in December 1976, it can be concluded that various centers now exist in the Soviet Union for the teaching of Hebrew.

Jewish culture is also transmitted by two unofficial publications, *Evrei v SSR* (Jews in the USSR) and *Tarbut* (Culture), both of which endeavor to familiarize Soviet Jews with their history and culture, as well as with Jewish culture outside the USSR and with problems of emigration. The attempt to hold a Moscow conference in 1976 underscores the expansion of Jewish cultural activities and the striving to make them part of the Soviet environment. This conference was banned but nevertheless attracted world attention. It showed that the problem was rooted in a Jewish will for identity, but with no desire to break with the non-Jewish world.

Because they are very well educated and stand high on the professional ladder, the Jews are unwilling to shut themselves off in a Judaism rooted in the past. They are seeking their identity in the language of their ancestors—not a substitute language for Russian. Likewise, the young Jews who gather in growing numbers in places of worship on Jewish holydays, especially for *Simhath Torah*, are not necessarily going back to the faith of their fathers. For many, worshipping represents a way of asserting their identity and regaining a history and culture that was lost.

Emigration is the most striking manifestation of the Jewish question. There are reliable figures on this. Since 1971, the year when emigration changed from an exception to a rule, more than 100,000 Jews have left the USSR to settle in Israel or, at least, to stop there before moving on.[62]

Judging by the emigrants' ages and geographic origins, we are struck by two facts which might seem contradictory at first sight. On the average, the emigrants are younger than the Soviet Jews—at least as recorded by the census—and closer to the Russian than to the Jewish population in terms of age structure.[63] Moreover, the emigration comes mainly from the Baltic countries and from Georgia where the Jews are less assimilated than in the Russian heartland, which furnishes but few emigrants.

These observations are contradictory inasmuch as younger members of the population are usually considered better assimilated. The fact remains that the Soviet Jewish emigrants are young and come from the less assimilated regions. But we cannot conclude from this that the Jews from the central regions are less inclined to express the wish to emigrate, or that this wish is only expressed where assimilation has been most incomplete. Moscow pursues a highly selective policy on authorizing Jews to emigrate, systematically trying to curtail the exodus of better educated and more Russified people.

In view of the difficulties and tragedies generally associated with it,[64] Jewish emigration is a phenomenon that cannot be taken lightly. It raises two questions: What separates the applicant for emigration from the nonapplicant? Is the desire to emigrate a reliable indicator of Jewish national consciousness? Zvi Gitelman has tried to reply to the first question in his survey of Soviet Jewish settlers in Israel. After subjecting them to many subtle questions, he came to the conclusion that there is no clear line separating the emigrants from their fellow Jews remaining in the USSR, either in terms of language or religion. According to Gitelman, the emigrants could have become well integrated in Soviet life on both counts, had they not been deeply troubled by the latent anti-Semitism in the USSR,[65] and especially by the fact that most of them felt rather alien to the country. In short, Gitelman concludes, while their motivation for emigration varies—rejection of the entire political system or certain aspects of it, Jewish national considerations, material factors—the Jews who emigrate demonstrate a deep sense of community. National yearnings or the desire to live in a Jewish cultural setting loom large in the aspiration to emigrate, but these are not the only factors. To understand this, one need only consider that in 1975 nearly 50% of the applicants for emigration chose not to go to Israel.[66]

The recent growth of those known in Israel as *Noshrims* may be more indicative of a systematic desire to emigrate than aroused nationalist feelings. These complex tendencies within the Jewish community actually express a highly exceptional situation and trend in the USSR. Because they are very well educated and urbanized, the Jews have been placed in conditions that promote their assimilation. Despite the existence of some professional discrimination, they are still well represented in intellectual and even political circles. In this connection, it is noteworthy that there were 294,744 Jews in the CPSU as of 1976, or 1.9% of the Party's overall strength. This means that over 13.7% of the Jewish community belongs to the Party; in other words, of all the national groups in the USSR, the Jews are the best represented.[67] Mixed marriages also represent a powerful means of assimilation.

In the absence of exact figures, it is generally estimated that nearly

30% of the Jews marry outside their community and that their children frequently adopt the nationality of the Russian parent.[68] Nevertheless, this social and cultural integration accepted by the Jews seems to be heading in two directions. Some are being totally assimilated, while others are turning toward their original group and its own system of values and allegiances. This explains why the synagogues are full of young people and have become the favorite places for identification with Judaism.

The rise of Jewish national consciousness, which has been an undeniable fact in recent years, is a problem for the Soviet government. This return to Jewish roots is particularly striking inasmuch as it involves a community that seemed to be following a single path just two decades ago, i.e., the path of acculturation. It is particularly striking too, because it concerns the most highly educated and urbanized segment of the Soviet population, and because its current trend runs counter to all assumptions about the link between modernization and the eroding of national consciousness.

This trend raises two issues. The renascence of a cohesive Jewish community appears to be based on religion. Is it, strictly speaking, a religious phenomenon? And does it come under the heading of the implicit emergence of religion in the ideology of contemporary Soviet society? Or is this reawakening, in fact, a case of religion being used as a criterion of national identity? It is difficult to find a clear-cut answer to these two hypotheses, both of which contain a measure of truth. On the other hand, it is evident that in the climate of religious stirrings which characterizes the USSR today, Judaism can only expand within itself as a national support. Moreover, the growth of Judaism actually serves to heighten the attraction of religion in the USSR.

A second question concerns the profound nature of this Jewish national feeling, which is on the rise. Annie Kriegel aptly notes that at one point the Stalinist policy had brought the Jewish community's evolution to an impasse. Can one deduce from this that it is discrimination, along with fundamental ambiguities in a Soviet policy creating a "legal" status for Jews while denying them national rights, which gave rise to a defensive or negative nationalism? Or are the Jews, in the course of modernization, seeking a return to their heritage and combining it in a positive way with the experience of modern life? Here, too, the answer comprises the essential elements of both hypotheses.

There is no question that the cultural discrimination to which the

Jewish community has been subjected has prompted this search for identity. Treated differently from others, the Jews have proudly asserted their differences and have tried to learn the real motivations for it. But thanks to their high educational level, which facilitated integration into the dominant culture of the USSR, the Jews quite naturally have sought to add to it their own values and the creations of their own genius. Even if the Jewish national sentiment is reduced to a negative reflex—an assumption which is totally unwarranted—the ever louder and increasingly vocal affirmation of this sentiment becomes an important part of contemporary Soviet reality. The Soviet Jewish issue demonstrates that a community stripped of its territory and culture, standing to gain by total assimilation, can remain a nation or become one again, and that national consciousness and the feeling of belonging to a particular group are criteria of nationalism, admittedly subjective, but just as powerful as objective factors such as territory and language which Soviet ideology stubbornly considers the only decisive ones.

The stateless citizens of the USSR, whether Jews, Tatars, or Germans, all serve to illustrate that national integration is not promoted by the regime's contempt for national rights. In different ways these stateless peoples show that contempt leads not to resignation but to self-affirmation and confrontation.

The Rebels

Of all the Soviet nations, the one that has best preserved its national features is the Georgian nation. Georgia was also the nation that rebelled the most openly and violently when it perceived Moscow's intent to destroy its heritage. The strength of the Georgian nation is based on various elements. First of all, there is its cohesiveness on its own soil. The 3,130,741 Georgians counted within Georgia in 1970 represent 66.8% of the republic's total population. This figure also represents the major part of the Georgian nation, whose diaspora is limited to 3.5% of all Georgians.

A long history, with Christianization begun in the fourth century and its independence under continual threat, has forged a nation deeply attached to its traditions and culture. This national feeling is clearly evident in Georgia's linguistic situation. All Georgians living in their republic and 62% of those outside remain loyal to their mother tongue. In sum, 99.4% cling to Georgian while 20.1% also boast a good knowledge of Russian. Their national life is strengthened by the largely national character of the education given to the Georgian elites.

In terms of the number of students receiving higher education, Georgia ranks at the top of the scale.[69] That higher education, even technical, is often dispensed in Georgian constitutes a remarkable fact. In addition, the Georgians along with the Armenians are the only nations to have preserved their alphabets, so it is easy to understand why the national elites are closed to all outside cultural influences. Since 1972 many signs of a serious conflict between Georgia and the central regime have been accumulating. Comprising a latent crisis, purges, outbursts of anger among the people, and even terrorism, the situation is relatively uncommon for the USSR.

It all began in 1972 with a political purge carried out on the pretext of corruption among the Georgian leaders. There was no thought of concealing corruption or illegal financial practices in Georgia; that was common knowledge in the Soviet Union. The Georgian situation was not very different from widespread illegal practices in the USSR in general,[70] but it could also be attributed to the defiant spirit and capricious southern temperament of Georgians. In the spring of 1972 the CPSU Central Committee suddenly realized that everything was going wrong in Georgia and issued a decree criticizing the republic's leaders.[71] This led to the fall of the First Secretary in Georgia, Mjavanadze, a man who was indeed corrupt and notoriously so. He was replaced by a man having an extensive police background, Chevarnadze, who immediately embarked on the suppression of illegal practices.

Despite a massive purge of political and economic cadres, the new First Secretary hardly seems to have satisfied the demands of the Central Committee. In June 1976 the Committee issued a new decree which, though full of praise, observed that "there was still a great deal to be done to politically and ideologically upgrade the Communists and other workers."[72] Furthermore, K. Ketiladze, the republic's Minister of the Interior, admitted at the time that corruption in every form was still rife.[73] Four years of investigations, criticisms, and purges seem to have done so little to alter the Georgian scene that, in November 1976, the Central Committee of the Georgian CP held a two-day conference to examine how organs of administration had participated in this cleansing of Augean stables. The conclusions drawn from these sessions had a strangely pessimistic ring. The organs of administration were far from having made a decisive effort in the "struggle against crime and the restoration of public order."[74] With each passing year the Party's concern grew. In 1972 it was a matter of corruption; in 1976, of public order. By February 1977 order seemed so threatened that the Georgian CC again held a new two-day meeting to evaluate the administration's progress, and convened all those responsible for taking action, namely, the Procurator of the Republic, L. Talakvadze; the Minister of the Interior, Ketiladze; the Minister of Justice, Chuchanachvili. Like the previous meeting, this one concluded that there was little desire to restore order in Georgia, and that the individuals and administrative bodies involved were very guilty.[75] It is interesting to note that even the police and the courts came under fire and were accused of leniency toward those threatening public order.[76]

What justification is there for this relentless denunciation of illegal practices in Georgia? There undoubtedly were serious incidents. The first goes back to 1973, when on May 9 a fire ravaged the Tbilisi opera house. While there was nothing sensational about the fire in itself, the mystery surrounding it attracted attention. First of all, there had been great silence about the incident, and the fire was not revealed until seven arsonists were brought to trial in 1977.[77] While this trial received a great deal of publicity, no one has ever explained why these people committed arson,[78] who had organized the incident and what were the reasons behind it. The absence of information is particularly noteworthy when we consider that this trial fitted into a series of three trials, two of them involving extremely serious matters. The first of these, the case of V. Jvania, had led to the execution of a man accused of placing bombs in public buildings.

While the press said nothing about Jvania's reasons for terrorism,[79] it was rumored in Georgia that he had explained his actions as protests against his country's Russification. At about the same time, two death sentences followed the trial of a "gang," made up of "bandits and drug addicts," who had assassinated a lieutenant of the militia. Here, too, the explanations were quite simple: drugs, deviant behavior and the lack of "good influence in the family."[80] A disturbing reality lies behind these three Georgian trials. Policemen were indeed killed; explosives were placed in public buildings; arson was committed at the opera house, which happens to be located across the street from Central Committee headquarters. As individual happenings these events are not extraordinary, but taken together they are ominous. They demonstrate the uneasiness of the Georgians over an "anti-corruption" campaign, which they regarded as a pretext designed to weaken the morale of the Georgian nation, thereby rendering it vulnerable and enabling Moscow by a purge of their cadres to proceed with the systematic substitution of cadres more amenable to the central government—possibly even Russian cadres.

How such changes could take place becomes apparent when the example of the chairman of the Georgian Supreme Soviet is considered. In January 1976 the chairman Dzotsenidze, who had held office since 1959, was relieved of his duties and replaced by his compatriot, Guilachvili.[81] By all outward appearances this was a routine operation, inasmuch as Dzotsenidze had just been named[82] to the Presidium of the Academy of Sciences. Nevertheless, it implied a demotion in the social hierarchy for one man and a promotion for the other. The one irregularity here lies in the fact that this change occurred in a general climate of dismissals and promotions, and barely a month after the session of the Georgian Supreme Soviet, which normally would be the most appropriate time for such revisions of posts. Considering the record of the two men perhaps sheds light on this affair. Dzotsenidze was the prototype of the national political cadre who had served in Georgia throughout his career. Guilachvili was more closely tied to the center and had spent several years in the Central Committee of the CPSU, where he had been responsible for the Moldavian CP.

While the Georgians can hardly not be alarmed by such changes in the leadership of the republic, there is one area that makes them rise en masse—the defense of their linguistic rights. In 1976, Georgian intellectuals made several protests against the rising Russification. The Constitution had given them the opportunity for a confrontation, from which they emerged victorious. Here, too, the facts are quite simple.

In mid-April of 1978 a crowd of demonstrators invaded the streets of Tbilisi. The demonstration took on such massive proportions that, shortly thereafter, the assistant director of the KGB, K. Piliouguine, was relieved of his duties.[83] A few hours of noisy demonstrations forced Moscow to drop its plans for eroding the status of the Georgian language. The draft republican constitution, published in March 1978, had eliminated the clause appearing in the previous constitution (Article 137) which stipulated that Georgian was the republic's official language. The Georgians saw the omission as a clear-cut diminution of their rights. And they chose the very day when the republic's authorities were discussing the new clause to express their hostility toward this draft. Faced with the vociferous protests,[84] the

Government yielded and inserted the following provision (Article 75) in the final text:[85] "The State language of the Georgian SSR is Georgian."

The Georgian victory in the constitutional conflict carried over to their Caucasian neighbors, who also obtained official confirmation of their linguistic rights. The case of Azerbaidzhan is particularly noteworthy in this connection. Despite the considerable effort made to impose Russian at every level of education,[86] this republic retains a very deep attachment to the Turkish cultural world. Thus, in spite of differences in national cohesion, the whole of the Caucasus remains a poorly integrated bastion. This rejection of integration is demonstrated in many ways: terrorism, mass demonstrations, economic practices forbidden by socialism,[87] attachment to local, religious, or purely popular traditions,[88] as well as sabotage of official directives by the cadres.[89]

Enemy-Brothers

The stateless citizens of the USSR and the rebel Georgians are all characterized by a high degree of education and by the fact that they belong to a cultural world totally alien to the Slavic, with the exception of the Jews. But do Slavic solidarity and a socio-cultural level comparable to that of the Russians suffice to produce easier assimilation? The trend of Ukrainian nationalism leaves room for doubt.

Ukrainian nationalism, unlike Georgia's, is a recent phenomenon. Unquestionably the 1917 Revolution gave free rein to a national movement that nineteenth-century romanticism had encouraged and shaped. But in 1917 nationalism remained a confused mixture of ideas that suited a tiny intelligentsia and the vague aspirations of a society made up mainly of peasants. The cities, on the other hand, grouped a more modernized, Russified population, which looked upon nationalist aims as a factor hindering social progress. This relative lack of national cohesion and the policy of "Ukrainization" pursued by the Soviets until the early 1930s contributed to the Ukraine's gradual integration into the federation. Despite the calamities of collectivization and war,[90] the Ukraine by degrees acquired the status of a privileged partner of the USSR in the federation, especially after 1954 when Khrushchev—and later Brezhnev—gradually Ukrainized the central administration by bringing into their entourage men who had served with them in the Ukraine. The "elder brother" of the Soviet people seemed thus to have a brilliant younger brother closer to it in terms of size, social structure, and culture than the other peoples.

Without doubt, by the mid-1960s dissident voices were being heard in the Ukraine. These were important not because they expressed disagreement with Moscow on general issues, but because they raised a fundamental question in both theory and practice, that of the Ukrainian nation and its aspirations—what separates Ukrainian nationalism from the goals of Soviet leaders.

In December 1965, a young Ukrainian writer, Ivan Dziuba, sent a long memorandum entitled "Internationalism or Russification"[91] to two of his illustrious compatriots, Pierre Chelest, then First Secretary of the Ukrainian CP and member of the Presidium of the Central Committee of the CPSU, and Vladimir Chtcherbitski, chairman of the Ukrainian Council of Ministers and substitute member of the Presidium of the CPSU's Central Committee.[92]

Reviewing Soviet and Ukrainian history over nearly forty years, Dziuba demonstrated that the Ukrainian nation was on the way to being suppressed for the benefit of a Russia decked out in the colors of internationalism. A few months later, in 1966, a Ukrainian journalist, V. Chornovil,[93] also wrote to the Supreme Procurator of the Ukrainian Republic to discuss not the nation's general problems, but rather the fate of those who claimed to speak in its name and have its rights respected. From this point on, the Ukrainian intelligentsia became subjected to a veritable onslaught.

By 1972 a political crisis had been added to the one created by the intellectuals. The most commonly known aspect of this crisis was the downfall of Pierre Chelest in 1972. Powerful in both Kiev and Moscow, he had undoubtedly been eliminated for trying to re-Ukrainize his motherland's political apparatus. Chelest's case is in fact typical of the Ukraine's recent trend and therefore deserves to be examined more closely.[94]

Until he assumed leadership of the Ukrainian CP in 1963, replacing Podgorny, Chelest behaved like a perfectly assimilated Ukrainian. As soon as he took command of the UCP, Chelest used his authority to bolster the UCP and to enhance the Ukrainian role in the CPSU. The membership of the UCP was to grow much more rapidly than that of the CPSU, something that was to give the Ukrainian organization considerable weight in the CPSU. Furthermore, Chelest opposed the assignment of non-Ukrainian cadres to the Ukraine and the dispatch of Ukrainian cadres outside their boundaries, which the central government advocated in the interests of Soviet solidarity and mutual exchanges of experience. Chelest's position might well have been rooted in a simple desire to secure a political foothold and a constituency. In two other domains, however, he clearly showed a tendency to being more Ukrainian than Soviet.

In the economic sphere Chelest tolerated increasingly bitter criticism of the economic exploitation of the Ukraine and the subordination of its interests to those of Siberian progress. In the domain of culture, although unable to protect the intellectuals, and although education was being rapidly Russified, he nevertheless insisted on the expansion of publications in the Ukrainian language. Yet up until 1970, nothing about this good administrator in the Ukraine gave him away as a fervent nationalist. One can imagine Moscow's surprise when this prudent man suddenly took it into his head to publish a book glorifying his country, which in the context of the Ukraine's national tensions marked him as one of the most ardent nationalists.

In this book, *Our Soviet Ukraine*,[95] Chelest acknowledges that the Ukraine is "an integral part of the USSR." But after this preamble he devotes page after page to glorifying the Ukraine's history, culture, and development. He states that the framework of this past and present is a national state which has become modernized, and which he seems to regard as permanent. He doesn't breathe a word about the doctrine of the continuous development of the nations toward fusion, a thesis repeated continuously by the Soviet leaders of the time.

The central government was quick to draw conclusions from this spectacular trend toward National Communism, a renascence of which it still feared in the Ukraine.[96] Y. Bilinsky emphasized that in the final analysis crises of that type were always settled in Moscow. Although in command of a powerful Communist apparatus, Chelest was removed from his Ukrainian functions in Moscow, not in Kiev, as if the central regime wanted to prove that decisions were made at the center when such crises arise.[97] Chelest's downfall paved the way for changes in the Ukrainian leadership that seemed limited but which actually cost the Ukraine part of its preferential political status. It should be noted that while Chelest's replacement, V. Chtcherbitski, is obviously a Ukrainian, the post of UCP Second Secretary was given to a Russian, although since 1949 the post had always been held by a Ukrainian.

Does the national crisis which has been smoldering in the Ukraine since the mid-1960s mark the limits of integration? Or is it a desperate outburst aimed at slowing down the process of integration? While the crisis is clear, the future is much less so. Significantly, experts on the Ukraine hold highly conflicting views on what the future holds in store. For some, the fact of being a "second elder brother" and of participating actively in the central regime and in other republics is indicative of integration. Others see mounting Ukrainian dissidence as a new and irreversible factor in Soviet history. Before making any judgment in this regard, it is necessary to consider the demands which are central to Ukrainian nationalism.

These demands are clear. They range from the preservation of cultural rights, and the rejection of a policy of ethnic fusion by migration, to a will for total independence. But this last extreme demand is difficult to express. On the other hand, the Ukrainians will fight unhesitatingly for the right to be Ukrainians culturally.

Are they threatened in this regard? Probably so, for the census reveals a downtrend in the use of the Ukrainian language. Without doubt, after Russian, Ukrainian is the most widespread language since 37.5 million people speak it, of whom 34.9 million regard it as their mother tongue. In the republic of the Ukraine, however, the number of people speaking Ukrainian dropped from 73% in 1959 to 69% in 1970, while the number speaking Russian increased. The causes of this downtrend are connected chiefly with the Soviet government's educational policy. In principle most of the schools—22,000 out of 27,000—teach in Ukrainian, while fewer than 5,000 teach in Russian. But this situation, which appears to favor Ukrainian, must be modified by various factors for which no exact figures are available but whose impact can be perceived.

First of all, the imbalance in favor of Ukrainian schools was smaller in the early 1970s than at the end of the 1950s. Time seems to be on the side of education in Russian. Furthermore, these figures lump together into a single category the urban schools which often have a ten-year program of education for a large number of students, and the rural schools with a shorter program for a limited number of students. Then, too, urban schools are often Russian, while rural schools are mostly Ukrainian.

Considering students rather than schools,[98] Ukrainian education has evolved as follows: in 1955–1956, 72% of the students studied in Ukrainian and 25.9% in Russian; in 1964, instruction in Ukrainian fell to 70%; in 1974, it dropped to about 60%. The situation of higher education is even worse, since almost all instruction there is given in Russian.[99] The Ukrainians are obviously more threatened by the Russian upswing than any other peoples. This stems primarily from the similarity of the two languages.

Since a knowledge of Russian is a prerequisite for social advancement and access to leading positions, Ukrainian parents are tempted to send their children to Russian schools, all the more because they will not feel too much cut off from these Russified children, hoping also that they will switch easily from Russian to Ukrainian. The role played by Ukrainians outside their own republic, which is a source of nationalist pride, also encourages the group to study Russian. This trend explains why the Ukrainian intelligentsia grows uneasy at seeing a certain kind of bilingualism take root in the republic, Russian being the language of the elites and cities, and Ukrainian that of the countryside and folklore. The question raised by the elites concerns the gradual reduction of their culture to the rank of a sub-culture which would only be used in less intellectually advanced circles and in certain theatrical productions.

Clearly, the Ukrainians feel that their ability to resist in the linguistic sphere is limited. Perhaps this is why they are so determined to defend their history and to give their national feeling an ethno-territorial dimension transcending Soviet borders. This interest in history is also a bone of contention with the Kremlin, for whom Ukrainian history is largely the issue of union with Russia.

By enlarging Ukrainian territory with lands taken from Poland, Rumania, and Czechoslovakia just after the war, Stalin was probably trying to unify Russians and Ukrainians. However, these territorial acquisitions only served to bolster nationalism. The Catholics brought into the Ukraine in 1945 were a source of agitation, and they kept their eyes fixed on the countries from which they had been taken. In a general way, the western Ukraine, unmindful of old Ukrainian-Polish conflicts, showed special sensitivity to all the heterodox movements that were shaking Poland and Czechoslovakia.

The expansion of the Ukraine created new links between this part of the Soviet Union and socialist Europe, which forced Moscow to use a harder line on any Eastern European nation wanting to diverge from the Soviet model of socialism. Had the Ukraine not been so alive to the nationalist hunger of the neighboring countries to which she is historically bound, would the "Springtime" of Prague in 1968 have been totally condemned in Moscow?

In the final analysis, the Ukraine is the most paradoxical of the Soviet nations. Very close to Russia in terms of size and interests, and committed to Russification—thereby serving the general functioning of the system—the Ukraine is being renationalized as quickly as it is apparently being denationalized. In this connection, one may well wonder if the Ukrainian elite will not generate Ukrainian nationalism, over and above the support offered by the local language. Whether this represents a new definition of national feeling, one based on political integration and the modernization of society, or, on the other hand, assimilation struggling with the last gasps of a waning nationalism, is a question that will be answered in the near future.

Nationality crises erupt sporadically from one end of the Soviet Union to the other. What is there in common between: (1) a community's refusal to go on suffering discrimination; (2) the aspiration of some 300,000 people to regain their native land; (3) preventive terrorism in a nation which has yet to yield on either its rights or its particularism; and (4) an ambiguous trend in the Soviet Union's second largest nation, one which serves as Moscow's right arm in the other republics, and at the same time protests any Russian meddling in its own republic?

These crises simply prove that the USSR is not one big happy family in which all differences have been erased, and where the feeling of belonging to a particular land and a particular culture is no more than a mere memory. These crises attest to the fact that the Soviet people is still a conglomeration of peoples. And that the thing they have in common, in spite of their different sizes and situations, is that these crises set them in open opposition to the central government. In their desire to realize their aspirations, it is clearly the central power to which they turn and which they attempt to convince or to intimidate.

In the final analysis, the crises share certain features. They take place within the Soviet political system and are in accordance with the values of the USSR. Do these crises affect the entire system? Apparently not. Judging by visible data—open manifestations of disagreement—an important part of non-Russian society has been spared such outbreaks. This seems to be the case for the large and dynamic Moslem society. Is Moslem society the stabilizing element in the system, the element which offsets the crises noted here? Or, on the other hand, does this stability conceal a latent crisis of another dimension, one even more dangerous for the cohesion of the Soviet Union?

CHAPTER VII

Religion and National Sentiment

The persistence of religious feeling in the USSR, or its revival, is a socio-cultural reality acknowledged both by the Soviet authorities and foreign observers. For the regime this reality has two aspects. At times, Moscow boasts loudly about this phenomenon as tangible proof of its democratic attitude toward all religious beliefs.[1] At other times the Soviets grow quite uneasy about religious sentiment, and then the organs specializing in antireligious propaganda are mobilized.[2]

Specialists in atheistic propaganda are urged to step up their efforts,[3] while the press makes many appeals for vigilance. The main targets for these campaigns are the educators, who are reminded that the school's primary task is to train Communists, hence, to keep future Soviet citizens away from the dangerously retrograde and anti-Communist ideas conveyed by religion.[4] More and more antireligious publications, which not so long ago contented themselves with attacking religion and predicting its inevitable demise, are stressing the capacity of religion to survive[5] and its ability to adapt to a society transformed by socialism.[6] Slowly, the Kremlin is becoming aware of the attraction that religious ritual can have in a society where uniformity prevails. The government also recognizes that in a society where urbanization leads to increased delinquency, religious morality goes side by side with socialist morality and may even replace it.[7]

Nevertheless, in their discovery of the facts of religion, the Soviet analysts are anything but unanimous. They tend to divide believers into two categories: the "traditionalists," whose religious feelings go back to childhood, and the "converts," for whom religion is a deliberate choice.[8] In the first category they place the members of the principal faiths, the Orthodox and apparently the Moslems. In the second category are placed the followers of religions less important in the historical Soviet context, Baptists and Roman Catholics. Is there any justification for such a classification? There is no quick answer to this without having recourse to extended socio-religious surveys carried out in the USSR. What is most important is the conclusion Moscow draws from these inquiries. For the regime, religious faith—seen as a manifestation of the attachment to tradition—is a survival of the past.

Thus, religion, which is so widespread in the Soviet Union, is regarded as the persistence of confused beliefs, due to insufficient education. Implicit in this conclusion is the view that religion is a specific phenomenon whose national-political repercussions are not clearly understood. But these hasty conclusions raise a number of questions. Is religion only a survival of the presocialist past, one that will be destroyed by the march toward Communism and by education? Is religion, as it is manifested at present, alien to the political culture of each nation? This being the case, is religion alien to the issue of nationality? Two examples, very different in their sociological and historical contexts, come to mind when these questions are raised.

At one end of the world of Soviet nationalities are the Balts. Steeped in European tradition, highly developed culturally and economically, they sometimes show a special attachment to religion. At the other end are the Moslem peoples of the USSR. Turned toward the historic world of Islam, less urbanized and less economically developed, they are undergoing a religious revival that above all bears witness to the diversity of political culture in the USSR.

Catholicism and National Identity

As always in the Soviet Union, it is the government itself which undertakes to point out facts whose existence it denies. According to them, religion is dying. For more than half a century, generations of young Soviets have been taught to pass a death sentence on God. And yet suddenly the authorities have become alarmed and are seeking ways of strengthening antireligious institutions in an effort to stem the rising tide of believers.

For instance, in 1975 Moscow suddenly decided to breathe new life into Lithuania's Museum of Atheism, asserting the need to mobilize militants of atheism in a struggle against religion, which stubbornly refuses to die.[9] The juxtaposition of contradictory elements can be noted here. To the well-known contradiction of a policy which maintains that *Homosovieticus* is an atheist, or at the least nonreligious, and which mobilizes considerable forces for the antireligious struggle, is coupled a second contradiction at the grassroots, duplicating the first. Partial surveys lay stress on an indisputable apathy, if not actual hostility, to religion. One survey carried out in the early 1970s in Latvian schools[10] showed that the majority of adolescents were indifferent to religion (56.2%), 17.1% were found to be inactive atheists, and 3.5% were militant atheists. Without doubt, the proportion of those modestly referred to as "superstitious" (21.1%) is far from negligible, especially as added to these are 2.1% listed as "undecided," whose refusal to take a stand on religious beliefs suggests that they might simply be afraid to declare their faith too openly, and could be classified among the believers.

Does the fact that 21% or 23% of Soviet young people in Latvia describe themselves as believers warrant the ideological campaign which has been mounted chiefly in Lithuania? Here another factor comes into play: attitudes toward religion vary from one republic to another, consequently from one religion to another. The surveys carried out in the USSR show that there is no uniformity of attitude toward religion in the three Baltic republics. The highest degree of religious life exists in Lithuania, which raises the question of the causes for these differences in a region which happens to be fairly homogeneous.

All the major Christian sects are found in the Baltic states. But Lithuania stands out in being predominantly Catholic, whereas most of Estonia is Lutheran, while in Latvia Catholics are a definite minority compared to a closely knit Lutheran group.[11] Of the three countries, Lithuania has traditionally been the most homogeneous in religion. There, too, in the course of history, religion has played the most important role in shaping the nation. In this country, where the conversion to Christianity at the start of the thirteenth century had been voluntary, the Church soon assumed the responsibility for training a national elite, which was to oppose Germanic penetration.

During the period of czarist domination, the Russification policy came into conflict with the Catholic Church and its educational institutions. Their cultural integrity threatened by Russia's unifying aspirations, the Lithuanians expanded their national consciousness around their Church, which was the basis of their cultural development. In these conditions, it is little wonder that the years of independence were marked by the emergence of an important Catholic party in political life, namely the Christian Democratic Party, which played a role in all the political combinations of those years.

In contrast, religion played a much more diffuse historical role in the other two Baltic states. There, the Lutheran Church served as a vehicle for German culture instead of forging a clear-cut national consciousness. In Estonia and Latvia, Russification was not directed against traditional native values but, rather, against the cultural influence and authority of Balts of German origin. Far from resisting, the educated classes in those two countries were immediately divided, not knowing whether their interests lay in defending the German culture against the Russian or, on the contrary, in trying to use Russification to weaken German influence in favor of an eventual national culture.

Regarded by Catholic Lithuania as a threat to its national-cultural integrity, Russia was perceived in Latvia and Estonia as a possible ally for the development of national autonomy. The years of independence perpetuated the various roles played by the churches. In Estonia the Christian Democratic Party had only minor importance; in Latvia there were many political parties based on religion, but their influence was virtually nonexistent owing to the fact that they were so divided.

The Sovietization of the Baltic republics therefore takes place in a setting which is highly heterogeneous, both religiously and politically. Everywhere in the Baltic countries, antireligious propaganda and education have been all the more persistent because the delayed entry of these republics in the USSR jeopardized—at least in the areas next to the Baltic countries—the work of destroying religion that had gone on between 1917 and 1945.

In Estonia the Orthodox Church enjoys a slightly more favored position than the other churches. There are more parishes,[12] and even a convent. Likewise, in Lithuania, the Orthodox churches in Vilna and Kaunas remain open—while in Vilna alone 23 Catholic churches have been closed since 1945, convents are forbidden, and nuns are persecuted. This preferential treatment is not limited to the Orthodox Church, but is extended to the Lutheran Church in certain cases. This becomes perfectly clear as regards training of the clergy. In all the Baltic republics Moscow limits admissions to seminaries. But the number of applicants authorized to enroll in the Riga religious academy, which theoretically meets the needs of the Lutheran communities in Latvia and Estonia, is proportionately five to six times higher than the number of students allowed to enroll at the Kaunas Catholic seminary. Consequently, the Lithuanian Catholic church now finds itself in a particularly difficult situation. In 1974, there were 628 Catholic churches in Lithuania, but only 554 had a priest. The average age of the clergy is sixty, and their numerical strength is declining all the time. In ten years the number of clergy fell from 850 to 759, among whom there is a growing proportion of retired priests. The particular harshness of the authorities toward Catholics is of course rooted in an antireligious policy that applies to all Soviet citizens, but especially in Lithuania because of the important place that religion has there, and the political meaning of religious observance.

Let us consider the importance of religious life first of all. In Estonia, despite a religious decline, the Soviet government recognizes that there are still actually 450,000 believers, or one-third of the entire population. Participation in religion varies with the different stages of an individual's life: about 12% of the children are baptized; 2.5% of the believers have church weddings, but nearly half of the burials are conducted by clergy. The relatively high number of confirmations—2,000 in 1969—shows that religious practice affects not only the elderly, is not prompted merely by the fear of death, but also attracts youth despite the regime's advice and threats.[13] In 1972 a delegation from the World Lutheran Federation published a series of official reports based on a fact-finding mission to the Baltic republics. This information enables us to conclude that religious observance is rising despite reductions in the number of places of worship and of ministers.[14]

In Latvia the effects of Moscow's antireligious policy are also ambiguous. The number of believers in the Lutheran community has been estimated at 300,000, which is not very large (scarcely more than one-tenth of the total population). However, the development of atheistic propaganda in the course of recent years in Latvia[15] suggests that these believers also make the Kremlin uneasy. After all, the churchgoers in that republic are the most active politically.

But Catholic Lithuania is the real problem. The Lithuanians' attachment to their religion is a fact acknowledged by the Soviet authorities and confirmed by all Lithuanian religious sources. Recently, the chairman of the republic's Council on Religious Affairs declared that at least half of the Lithuanians were practicing Catholics. All the sacraments are administered to a degree unknown in the other Baltic states; 50% of the children are baptized; 25% of the marriages are celebrated in church, and more than half of the funerals; and in 1974 there were nearly 18,000 confirmations. These figures are the more remarkable in view of the particularly repressive legislation in Lithuania. Since the early 1960s the republic's Supreme Soviet has issued a large number of decrees aimed at halting religious observance among the young and cutting them off completely from religious authorities.[16]

Despite restrictions, the Soviet regime must recognize that the Catholic faith of the Lithuanians seems ineradicable, even when they are uprooted from their native land and isolated in a foreign environment. That is the case of the Lithuanians who have settled, voluntarily or under compulsion, in Kazakhstan, where they retain the same religious habits as their coreligionists remaining in Lithuania.[17]

The attachment of the Lithuanians to their religion is reflected in special behavior patterns, notably in the demographic sphere. Of all the western peoples in the Soviet Union, the Lithuanians show the least unfavorable population trend. In spite of wartime losses, the aging of the population, and a consequent rising death rate, the child/woman ratio in 1970 showed a slight uptrend compared to 1959 and was definitely higher than those of the other Balts, the Russians, the Ukrainians, or the Belorussians. While all the other European peoples except the Russians are declining, the Lithuanian population is characterized by relative stability.

The Catholic hierarchy's firm stance on birth control, compared with the other Christian denominations' tolerant attitude, has a definite bearing on the particular character of Lithuania's demography. This connection is all the more evident in view of the position of the Catholic Church as a rallying point for national aspirations in confronting the central government. The Lithuanian National-Catholic identity appears clearly in all its political or cultural activities. This identity, which is largely due to the role of the clergy in political life, was underscored by the Soviet regime when it accused them of participation en masse in armed resistance against the USSR during the 1940s.[18]

Antigovernmental political activity in Lithuania is rooted largely in the difficulties confronting Catholicism. Since 1968, petitions have been coming from the dioceses protesting measures that restrict religious life, measures that the Lithuanians consider to be violations of the Constitution. Two features make these campaigns of petitioning noteworthy—first of all, their extent. From 1968 to 1974 nearly thirty appeals of this type have been counted, some bearing as many as 17,000 signatures.[19] Secondly, the role played by the clergy in these campaigns was extensive. In 1974 it was estimated that at least half the Lithuanian priests had signed one or more protests. In 1970–1971 the conflict between Moscow and the believers took a sinister turn with the arrest of two priests accused of preparing children for communion. During the trial of one of them in 1971, a violent demonstration broke out involving a crowd of believers estimated at nearly a thousand. The following year, in Kaunas, a young student immolated himself by fire. He was a member of the Komsomol but had been attracted to the seminary, and chose suicide as a way of protesting the fate of his church and his homeland. His self-immolation gave rise to a wave of student demonstrations rarely equaled in the USSR, and to a deepening of the religious movement, which was to link the issues of faith and nationality even more closely. This was reflected in groups that sprang up despite all proscriptions, such as the Lithuanian Catholic Association.

This mingling of the church and state emerged most vividly from the pages of a clandestine publication[20] which was started in 1972 and which, having managed to reach the West, makes it possible to follow Lithuanian political developments. Begun as a religious protest against restrictions placed on freedom of conscience, this journal from 1973 on devoted more and more space to infringements of national rights.[21] In the pages of this publication are revealed all the anxieties of a society faced with what appears to be a continuous program of national dispossession—educational discrimination against believers or the children of believers, progressive imposition of the Russian language, economic sanctions. Included also is a detailed account of arrests and trials of dissidents without distinction as to the cause involved, whether religion or human rights; to that are added references to national events regardless of the occasion, ranging from sports to court trials. This Catholic paper even went so far as to applaud a deeply anticlerical film, *Herkus Matas*, because its theme evoked one of the most revered chapters in national history, the defeat of the Teutonic Knights in the thirteenth century. This shows how powerful the bond between religious feeling and national sentiment in the Baltic states can be. The fact that religion is the most alive in Lithuania exemplifies this bond. Catholicism, a religion affirming the nationality of the peoples living on the borders of Protestant Germany and of Orthodox Russia, has quite naturally assumed the function of unifying the communities that adhere to it. It is not irrelevant to note that Poland and Lithuania, the two Communist countries in which national sentiment is most strongly manifested through religion, are bound by history—a history in which religious struggle and the struggle for national existence have always been intertwined.

That Catholicism, more than Lutheran Protestantism, the Baptist Church, or the Orthodox Church, is the focal point of national protest in the Baltic countries, can be explained both by history and by the status of the religious groups within each country. The Orthodox religion, for the Estonians who demand it, can become a factor for rapprochement with the Russian people who, in turn, are slowly coming back to a faith long forgotten. At any rate, the Orthodox religion contributes to the heterogeneity of the Estonian people, not to its unity. The Baptist Church, whose adherents demonstrate an incredibly courageous will for spiritual emancipation from the regime—far from crystallizing national feelings—serves to weaken or transcend them. Therein lies its strength, as a transnational religion.

Only the Lutheran Church, because it is totally alien to Russia, might be able to assume a national role. In this connection, however, history suggests that the separate and local character of Lutheran churches, two factors which were formerly favorable to their survival, may well affect them adversely today. Having been less opposed by Russia in the past, the Lutheran churches have also been less symbolic of the struggle against national oppression.[22]

Nevertheless, in recent years a new trend has been seen in Estonia and Latvia. No one would deny the gains made by every religion in these two republics. It is still too soon to say whether this movement is a purely religious phenomenon, a way of becoming more deeply rooted in national culture as a reaction to Moscow's drive for integration, or the consequence of a climate of national protest in which citizens find the courage to acknowledge convictions that diverge from the official ideology. Essentially it is a question of the novelty of the religious phenomenon in the Soviet Union. A survival of the past, the government maintains; but a survival which attracts attention because the Party's tolerance allows it to be displayed in broad daylight. While these arguments are contradicted by official surveys among the youth of the Baltic countries, and by the hazings and persecutions suffered by the believers, one question remains. Is it a purely religious phenomenon, a new start for Christianity? Or is it a political phenomenon as well?

Islam, Cement for Political and Social Organization

For the Soviet regime the persistence of religion simply indicates weakness, a lag in "political modernization." This argument, which denies any political significance to religious "survivals," is used by Moscow especially in the Moslem borderlands at the other end of the Soviet Union. Denouncing the persistence of religious practices, the government claims that they generally take place in remote areas such as isolated rural districts or villages in the Caucasus, interpreting these religious manifestations as a certain delay in the penetration of the Soviet social and ideological model.[23]

However, while minimizing the impact of the Moslem phenomenon, the Soviets admit that it does survive in some sectors of the population, and to rationalize this, the regime divides believers into three categories: (1) "fanatics," rather limited in numbers but perpetuating a purely Islamic ideology in society; (2) "ordinary believers"; and lastly (3) "waverers."[24] The juxtaposition of these three groups is significant. Classifying the waverers with the believers suggests that in the final analysis everyone claims some degree of affiliation with the Moslem religion. This extended definition shows that Islam, unlike the other religons, is both a spiritual and a social world, which can cover all aspects of Moslem life. We shall concern ourselves with that strictly religious world here before returning later on to the social reality bound up in the religious one.

Islam's power in society cannot be measured in the same way as that of a Christian church. The traditional criteria—the number of houses of worship, their attendance, and even clear-cut replies to the question of personal faith—are inadequate yardsticks. Hence, we must either replace these indicators or add new ones. If these criteria are used, a disconcerting picture of Islam in the USSR is obtained. Few places of worship are open for the mass of over 50 million people of Moslem origin. While it is impossible to obtain complete official information on the number of mosques open for worship, partial information reveals absurd figures.

About 200 mosques are officially open in the USSR, of which 146 are in Central Asia and Kazakhstan, 27 in the Daghestan and Chechen republics, and 13 in the Tatar republic.[25] However, their distribution often has no correlation with the size of the local Islamic community. In Azerbaidzhan, only 16 mosques serve an Azeri population of nearly 4 million. In Kirghizia, on the other hand, 33 official mosques were counted in the late 1960s for barely 1 million inhabitants.[26] These two figures, representing the extremes of concentration of places of worship in all the Moslem republics, have little meaning of themselves. At any rate, they do reflect the very small number of places of worship officially open. The figures do not take into account unofficial houses of worship where lay elders officiate, which are numerous in all of Central Asia and in the Caucasus. The very low attendance figures at mosques and the almost exclusive presence of elderly believers characterize religious life in the Islamic lands of the Soviet Union.

All of this information would seem to suggest that Islam is gradually dying out in the USSR along with the older generation, untrained in Soviet ideology. But this picture is contradicted almost immediately by conflicting data. The growing number of sociological studies being carried out on this subject in the USSR shows that Moslem society remains attached to its beliefs.[27] Generally speaking, in rural areas, nearly half the people surveyed answered that they were believers.[28]

In the Karakalpak Republic, which is part of Uzbekistan, a survey showed that in 1972 only 23% of the men and 20% of the women reported that they were atheists. The rest, i.e., 77% of the male population and 80% of the female population, can be broken down as shown in Table 39.

Table 39
Followers of the Islamic Faith in the Karakalpak Autonomous Republic

	Men	Women
Devout believers	11.3%	11 %
Believers by tradition	14	15
Waverers	13.3	14.3
Non-believers, but observing Moslem rites	17.2	19.3
Non-believers, but observing Moslem rites under the influence of their families	21.2	20.2

In the region of North Caucasus, only 20% of the population indicated that they were atheists in 1974.

But here again, the figures reflect a highly complex reality. Can-
vassers working in Moslem areas, even when they are Moslems themselves, have often noted the extraordinary reticence with which re-
spondents speak of their religious faith. When the question becomes
at all complicated, the answer is often reduced to a paradox or a
joke. The most frequent reply to the question, "Are you a Moslem?" has been a decided "yes." However, to the supplementary
question: "Are you a true believer?" the answer suddenly grows
more shaded. In rural areas the reply is often affirmative; in urban
areas it is less frequently positive, and much less so among the national elites.

How then can one describe this Islam which has nearly 50 million
adherents, a considerable proportion of whom are not believers and
the majority of whom do not practice the religion? And yet, Islam is
present everywhere in the Moslem republics. To deal with this contradiction which shows that those who declare themselves Moslem
have really nothing in common with those who declare their Christian faith, it is necessary first to look at organized religion and then
try to understand what being Moslem means for a Soviet.

Like Christianity, Islam has several "churches," and several of
these exist in the USSR. While the majority of Soviet Moslems come
under orthodox Islam—the Sunni—, there is also a important group
called the Shiites, which, in turn, is subdivided. In addition, we find
adherents of smaller, heterodox sects.[29] However, unlike the Christians, who define themselves as Catholic or Orthodox (can one imagine a Lithuanian who would not proclaim himself Catholic?), the
Moslems of the Soviet Union never indicate that they are Sunnites
or Shiites. They are, they maintain, Moslem. The implication of this
reply is obvious. Islam in the USSR is not an aggregate of different
religions but primarily a community, the "Ummah."

Whether orthodox or heterodox, all Moslems who declare themselves such are members of the community of believers. This sense
of sharing membership in the Ummah is in basic contrast to the division of the Christian churches and to the Christian's more personal
relationship with his church—in the Soviet Union, at least. The very
organization of Islam in the USSR reflects the community's existence. Four "spiritual leaderships"—*Muftiates*—dominate the whole
of Soviet Islam. The Ufa leadership extends its authority to the Sun-

nite Moslems in European Russia and in Siberia. The authority of the Tashkent leadership, again covering Sunnites, takes in Central Asia and Kazakhstan. In the Caucasus the Buynaksk leadership extends over the Sunnites of the northern Caucasus and Daghestan. Finally, there is the Baku leadership, which has jurisdiction over a mixture of Sunnites and Shiites.

The existence of a mixed spiritual leadership bears witness to bonds, not divisions, between the two great Moslem families. These spiritual directorates, in much the same way as the Patriarchate of Moscow for the Orthodox, deal with the Soviet government on matters of religion and are responsible for organizing the religious life of the believers. The most powerful of all is the Tashkent spiritual leadership, for it has jurisdiction over the only two Moslem universities in the USSR, the Medress Mir Arab in Bukhara and Baraq Khan in Tashkent. Islamic dignitaries, about fifty a year, are trained at these universities.

The Tashkent leadership uses—and this is comical—the printing press of the Party's own newspaper, *Qzyl Uzbekistan* (Red Uzbekistan), to print the Koran, and the Moslem calendar; also a publication which serves as a link for all the Moslems of the USSR and in a general way as the community's official journal, *The Moslems of the Soviet East*, published in Uzbek, Arabic, French, English, and Russian. In addition, the Mufti of Tashkent is the primary agent for communication with the Moslem world outside the USSR. He receives foreign Moslem delegations and speaks to the outside world in the name of the Soviet Moslem community, of which the Mufti is the embodiment.

From the outset an obvious ambiguity can be seen in the status of Islam in the USSR. The Soviet State, in accordance with its ideology, recognizes only the existence of individual believers. It tolerates religious life for these believers and, hence, institutions such as the Muftiates. In the eyes of the regime, however, these institutions should be territorially based administrations. In reality, nothing could be further from the truth, insofar as the Soviet Moslems are concerned. The Tashkent leadership covers the area of ancient Turkestan. In fact, like the Orthodox patriarchate, the Moslem spiritual leaderships do not come under the severe Soviet ruling on territorial divisions.

Another peculiarity of Islam further complicates the situation. Unlike Christianity, whose doctrine separates the spiritual and the temporal, Islam by its very definition merges both spheres. Moslem doctrine, the product of the Koran and of tradition, imposes on the faithful special institutions which, despite variations from one culture to another, characterize Moslem lands and dominate social life. Here again, the Soviet State's designs for uniformity could not accept a special status for the Moslem community, and in their first few years in power the Soviet leaders abolished the fundamental elements of that community, namely the juridical system,[30] the legal institutions, and the financial bases.

Reduced to being the religion of private individuals and not of a community, stripped of its institutions, excluded from the temporal sphere, does the Moslem religion in its organized form really still exist? Or is it nothing more than a semblance, a skeleton about to collapse with the death of the last believers?

Numerous glaring facts show that although such a negative hypothesis about Islam's future might well have been plausible in the recent past, there is no longer any basis for it. On the contrary, everything suggests that Islam in the USSR is undergoing a rebirth amid new conditions,[31] and that this renascence is conscious and desired. It is being aided and guided by the Moslem hierarchy, which is directing its efforts to two particular areas: facilitating the practice of Islam by adapting it to the needs of modern life, and giving it temporal power by uniting it with Soviet ideology.

The question is whether being a good Moslem in Soviet society is more difficult than being a good Catholic. Judging by the obligations that it imposes on its adherents, Islam seems most ill-suited to a social system which is hostile to it. Of the five obligations of a Moslem believer, two of them—reciting the profession of faith and giving alms—come completely under the heading of private life. The other three—the five daily prayers, fasting, and pilgrimages—necessarily interfere with the outside world. Anyone, of course, can say prayers within the confines of one's heart, but Islam imposes a ritual of ablutions and postures that requires Moslems to interrupt their work each time they must pray. In addition, the noon prayer on Fridays is supposed to be said at the mosque. But the Soviet State does not allow daily occupations like school and work to be disturbed by religious practices. Freedom of conscience in no way implies the right to allow religious beliefs to intervene in the obligations of citizenship. For the same reason, and because of the "economic imbalance" that it produces, the fast of Ramadan has always been vigorously contested by the Soviet regime. As for the pilgrimage to Mecca, it is obvious that that is out of the question for Soviet Moslems. Given these conditions, it is easy to understand why few Moslems list themselves as being devout, and that so few go to the mosques. But the difficulties involved in scrupulously observing the Islamic faith are not limited to the Moslems of the USSR. In all Moslem countries undergoing modernization, strict observance of the rules of Islams runs counter to the demands of daily life and economic development. Frequently, Islam gives way to modernity, even without external pressure.

In the USSR, after a long phase of inertia in the face of this problem, the Moslem authorities are suddenly seeking solutions. They are attempting to make the practice of Islam possible for all believers by reforming it and adapting to the Soviet framework. More importantly, they are trying to give modern meaning to the Moslem community and its duties.

How Can One Be a Moslem in the USSR Today?

One can be a moslem simply by practicing the religion and doing so as best one can, reply the Moslem authorities. In other words, by saying the prayers five times a day and going to the mosque on Friday, if one is free to do so. But if social duties stand in the way, the believer may reduce his prayers to only one a day, saying them at whatever time suits him.[32] This understanding attitude on the part of Moslem authorities is also found in their new approach to the question of fasting.

Because fasts meet with the regime's violent and open opposition, believers have long had to choose between resistance to the regime and a submissiveness that seemed to imply abandoning their faith. The solution to this dilemma now lies in an interpretation which favors the spirit and not the letter of the law. The Imam of the Mirza Yussof mosque in Tashkent, P. Abdurrahimov, recently indicated what fasting was to be.

Fasting, he said, has two final goals: To enable each Moslem to transcend himself by depriving himself. But at the same time, to enable every Moslem, whatever his or her station, to have a common awareness of deprivation, of hunger. By stressing the spiritual impact of Moslem laws more than their formal aspect, the Imam of Tashkent was not really making an innovation. Actually, he was following the ideas of Central Asian reformers who early in this century had tried to renew Islam and form a strong Moslem community capable of resisting Russian domination. For decades Soviet constraint had prompted Islamic dignitaries to give up innovative ideas and take refuge in a formalist, rigid Islam which indeed survived persecution but actually made it a religion of the elderly.

At the present time an organized Islam is taking up these reforms once more and is endeavoring to show that the Moslem must understand the ritual as an effort to be made, but that the nature of this effort may vary with the circumstances, particularly because of the obligations that a political society imposes on its members. Exemptions from fasting, traditionally granted to special categories of individuals—children, the elderly, the sick—are now allowed for workers.[33] The spiritual authorities give them a choice, either to set aside one day in the Ramadan period for fasting and thereby join in the common observance, or to replace the fast with a special effort in their spiritual life or in their work.[34] The important thing is that the individual Moslem should have a consciousness of participating in the community's obligations.

The meaning of the policy which they follow becomes still clearer in the directives issued by the spiritual authorities with regard to Ramadan. Having both the regime and the faithful in mind, these directives are meant to show Moscow that the practice of Islam does not run counter to the Soviet State's economic interests. At times, to achieve this end, the directives make use of more specious arguments aimed at demonstrating the physical benefits of fasting: "It improves the health. It may even lessen the risks of certain diseases such as cancer."[35]

But mainly the efforts are directed toward the believers, whom the religious leaders try to unify in a homogeneous community. In fact, the Soviet regime has divided the world of Islam—as it has for the other religions—into practitioners and nonpractitioners. It was hoped that the importance and obligatory nature of the Moslem ritual would deepen this division to the point where practitioners would appear as survivors of a lost world, totally alien to the USSR. Conscious of this danger, the Moslem authorities are trying to bridge this gap by recreating an Islamic community in which practicing and nonpracticing members have a place and participate in one common spirit but in different ways. To achieve this, the Islamic leaders clearly explain that both groups are Moslems, but that one observes Islam by praying regularly and fasting according to the rules, while the other fulfills its self-denials through work.

Islam's holiest festivals, daily prayers, and fasts, far from being eliminated in this concept, are employed to help in this restructuring of the Moslem community. What the spiritual authorities wish is that during each festival their coreligionists be aware that they belong to the community, and that they regard each of their acts and each of their efforts as a participation in the united effort of the community. To further heighten this sense of participation, the Islamic leaders invoke the numerous feast days in Moslem spiritual life. For instance, breaking the fast at the end of Ramadan becomes the occasion for gathering together those who have fasted and those who have pursued their regular lives. This joyous ceremony, the *Iftar*, tends to symbolize the different attitudes toward the ritual. The Soviet regime itself has not been blind to the effects of modernization in Islam. Many indications of this development can be found in the press of the Moslem republics. Judging from these reports, it would seem not only that the sense of Moslem solidarity has been strengthened, but also in particular that "the believers are having a growing influence on that segment of the population which does not practice religion."[36]

The importance assigned to religious festivals for welding the community explains the fact that, for most of the festivals, an effort is made to adapt to Soviet conditions. This is the case for the Festival of the Sacrifice, *Kurban Bairam*, in which each Moslem must sacrifice an animal and distribute it to the poor. Here again, the ritual runs counter to the economic interests of the Soviet State, which does not allow the mass slaughter of animals for religious purposes, even if they are privately owned. But the Moslem spiritual authorities are particularly attached to this rite, which heightens the feeling of community and sacrifice.

In 1945, aware of the political objections to this practice, the Moslem spiritual leadership in Central Asia issued a *Fetwa* emphasizing that this sacrifice was desirable but not obligatory. In 1969, to still the uneasiness of the Soviet regime, which had found that the sacrificing of animals remained a widespread practice, even though not obligatory, all the spiritual leaderships came out in favor of a modification of this practice. Animal sacrifice could henceforth be replaced by an offering equal to the animal's value, an offering that the mosques receive and either use for their own purposes or distribute.

In this way Soviet laws are respected, and the mosques derive considerable income therefrom.

Another adaptation no less beneficial to the life of the community involves the feast of *Mavlud*, commemorating the Prophet's birth. Because it may be difficult for believers to go to the mosque, there is a growing tendency to organize this celebration in various private houses. This practice produces a considerable gap between the official number of people celebrating this feast in a half-empty mosque and the actual number participating in the many private ceremonies. For example, in 1968 the official ceremony at the Mardzhani cathedral-mosque in Kazan was "supplemented" by more than eighty private ceremonies combining the actual ritual—prayer, sermon, stories from the life of the Prophet—with a feast. A Soviet expert calculated that in this one case those officiating gave far more sermons than they had all year in the mosque.[37]

By adapting to the timetable of the active Soviet workers and by combining religious ceremony with festivals, the Islamic dignitaries attract throngs to their ceremonies out of all proportion in terms of number, age, and social level to the small group of officially practicing Moslems. It should also be emphasized that this combination of religious ceremony and festival offers the advantage of attenuating the illegal character of these privately held religious celebrations. It is significant that these ceremonies take place, that they attract large numbers of participants, and that the Soviets authorities feel helpless to cope with these new and almost uncontrollable forms of religious practice.

More, so even than Ramadan, pilgrimages raised a thorny problem for Moslem authorities, inasmuch as they were trying to combine an attitude that the State could not criticize with an expansion of Islamic religious practice. Very seldom have Soviet Moslems been authorized to travel to the holy places. In those rare instances, it was more a case of operations related to Soviet foreign policy than any regard for freedom of conscience. As a matter of fact, this problem is not restricted to the USSR, even though it is more acute there.

The practice of pilgrimages by proxy[38] has been a longstanding tradition in the Soviet Union as elsewhere. But here also, Soviet Islam tries in many ways to involve the whole community in an obligation that is particularly hard to fulfill. The pilgrimage to Mecca represents an exceptional opportunity for the Soviet Moslem community to make contact with the entire Islamic world. For this reason the spiritual leaderships endeavor to use these rare opportunities for the benefit of those best qualified to represent the community. Only the Islamic dignitaries have the canonical and linguistic ability to satisfy these requirements, so they alone are given special permission by the Soviet government to travel to other Islamic countries. Inasmuch as it is in the interests of the Soviet State to demonstrate to the Third World that the USSR is *also* an Islamic country and that, contrary to what takes place in China, all Moslem rights are preserved, it can be seen that the Kremlin's interests at times coincide with those of the Soviet Moslem community and actually promote them.[39]

Yet the ordinary believer is not totally excluded from pilgrimages. In the USSR the impossible journey to Mecca has been replaced—and tradition actually encourages this—by pilgrimages to local holy places, of which there are many. The most famous of these are the tombs of Iassawi and Shah-i Zinda. However, the Moslem authorities are divided on this point. In Central Asia, where pilgrimages to the tombs of saints are frequent and take on the quality of a popular festival,[40] the Tashkent Muftiate attempts to limit this practice to a spiritual interpretation of the pilgrimages. Emphasis is placed on effort and a sense of community, rather than on formal practices which often lose their spiritual meaning and become mere holidays.

In the Caucasus, on the other hand, Islam is moving in other directions. There the cult of sheikhs, both living and dead, is quite widespread and tends to isolate the religious community from any outside influence.[41] Another phenomenon, shamanism, on the fringe between religion and popular beliefs, adds another element to the image of the Soviet Moslem world.[42] Shamanism is a name applied by the Soviet regime to any mystical cult, whether organized or not, which derives from Sufism and which frightens the regime. As the mosques are unable fully to perform their function, Moslems turn to Sufi practices, just as Christians turn to radical sects. It is a religious phenomenon but a socio-political one as well, the equivalent of a political party. This point will be taken up later on.

Whatever the criticisms or reservations in the Moslem community regarding pilgrimages to the holy places, the crucial point is the fact that significant crowds gather in contempt of all the regime's warnings. These public gatherings, held at regular intervals, reveal that religion constantly leaves the sphere of individual life and becomes primarily a manifestation of collective conscience. In this way, Moslems—whether believers or not—show their sense of belonging to a group transcending their individual destiny.

Even when the spiritual authorities do not always go along with the popular response, the idea of integration in the group still lies at the heart of the Islamic attitude and the interpretations offered by these same authorities. In every case, they emphasize that Islam is synonomous with community and collective education. But at the same time they endeavor to bring this religion into the Soviet framework, and with this in mind to reform practices unacceptable to the regime or to show that some of those practices considered unacceptable actually coincide with the State's interests. This is the case with the idea of holy war, in regard to which a sermon delivered at the great mosque of Moscow ran as follows: "Islam obliges us to engage in holy war, namely, to build a social life founded on love, fraternity, and a concern for all; an international life founded on peace."

When defined as a personal struggle for the happiness of all, can holy war be condemned by Soviet ideology? By underscoring the role of education and the practice of Islam in building a society that cannot be repudiated by Communism, Moslem leaders are legitimatizing Islam.

It is still too soon to say whether this more modern approach to Moslem life has increased religious practice. On the other hand, its impact on the people's way of thinking can already be seen. In this way, Moslem authorities have restored meaning to the *Ummah*, making it accessible to everyone. In asserting Moslem solidarity beyond religious ritual and professed belief, the existence of an Islamic sphere has been affirmed, and all Soviet citizens with ties to this sphere have been brought back into the Islamic community. The change is qualitative. It consists of the continuous creation, within a modern, educated society, of a collective consciousness based on the feeling of belonging to a common world.

In Soviet society collective consciousness is supposed to be unique, namely, the Communist consciousness which the Party attempts to instill by every means at its command. At a lower level, and by way of transition, the Soviet State and the Party allow feelings of belonging to a nationality to subsist, for they think that the fragmentation of nationalities renders such feelings harmless. The emergence above national sentiments of a collective Moslem consciousness, often with a content more pan-cultural than religious, is a new phenomenon in the USSR, and probably irreversible. The phenomenon can be called irreversible because it is not a question of intellectual backwardness rooted in an implicit awareness of a common world, but rather an evolution going along with intellectual progress and in an explicit way.

But this activity on the part of the most conscious segment of the Soviet Moslem world goes beyond mobilization of a purely Islamic collective consciousness. It is gradually linking up with efforts for integration in the sphere of politics, which is the most original aspect of this Moslem effort at modernization.

Islam, Another System of Values in Soviet Society

The immediate aspect of this political integration is the reconciliation of Islam with Communism. The Soviet regime has always maintained that only its ideology is legitimate because it coincides with the historical interests of humanity. Communist ideology, opposed to all other systems of values, makes no relative judgments—it simply excludes all others. Contemporary Moslem thinkers are trying to weaken that absolutism by denying the originality of Communism and demonstrating that, up to a point, Islamic and Communist principles are quite compatible.

Islam cannot oppose the principles of Communist ideology, simply because both are steeped in the spirit of justice, say Moslem leaders in the USSR. At the 1970 Tashkent Congress of Soviet Moslems, M. Hazaev, an Azeri religious dignitary, declared: "We can categorically affirm that the capitalist system, built on injustice and exploitation, must disappear and be replaced by a socialist system based on just laws. In this regard, the divine laws are unequivocal: justice triumphs in this world."[43]

Therefore, it can be seen that the domestic system of the USSR, just as its foreign policy, is carrying out a task held to be decisive by Islamic ideals; there is a clear-cut parallel between the Communist doctrine that the USSR "fights for peace, because war is rooted in injustice," and the Moslem doctrine that "Islam also fights for peace and justice."[44] This being the case, what separates Islam from Communism? One might be tempted to conclude that the Kremlin is simply exploiting Islam and its hierarchy, and to add that, in a society still marked by differences, it is shrewd to put Islam in the sphere of official ideology. But this would be overlooking Soviet reality and

Moslem reasoning. Soviet reality is a mono-ideological and mono-organizational system in which Islam, not Communism, must defend itself.

However, exploiting Islam amounts to recognizing its existence and its impact on the Moslem masses. Any dialogue between the official ideology and the others would represent a retreat on the part of the regime. Therefore, it is not in the interest of Communism to take the initiative, which must come from Islam. By taking the first step, Islam can make a place for itself in a mono-ideological context, which it is gradually transforming into one of competing ideologies.

This competitive aspect becomes particularly apparent in the light of the arguments used by the Moslems. They recognize that Islam and Communism can coexist, but that this coexistence must give Islam a privileged place. The Moslem dignitaries said just that at the 1970 Tashkent Moslem conference: "Soviet leaders who believe neither in God nor his Prophet . . . nevertheless apply laws that were dictated by God and expounded by his Prophet."[45] They went on to say: "(We) admire the genius of the Prophet who preached the social principles of socialism. (We are) pleased that a great number of socialist principles implement the orders of Mohammed."[46]

The meaning of this speech is clear: socialism is acceptable to the Moslems because it is pursuing their own goals. In this connection it is appropriate to mention the interpretation of Communism by the Libyan leader Khadafi, who holds that Marx, in his knowledge of history, was inspired by the precepts of Islam, and to the extent that he was so inspired, Marx is acceptable to a Moslem.[47] Will it be said that Khadafi glorifies Marx by coldly appending him to the heritage of Islam? This relationship between the Libyan leader's intransigent, militant Islam and the modernism of Soviet Moslem dignitaries should make them reflect on the meaning of their actions. The Soviet authorities, for their part, see things quite clearly, underscoring the dangers in this modernism against which their antireligious propaganda becomes ineffectual.[48]

Having affirmed the compatibility of Islam and Communism, and therefore the right of Islam to exist and act in a Communist society, the Moslem leaders go further still. They are endeavoring to make Islam an active component in the new society. They ask Moslems, whether believers or not, to take part in the socialist life, not simply as citizens, but as Moslems. The organ of the Tashkent Muftiate leaves no doubt on this point: "Those believers who are good Moslems . . . must take part in building a new life and a new society in their own country.''

It is not only the participation of adults in socialist organizations that the Moslem leaders are calling for, but—and this represents a crucial aspect in their position—the active participation of children and adolescents, trained in Moslem ways, in the organization responsible for socializing them. This stance is interesting in several respects. First of all, it contrasts with the position of other groups of believers, particularly that of the Baptists, who endeavor to keep their youth apart from Communist organizations and maintain that Christian training is incompatible with the process of socialization such as it is conceived in the USSR. The Moslems quite explicitly oppose this view, saying: "Our children must be pioneers, Komsomols, Party members. They must take leading positions everywhere."

The second noteworthy aspect of the Moslem leaders' position is their clearsightedness concerning the process of socialization. They perceive the importance the Soviet system attaches to the socialization of youth and beyond this to the permanent socialization of the individual. Aware of this tendency and unwilling to keep in the background, Moslem leaders declare their commitment and want their people to be "joiners" with regard to all organizations responsible for socialization. But they are entreated to "join" not like other citizens but as Moslems, who will thus belong to socialist organizations everywhere *as Moslems* and represent their community there.

Before analyzing the full implications of such an attitude, it is worthwhile to see how the Moslem stance is perceived by the Kremlin. Reading the newspapers of the Moslem republics, or the publications specializing in religious questions, and seeing the number of conferences held on this theme, one comes to a startling conclusion. The times are over when Soviet leaders nonchalantly dismissed religious manifestations in the expectation that they would soon go away. The findings of insightful analyses have prompted Communist officials to admit that Islam is a problem not of the past but of the present and future, that Moslem trends represent a real threat for the future of Soviet society as a society in the process of integration.

In addition to Islam's vitality, two related facts trouble Soviet authorities in connection with the situation prevailing in the Moslem territories. Young people are aware of this religious revival, and the new elites, if not actively involved, are at least passively interested.

The "perversion" of youth is a constant theme in the Soviet press.

It is easy to understand Moscow's anxiety, considering the networks of influence and control surrounding Soviet youth. No moment in the life of a young Soviet can be called "neutral," as far as his education is concerned. The family is responsible for preparing the child from infancy for a Communist education. Along with the schools, the organizations of socialization—the Octobrists for preschoolers, the Young Pioneers, the Komsomols—are there to take hold of a child and make him the New Man of Communist society. Coupled with this network for mental development is a mass of legislation intended to preserve the child from any influence not contributing to the spread of the official value system.

Children are not allowed to take part in religious ceremonies. Collective religious education is out of the question. In addition, parents are kept under surveillance by their own children,[49] thereby preventing them from assuming the task of religious education themselves. What is the purpose of these restrictions? The question is all the more pertinent after reading that Soviet citizens interpret the notion of freedom of conscience in reverse, not only exploiting this concept to bring religion into the life of young children and adolescents, but even to involve them in spreading religious ideas and literature.[50]

At best, the young people show their indifference—not to religion but, rather, to the antireligious precepts instilled in them by their education. They fail to see the "negative, dangerous" aspects of religion, and therefore are prepared to submit to its influence.[51] The continuous growing hold of the family on young people is such that there have been cases where a member of the Komsomol has actually been praised for the noteworthy accomplishment of giving up his religious practices in defiance of family pressures.[52]

In short, it appears that the restriction on involving youth in religious ceremonies is deliberately ignored in Moslem society. This contempt for Soviet rules is sometimes carried to extremes; for example, in the Shiite communities during the celebration of the Achura,[53] the fight between Hussein and Yazid, and Hussein's martyrdom, are re-enacted in a spectacular manner despite all restrictions, with children taking part in the pageant.[54] All this is the subject of deep concern for the regime's official observers—the hold that Islam has on children, the hold of traditions shaping intellectual models, and even children's games. Instead of classic battles, schoolboys in Moslem areas often act out chapters from Moslem history—

for example, the Achura, something that imbues them with traditions and values totally alien to those of the overall society.[55]

Winning over youth has now become the primary goal of Moslem authorities. For Moscow these are anything but the aspirations of a dying religion.[56] Should Islam also become the religion of youth, the regime's entire educational program, and its entire campaign of social transformation would be compromised.

Who is responsible for this situation? Undoubtedly, the Moslem dignitaries, although prime responsibility must fall on the local elites, the very leaders the Soviet regime has educated and shaped ideologically so that they might contribute to the transformation and modernization of the whole Moslem society. In every Moslem area the "ideological weakness" of these leaders has been detected in their tacit approval of a world that they were responsible for modernizing. Faced with the activism of the official or clandestine Moslem clerics, the Party members, Komsomols, and cadres of the State go along with this activism when not actually participating in it themselves.[57]

The acknowledgment of Islam's vitality represents the Kremlin's first reaction to the situation. But while it sees the facts clearly, its reaction has been both slow and confused. The regime's appeals for more effective atheist propaganda smack more of magic remedies than a realistic view of the facts. It is illogical to admit that the elites are indifferent to Islam's progress and even help it along by their silence, and then ask them to combat that progress. Sending professional propagandists into Moslem areas from the outside might mobilize the society against what is bound to appear as meddling on the part of the center. That would only be courting failure.

The regime's inability to find a suitable retort appears clearly in the weakness of Moscow propaganda. It has become difficult for the regime to forbid the fast of Ramadan on grounds of productivity since the Moslem authorities exempt workers from the need for strict observance. Then why should Ramadan be considered undesirable? Throughout the countless articles that appear each year just before Ramadan, denouncing the "reactionary" character of that festival,[58] a new approach has emerged. The Soviets are now saying that Ramadan should be banned because it is not purely Moslem but stems from a pre-Islamic Arab custom later adopted by Islam.

The regime sometimes portrays prayer as a magical, non-religious practice, a legacy from an era predating Islam.[59] In the same way,

Soviet propaganda attacks the cult of saints, denouncing it as a survival of primitive cults and totally opposed to monotheism.[60] There can be no doubt that certain practices extant in Soviet Moslem society are borrowed from pre-Islamic cults. On the other hand, it is surprising to see Soviet propaganda champion a purist Islam, condemning the cult of saints in the name of monotheism.

Does this mean that atheism and the rational criticism of all religion no longer suffice to convince generations educated in the socialist way? Another argument seems just as ludicrous although it emanates from the top echelon of the Kremlin's propaganda department. This line of propaganda condemns Ramadan by quoting directives from the Grand Mufti of Tunisia, who in the 1960s acknowledged that economic necessities could lead to restricting the fast.

This astonishing argument is dangerous for two reasons. First of all, by availing itself of Islam's wise men, Moscow is actually admitting once more that its own ideology cannot cope with the problems of Islam's evolution in the developing world. Furthermore, by invoking Islamic doctrine from abroad, the Kremlin emphasizes the fact that there exists an Islamic world, a world of its own transcending Soviet borders. By using this propaganda approach, the Soviets are actually contributing to Islamic solidarity, at a time when the regime is well aware that the proximity of other Moslem states is precisely one of the main factors in Islam's vitality in the USSR.[61]

Yet, this ineptitude and vacillation in dealing with the challenge can be explained. The Kremlin has very accurately gauged the extent of the Moslem problem, and realizes that Islam's strength lies in the fact that the religious issue is closely intertwined with the nationality issue. Therefore it is not a question of religious beliefs, but of national will and sensibilities which raise political problems as well.

When Communism Becomes a "By-product" of Islam

Having for decades maintained that religion had no roots other than social ones—that it was a means of oppression used by the powerful against the underprivileged, that it was the consolation of the underprivileged, still unaware of class solidarity—the Soviet regime is now admitting that the national foundations of Islam probably explain its continuance. Of course, this does not represent an absolute acknowledgment of the religious character of some cultures. Islam is always represented as a negative part in the history of the peoples, as oppressive as czarism. Islam's fundamentally "reactionary" character, closed to other civilizations which, like that of Europe,[62] spell progress, is unceasingly criticized by the Soviet government, at least within the frontiers of the USSR. But, while attacking Islam and maintaining that it cannot cope with the problems of the modern world, the Soviet regime acknowledges that Islam and its dignitaries are capable of appealing to historical tradition and national sentiment: "The Moslem clergy idealizes the historic past of the eastern peoples . . . it makes use of the attraction that history has for these peoples. Furthermore, it presents the facts as if Islam had embodied and still embodies the special national features of the peoples in the Soviet east and their common life."[63]

This is, in effect, a very clear statement of the problem. The Islamic clergy have two strings to their bow, the appeal to national sentiment and the appeal to a purely Islamic common consciousness. The writer of the foregoing passage underscores a penetrating point regarding the attitude of Moslem leaders. In the monthly organ of the Tashkent Muftiate, *Moslems of the Soviet East*, there is a column entitled "National and Religious Traditions and Rites." Everything related to the national and religious spheres and almost every aspect of social life appears in this column, as will be discussed later on. The link between religion and nationalism is the element which attracts to Islam all those bound to their ethnic community, and who consider the celebration of religious festivals as a way of expressing their attachment to their compatriots.

Soviet leaders have accepted the fact that national consciousness is defined primarily in religious terms, that the attachment to Islam is a way for Moslems to root themselves in their native group, and that the Islamic leaders base their entire program on this fact. Therefore, the Soviets must admit that confusing nationality and religion leads to a uniformity in the behavior of believers, both of Moslems scattered among other groups and those living in compact communities. Surveys carried out in Tatar regions show that, for the Tatars, their collective conversion to Islam represents a national event, which is commemorated each year by believers and nonbelievers alike in what they view as a true Tatar national festival.[64]

The consequences of the "nationalization" of Islam have been denounced by the Soviets even though its implications are played down by Communist analysts. Everything about this nationalization, they say, tends to foster a sentiment of national "specialness" which is also Islamic. But this feeling of being special is seen as curbing relations between nations and hindering the integration process, while encouraging nationalist behavior. Among these special behavior patterns should be included the demographic patterns which, despite transformations in Moslem lifestyle, remain traditional.[65] The weakening of religious consciousness has been offset by integrating Moslem religious teachings with national traditions. This is the principal reason for the lag in social awareness among the Moslems of the USSR, which is reflected primarily in their population trends.[66]

Another result is that "gradually, a negative attitude toward the values of Soviet society is developing among some people." To deal with this, the regime has called on its specialists to mount a campaign of study into the way of life, beliefs, and behavior patterns of the Moslems in order to determine which of these can be accepted as being truly national—i.e., mere folklore—and which are religious and therefore improperly connected with national values. This direction given to the anti-Islamic campaign reveals the regime's confusion when confronted by an overwhelming situation which forces it to give up the offensive and, put on the defensive, to choose what now seems to be a "lesser evil." In identifying and evaluating so-called purely national traditions, ones said to be independent of religion, Soviet authorities run the risk of encouraging Moslem nationalism, already so deeply rooted. Is this really a solution? And are not greater risks involved? To understand the question we must take up the position defended by the Islamic dignitaries and see where it would lead and what its full significance is.

Moslem dignitaries undoubtedly resort to national sentiment to keep Islam alive and to attract a greater number of worshippers. But the term "national" means one thing to Moslems and another to non-Moslems. For the Moslems, the various nationalities coexist in a broader community, namely, that of Islam. All the work accomplished by Moscow since 1920 toward consolidating the different nations and cultures, all the effort aimed at breaking pan-Moslem solidarity and replacing it by identity with local communities has been challenged by the action of the Moslem authorities. The restoration of an Ummah, consisting not of those who are Moslems because they believe but those who are Moslems because they claim to be members of the community, has now become a reality in the Soviet world.

The Soviet experts are right when they say that the Moslem hierarchy is not concerned with the fate of the nationalities but rather with the fate of the Moslem group. But the experts are mistaken in their restrictive interpretation of nationality, for they forget that nationality is also defined by each individual's personal feeling of belonging to it. Very clearly, the Moslems have the feeling of belonging first of all to the *Moslem nation*, even if it hardly conforms to Marxist ideals, and only afterwards, as members of this nation, of belonging to the Uzbek, Tatar, or other nation. The Soviet experts are correct when they point out that Islam confers on its adherents a profound sense of their own "specialness"[67] and the feeling of being members of a different community, *separate* from the non-Moslem one. They are wrong, however, when they claim that this feeling has a religious character, when actually it is a question of a socio-political sensibility and a national fact.

But the action of the Moslem hierarchy is not limited simply to encouraging pan-Moslem tendencies and consolidating Moslem national consciousness. It also has an immediate political implication. It is a variant of the National Communism destroyed by Stalin, reborn from its ashes and profiting from the lessons of the past. The National Communism of the 1920s had been shaped by Communists of Moslem origin, in the forefront of whom stood Sultan Galiev. He tried to resolve the problem of the Moslem nationalities in Bolshevik Russia by urging the creation of parallel revolutionary organizations adapted to their cause and culture. Bolshevik monolithism and its claim to a monopoly of power and ideas doomed his undertaking. Galiev's failure taught all the potential National Communists (or nationalists using the Communist alibi) that the Communism in power would never tolerate parallel organizations and concurrent ideologies, even if these were merely national variants of the Communist ideology.

On the other hand, what should be done about the "joining" urged by the Moslem leadership? If all the political and social organizations were now to be invaded by citizens claiming to be Moslems, wouldn't they be transformed into Moslem organizations? Perhaps a system could be instituted for the purpose of eliminating or purging those who call themselves Moslems although they are nonbelievers. However, Soviet equilibrium is based on equal participation for everyone in the social organizations. This being the case, how can people be eliminated who have in no way violated Soviet law? A feeling of belonging to one's national community is perfectly legal; and the feeling of belonging to the overall community of Moslem origin is also perfectly legal, when it does not take the form of pan-Islamic propaganda or resolutions.

There is no question here of transforming social organizations into institutions different from what they are; but their content can change radically. Herein lies the fundamental problem confronting the Soviet regime in Islamic society, namely the overthrow of the cultural compromise hammered out by Lenin and Stalin to solve the national question. For them, that compromise was clear: the culture of the Soviet peoples, understood in the sense of political culture, was national in form and socialist in essence.

Now, what is happening with the Moslems is a profound transformation of national cultures, of the overall political life, and of ideology. Everywhere that life is being increasingly nationalized, is becoming steeped in profound national values, pushing everything socialist to its periphery, to the point of transforming essence into form. In the course of this change, and to preclude any criticism, emphasis is being placed on socialism, but merely for the sake of appearances. The same may hold true for social and political organizations in the Moslem states; with their primarily Moslem membership, these will remain loyal to socialism in form but will be totally transformed within.

This change is already taking place as far as ideology is concerned. In affirming the compatibility of Islam and Communism, but making the latter a historical byproduct of Islam, the Moslem leaders are reducing socialism to almost nothing. Like all compromises, the cultural compromise was not intended to last indefinitely, but to lead to the total victory of socialism over the national elements thus preserved. In this unequal coexistence of socialist values and national values the latter seem to be gaining the upper hand in a way that the promoters of the compromise had never expected. And the Moslem religion will have contributed to this evolution because, like all religions in the USSR, it represents the only organization existing outside the official framework and ideology, the only physical and spiritual gathering place, the only organized structure having the means to communicate with its members.

*
**

All things considered, Catholicism in Lithuania and Islam in the southern borderlands find themselves in highly similar positions.

Both religions are bound up with the history of the peoples in question. Both derive their present strength from past historical roles and their ability to embody national aspirations which exist everywhere but are fulfilled in varying degrees. However, there are already indications of what separates the destiny of the Lithuanian Catholics from that of the Moslems. Religion has helped the Lithuanians to survive better than their Estonian and Latvian neighbors; it has unified their aspirations and brought them together, but its role stops there. History and spiritual community draw Lithuania to Poland; but from the latter country, which knows all too well how hard it is to maintain an equilibrium with the USSR, Lithuania can hardly expect support in its struggle to preserve the special features of Lithuanian nationality.

The situation of the Soviet Moslem community is entirely different. The size of its population, its demographic dynamism, the geographic position of this community on the edge of a world where the Soviet Union is competing with the West, all these things contribute to the uneasiness with which the Soviet regime witnesses the changes occurring, but at the same time prevent the regime from invoking drastic measures and force it to act with caution. The balance of international relations must inevitably doom Lithuanian nationalism, along with its specific influence in the USSR. On the other hand, for reasons of foreign policy, the Kremlin must reckon with the Moslems, deal with them, and ultimately make use of them. One final difference is that in Lithuania the power of religion has not shaped a society differing basically from the rest of Soviet society. Whereas Islam, on the contrary—besides the fact that it unifies a total community all the more alarming because of its solidarity with the rest of the Moslem world, a part of which borders on the USSR—has fashioned a society whose behavior patterns and values are very different from those of Soviet society.

Assuming that the Soviet regime can control the Moslem leadership's attempts at political action—a logical assumption considering the organized, integrationist character of the Soviet political system—it will have to confront a broader problem. This is the problem of an intellectually and economically transformed society in which education and urbanization, far from eradicating the political culture peculiar to this society, actually seem to reinforce it. Behind "Homo Sovieticus" now looms "Homo Islamicus."

CHAPTER VIII

Homo Islamicus in Soviet Society

" "In the half century of the USSR's existence, a Soviet socialist culture unique in spirit and substance has been created and developed. This culture incorporates the most valuable elements and
traditions of the life of every nation in our motherland. Each of the
Soviet national cultures is not only nourished by its own resources,
but borrows from the spiritual riches of other fraternal nations, and,
in turn, has a beneficial influence on them and enriches them."

In so defining Soviet culture,[1] Leonid Brezhnev took for granted
the fact that in Soviet society contacts between individuals and
groups were part of everyday life. Without doubt in every modern
society, urbanization, improved transportation, education, and the
media all serve to break down barriers, to alter and standardize human thought. In the USSR, however, despite these factors which are
an integral part of modern life everywhere, despite a continuous effort by the political system to encourage interethnic contacts and dis-
pel differences in Soviet political culture,[2] it seems clear that in the
Moslem regions the attempt to transform human thought has run
into an almost impenetrable socio-cultural situation. The persistence
of a particular culture, one tied to Islam, manifests itself in the
sphere of interethnic relations, in private life, and in the relations of
the individual with the political environment.

Endogamy, the Refusal to Marry Outside the Group

Is endogamy simply a product of a high degree of national consciousness? Or does it result chiefly from circumstantial factors such

as social status and the chance of meeting a prospective spouse in another national group? Generally speaking, while the correlation between endogamy and national consciousness is not obvious in the USSR, the question of mixed marriages cannot be discussed in any framework other than national attitudes. This is because the Soviet regime has hoped that mixed marriages would create an ethnic melting pot, and because Moscow uses the argument of mixed marriages to demonstrate progress toward a supranational consciousness.[3]

Recent studies by Soviet sociologists show that, while Soviets sometimes marry outside their nationality, there is anything but a uniform attitude on this question among the different nations. In a survey of marriages performed in 1969 in all the Soviet republics except the RSFSR the nationalities of the USSR fall into three groups according to the percentages of endogamy. First, nationalities almost completely endogamous: Kirghiz (95.4%), Kazakhs (93.6%), Turkmen (90.7%), Azeris (89.8%), Uzbeks (86.2%), and Georgians (80.5%). Second, nationalities which lean toward endogamy: Estonians (78.8%), Tadzhiks (77.3%), Lithuanians (68.2%), Moldavians (62%), and Latvians (61.4%). Third, those in which there are more mixed marriages than endogamous ones: Belorussians (39%), Ukrainians (34.3%), and Armenians (33.4%).[4]

These data are interesting inasmuch as they reveal a division in matrimonial attitudes like that already noted on the question of attachment to languages. The Central Asian and Caucasian peoples (except for the Tadzhiks and Armenians) all appear in the most highly endogamous group. How is this attitude to be interpreted? Do the Central Asian nationalities practice endogamy from habit? Does it reflect a lack of different opportunities? Or are they endogamous for cultural reasons? Do the Tadzhiks, who are somewhat more inclined to marry outside their group, represent a future trend? To understand the meaning of endogamy as practiced among these peoples, it is necessary to take a closer look and see who is marrying whom.

In 1962, Abramzon, a pioneer in the sociology of interethnic relations, published an important study[5] on this subject. He pointed out three characteristics of mixed marriages: (1) those between Moslems and non-Moslems, which before the Revolution were the exception in Central Asia, continue to be exceptional because they collide with the weight of socio-religious traditions; (2) when such marriages do take place, they almost always involve the wedding of a male Moslem (i.e., from a nationality of Moslem origin) and a female non-Moslem, whereas young women of Moslem origin hardly ever marry out of their group; (3) in many cases these mixed marriages (which usually take place in urban settings), are met with hostility by the Moslem spouse's family.[6]

Since 1962 there have been changes in Soviet society, but everything seems to indicate that Abramzon's comments still apply. A fairly recent survey on mixed marriages in Daghestan—one Soviet author says these findings could be extended to Central Asia[7]—shows how the problem stands at the present time. Figures for 1959 showed that in Makhatchkala, the capital of Daghestan, 32% of the people were Daghestanis, and 51% were Russians and various other nationalities. Thus, there was a situation tending to encourage mixed marriages, resulting from urban living and a large Russian community. Several conclusions can be drawn from this survey,[8] which covered a period of ten years (1958–1968). First of all, there is extraordinary stability in the number of mixed marriages (25.2% in 1958, 25% in 1968). Then there is the fact that the expression "mixed marriage" is used even in statistical studies for unions between a Moslem and a non-Moslem as well as for those between a bride and groom from two culturally related national groups. Yet there is a big difference between these two categories.

In Makhatchkala, Daghestanis account for only about half of the mixed marriages, and only a quarter of the marriages are between Daghestanis and non-Moslems (Russians or Ukrainians). In these mixed couples the proportion of Daghestani women is very low, although it has increased slightly. Most of the women married to Russians have Russian given names, which suggests that they are themselves the offspring of mixed marriages. Significantly, the highest proportion of divorce is found among Daghestanis married to Russian women.

Another survey carried out in the capital of Tadzhikistan by Duchambe fully supports Abramzon's findings and the situation in the Caucasus.[9] In that situation also favoring mixed marriages (108,236 Russians as against 43,008 Tadzhiks, and 23,178 Uzbeks), Duchambe tried to determine how the probabilities of marriages between the different groups coincide with actuality, taking into account the population of both sexes of each nationality living in the city. The results were startling. In the case of marriages between Tadzhiks and Uzbeks, the curves of probable and actual marriages coincide just about perfectly. In the case of marriages between Uzbeks, the curve of actual marriages is higher than the one for probable marriages, but not as clearly as for marriages between Tadzhiks.

One may therefore conclude that the Tadzhiks have a considerable and growing inclination[10] to marry among themselves, even in conditions most apt to promote contact with other nationalities, namely urban living—especially in the capital of a republic where the most sophisticated and most bilingual segment of the population is to be found. This study also shows that the greater inclination of the Tadzhiks to marry outside their group must not be overemphasized, for the Tadzhiks do a good deal of their intermarrying with Uzbeks. Surveys also indicate that the proportion of marriages between Kirghizs and European Soviets hardly changed between 1927 and 1968; that for two-thirds of the Kirghizs, the mixed marriages involve Kirghiz and other Moslems;[11] and finally that Kirghiz women do not marry non-Moslems.[12]

Whatever the territory or the group considered, it is noteworthy that there exists a homogeneity in space and a continuity in time in the attitudes toward marriage of all Moslems in the USSR. In search of the factors that promote exogamy, sociologists have carried out surveys on such elements as urbanization, the multinational character of the territory, and the level of education, especially that of women. Comparing the position of the various peoples of the USSR, it appears that the Kazakhs, who are in the minority in their own republic, are among the most endogamous; that when it comes to urbanization, the Azeris are as highly urbanized as the Ukrainians and the Belorussians; and finally that intellectual progress in the Moslem republics has been very rapid in the last few years, and that differences between the educational levels of men and women are diminishing there—if not rapidly, at least very perceptibly.[13]

Diverse surveys carried out in the Soviet Union have shown that most of the nationalities surveyed on their attitude to mixed marriages were not opposed[14] and that their responses varied only with religious factors. On the one hand, therefore, there is apparent assent to mixed marriages; on the other, a contrary situation exists in the Moslem borderlands where mixed marriages very rarely include the union of a male Moslem with a non-Moslem female, regardless of the social conditions involved.

This raises another question. Are mixed marriages, although few in number, paving the way for a new type of society, where mixed marriages are common? This question can be answered by studying the nationality choices made by the offspring of such marriages. At sixteen years of age, when passports are issued, every Soviet citizen who has a choice of nationality—which is precisely the case of children with parents of different nationalities—is required to make a decision. In this regard, according to the case involved,[15] it is found that the choices follow definite patterns. When a Moslem man marries a non-Moslem woman, the child usually chooses the father's nationality. Generally speaking, among the Moslems, the father's nationality is considered dominant regardless of the social group or educational level involved.[16] Nevertheless, in isolated instances where a Daghestani woman had married a man from a non-Moslem group, the mother's nationality was selected by the children in 87.5% of the cases.[17]

On the other hand, in marriages between Russians and non-Moslems (Ukrainians, Jews, etc.) the Russian nationality prevails. One more category concerns mixed marriages between Moslems (Uzbeks, Tadzhiks), in which cases children tend to select the nationality of the parent who comes from the republic in which they live. Clearly, then, marriages between non-Moslems pave the way for changes in national consciousness; but mixed marriages between Moslems apparently do not lead into the world outside Islam. This is not to imply that these marriages have no influence at all on the children born of them. This influence is exerted mainly through language. In a mixed Russian or Ukrainian and Moslem family, the language spoken in the home is unquestionably Russian. Moreover, the children often have a Russian given name (girls more often than boys), and when they have a non-Russian given name, a European one is frequently added.[18] The Soviet authorities therefore are not mistaken in thinking that mixed marriages can destabilize nationalities in the long run. But they have long underestimated the resistance of national groups to such marriages, and their yearnings to preserve a particular socio-cultural world of their own.

Group Cohesion Through Lifestyle

Moslems are hostile or closed to matrimonial contacts with non-Moslems because they jealously preserve their way of life, which is bound up in socio-religious traditions. Furthermore, this traditional lifestyle is strongest in the area of the family. The three major events of human life—birth, marriage, death—are also the favorite areas for traditions. These are the times when the individual returns most readily to customs that bind him to the group. Respect for the ways of the group grows as the individual's life nears an end.

To some extent, customs related to birth are certainly dying out, inasmuch as more and more children are born in hospitals where traditions, often in conflict with the rules of hygiene, are not permitted. Notwithstanding this, it is significant that half of the urbanized Tatars, queried in this regard, replied that they observed the ritual connected with the birth of a child.[19] On one point, the social tradition connected with Islam is carried on in almost all national communities of Moslem origin: circumcision. Every survey shows that throughout the Soviet Union, without distinction as to attitudes toward religion, without distinction as to setting (urban or rural) and without distinction as to educational level or social position, practically all male Moslem infants are circumcised.

Soviet sociologists who have studied the question conclude that the continuance of this practice was a manifestation of belonging to a cultural community. In the USSR, circumcision—even though not one of the obligations of a Moslem—takes on an obvious meaning. It implies that the young Moslem is a member of an overall community, the *Ummah*, which he shares with his brethren and which is the world of Islam (*Dar Ul Islam*). Similarly, the newborn infant is marked by the choice of a given name, an area in which religious tradition continues to play an important part. It is for this reason that the Shiites go on banning certain first names—Omar, Osman, Aicha—and show hostility to those who bear them.[20] Another tradition common in Moslem society is the custom of giving the newborn infant a second given name, so as to divert the Devil's attention and trick him with this double identity.

Because it takes place in a private setting, marriage—more so than birth—provides an opportunity for Moslems to manifest their loyalty to the ways of their forefathers. Here again, the answers of urbanized Tatars are revealing: only 37% of them replied that they did not keep up traditions connected with weddings.[21] Several points trouble the Soviet regime in this regard. First of all is the religious character of marriages.

Disturbed at seeing young people of all faiths returning to churches for religious weddings, the regime in the early 1960s decided that this must be due to the uninviting, colorless, administrative aspect of civil ceremonies. To fight the attraction of the churches, rather elegant marriage halls were built in the Soviet Union, to give greater solemnity to the civil weddings. The long-standing practice of simply recording marriages at the town hall was gradually replaced by civil festivities. But this was apparently to no avail, and religious weddings continued to retain their attraction. Frequently in Moslem society, the civil ceremony is followed by another one at which the mullah performs a religious marriage.[22] Of course, the Soviets claim this is not typical but simply reflects the influence of elderly people, practically the only ones interested in religious weddings. It would appear, however, that in Moslem society children born of civil marriages may actually be considered illegitimate.[23]

Of even greater concern than religious weddings is the persistence of Moslem customs connected with marriage. What makes this particularly noteworthy is the fact that, while religious weddings come under freedom of conscience, some of the customs surrounding them are strictly prohibited for social or economic reasons. The marriage of prepubescent or unconsenting girls is forbidden; as also the "abduction" or the "ransom" of the fiancée, both being classified as feudal practices. In spite of laws to the contrary, marriages of prepubescent girls and marriages arranged by the parents against the girl's will are still quite common, even in circles close to the government.[24] The practice of the *Kalym*, the ransoming of the fiancée, not only seems fairly popular,[25] but is governed by rules and has established rates. In the mid-1960's the Central Committee of the Uzbek CP evaluated the *Kalym* at "500 rubles, 200 kilos of flour, 80 kilos of rice, 2 sheep and 9 sets of dresses." In all, one had to pay 2,000 to 3,000 rubles to acquire a wife,[26] and in case of incomplete payment one had to (and still has to) give her back to her family.[27] The abduction of the fiancée now usually takes the form of a brief symbolic ritual.[28]

In addition to these traditions, widespread in the entire Soviet Moslem society, there are other practices more local in character originating in the *adat* (unwritten law) prevalent mainly in the Caucasus. These complex ceremonies hinge around the presentation of the fiancée to her prospective husband's parents. The ceremonies underscore loyalty to Islam; the fiancée is required to keep her face turned toward Mecca at all times. Finally, the traditional rules of exogamy still prevail with many peoples—marriages are forbidden within a single tribal community—along with the *levirate*[29], which is the obligation of a man to marry the widow of a brother dying without an heir.

It is evident therefore that marriage preserves both religion—the wedding ceremony requires the aid of a religious official—and a body of rites, restrictions, and obligations, some of which are bound up with the traditions of Orthodox Islam, others with the *adat*, still others with tribal links to the past. In every case, marriage provides the occasion for peoples of Moslem origin to manifest a deep attachment to their traditions and to behave with a supreme contempt for Soviet laws and attitudes. Like circumcision, marriage gives rise to great festivities involving economic practices frowned on by the regime, notably the slaughter of livestock. At times privately owned livestock is involved, but often, in view of the extent of the celebrations, livestock from the collectivized farms is used quite unscrupulously to enhance so-called Moslem ceremonies. Further aggravating this misappropriation of public property, these ceremonies, whether circumcisions or marriages, are always conducted in the presence of the local authorities.

While all these events provide the opportunity for manifesting adherence to a particular culture, the ties between the individual and tradition are drawn most closely by death. Only 23% of Tatars in urban settings fail to observe Moslem ritual concerning death.[30] Clearly, if a survey were to be carried out on this question in Central Asia, and if rural and urban people were combined, the percentage would drop even further. Here, at the terminal point in life, the coexistence of Moslems and non-Moslems comes to an end. The Soviet author Achirov[31] writes: "People of diverse nationalities may live together in a united international family . . . But after their death it turns out that they cannot be buried in the same cemetery; and that their last journey is used for the propagation of religion and national particularism."

No one hesitates to show this will for difference in the face of death. When the director of the Tashkent Pedagogical Institute died in 1972, the authorities decided to bury him with the ceremony reserved for important Soviet figures and to hold an official funeral for him. Even this led to controversy. The family refused the ceremony and display of honors intended for a man who, judging from his office, had been a good Communist all his life. The family had him interred in the Moslem cemetery, giving him a Moslem burial.[32]

This particularism is also expressed by maintaining the custom of costly funeral rituals,[33] which provide the occasion for gathering together the community around its own socio-religious traditions. This also leads to commemorative ceremonies which the Islamic clerics contrive to hold as frequently as possible.[34] The Soviet regime attacks these rituals by underscoring the extravagances they entail; yet in fact it is perfectly aware of the integrative function served by these ceremonies, and this is what alarms Moscow most of all. Here again, the Soviets find themselves confronted by a tightly knit community in which many call themselves nonbelievers but attribute religious meaning to the rituals of family life.[35]

Generally speaking, the Soviet regime perceives that Moslem society has its own world of feasts and important dates. In the early 1970s an American reporter asked some Uzbeks just before the ceremonies commemorating the Revolution, what was the most important holiday in the USSR. Invariably the reply was, "The end of Ramadan."[36]

This explains the particular attention given by Moscow to festivals in Moslem society and its changing attitude toward them.

New Content for Traditional Holidays

For several decades all religious feasts and customs were systematically condemned in the USSR. Events dominating private life were secularized and religious celebration of them either forbidden or rigorously discouraged. At the same time the social practices surrounding these celebrations—the *Kalym*, meals in honor of the dead, and other customs—were prohibited as signs of attachment to "feudal traditions." When they couldn't actually stop these traditions, the Soviet authorities hoped that they would die out with progress, and at any rate regarded them as no more than folklore.

Since the early 1960s teams of ethnographers and sociologists have been carrying out extensive field studies. Their findings have shown the regime that what it lightly dismissed as "survivals" was actually a body of behavior patterns and loyalties that unified an entire society. This resulted in the government's sudden and more clearsighted attention to these phenomena. In 1960 a pan-Russian conference was set up to discuss Soviet holidays and ways of using them to surmount religious survivals. Another conference, held in March 1964, brought experts from the entire Soviet Union to Moscow in order to discuss what had become a growing concern.[37] The outcome of these meetings prompted the regime to admit that Soviet holidays, whether political or private, were having little success, and that to effectively combat traditional holidays, the problem had to be approached in two ways: clearly, to add excitement to the Soviet celebrations; and especially to try to graft them onto the traditional holidays in order to drain the latter of their national-religious content, and give them a Soviet meaning.

Generally speaking, the social organizations are responsible for purely Soviet celebrations, such as the official registration of newborn infants—a ceremony which is run by Komsomol. For such an occasion, for instance, the Palace of Culture in Samarkand would be appropriately decorated and music supplied; and under the combined aegis of social organizations and the Civil Service department, there would be a gathering of the family, the guests, the "heroine mothers," and a few other Communist personalities. The ceremony is intended to bring all those who are important in Soviet society together around the newborn infant.[38] Where can families find a more attractive ceremony and a more gratifying assemblage? Yet, despite Soviet efforts to officially celebrate the various stages of life—presentation of the passport, leaving for the army, marriage, work—despite the systematic participation of social organizations in ceremonies of this type, there remains an insurmountable attachment to traditional celebrations. This realization has prompted the authorities to try to divert the ritual embedded in Moslem society and incorporate it into Soviet culture.

For instance, unable to talk many Central Asians out of celebrating the Moslem New Year, the regime allows the *Nauruz* to be celebrated properly, but is endeavoring to turn it into "the feast of spring and peasants," in order to connect the event with socialized activities and divest it of its particular content.[39]

Another example of this Soviet policy of grafting Communist festivals on to Moslem ones is the ceremony aimed at celebrating old age. Traditionally, the peoples of Central Asia assign great importance to the sixty-third birthday. The Moslem, either man or woman, reaching this age (that of the Prophet at the time of his death) is fêted by a crowd of wellwishers, and the accompanying religious celebration is marked by the reading of the Koran, and ends amid feasting and gift-giving. The social organizations have been asked to use this occasion to celebrate purely civil events, generally retirement or some award. It hardly matters that retirement comes early in the Soviet Union; the main thing is to strip the *Paigamber Echi* ceremony of all religious content and include it in a series of celebrations marking the same events for the whole USSR.[40]

This is, in effect, the thrust of the Soviet regime's campaign. On the one hand, the program is aimed at depriving religion of its privilege of marking the great moments in human life. Besides that, Soviet action aims above all at standardizing rituals and tearing down differences of customs between all the peoples of the USSR. For this reason, the Moslem New Year has become a "festival of spring," whether celebrated in the Ukrainian countryside, the Siberian taiga, or Kirghiz cities and villages. Unable to suppress national customs, Moscow is accepting them while trying to Sovietize them.

Has this attempt to make use of national traditions fared any better? Probably not; there are many indications that the grafting process has not succeeded.[41] Moslem holidays exist alongside Soviet ones. Sometimes in the midst of new and purely Soviet ritual there re-emerge traditions that were thought to have been rooted out. At the banquets of civil weddings in Uzbekistan, for example, it may happen that the bride will cover her face, so what good are the "Houses of Happiness" the government has built for family ceremonies?[42] Under such conditions, what good is the continuous mobilization of the social organizations and all the political cadres of these past ten years if all this only results in confirming age-old traditions under the misleading pretext that their content has become Soviet? The old compromise of national form and socialist content is still the order of the day, despite the intellectual progress made by the whole of society.

A Special Pattern of Social Organization

One of the essential factors of progress in Moslem society is education for women. The Soviets have insisted on this because they knew that social change was impossible unless women participated in it, especially in a society that attaches decisive importance to the socialization of children. By all outward appearances the Soviet regime has succeeded in tearing the Moslem woman away from her traditional status and integrating her into social life through education and professional life. The statistics are very eloquent on this point. Many women hold salaried positions. In 1975 nearly half of the local soviets in Central Asia were made up of women.[43]

Behind these statistics, which reflect only a limited aspect, the actual situation is quite different. Girls in Central Asia often give up their studies before completing the secondary school program. This premature abandonment of school is found in sophisticated, apparently modernized families as well as those lacking in education. There is still considerable resistance in Moslem society to allowing women to join the work force, and the high birth rate found in those regions results in part from the fact that a woman's life is devoted to her family. As a result, the government, after trying forcibly to drag women away from the family setting, has begun to compromise with Moslem predilections. On collective farms an effort is being made not to separate couples and to avoid having a woman work with a man not related to her. Women's clubs are closed to men so as to avoid hostile reactions.[44]

Yet despite outward appearances, Moslem society remains dominated by men. This society is also surprisingly dominated by organizations totally outside the political system. It has already been noted that the regime endeavors to lump all organizations situated on the periphery of orthodox Islam into the convenient category of "shamans." Without doubt, these shamans—half witch doctors, half faith healers—are still found in the countryside, where their remedies attract many followers, often those despaired of by government doctors, especially sterile women. Sterility is seen as an actual curse among the Moslem peoples, and for them the cure is more supernatural than medical.

But behind the term shaman, behind the accusations of magic practices, there lurks an entirely different reality, an idea of which can be glimpsed in a book devoted to pre-Islamic beliefs and rites in Central Asia.[45] Several chapters in this collection of writings refer to "brotherhoods." One of the authors suggests that a good many beliefs and practices of this kind still subsist. Actually, concealed behind the shamans whom the government tries to ridicule, is the survival of Sufi brotherhoods, the Tariqats, whose existence today is attested by Soviet sources. According to these, two Tariqats exist in the USSR, the orders of the Naqshbandis and of the Qadyris.[46]

Soviet surveys give an insight into the extent of this phenomenon in the Caucasus, where the Sufi orders have always enjoyed enormous success. Depending on the Soviet authors—and there is no reason for them to exaggerate the size of the brotherhoods—more than half the believers in the northern Caucasus are members of a Sufi brotherhood. In view of the fact that more than half the inhabitants of the region give themselves as believers, and that more than two million persons live there, we can deduce that at least half a million Moslems in the Caucasus are members of Tariqats.[47] This reveals the seriousness of the situation. The Tariqats are secret societies with initiatory rites, extraordinary discipline, and a regular chain of command. In this regard, although we have no exact figures covering Central Asia, the existing data suggest that Sufism is on the rise.

This is far from being merely a religious problem. The Soviet State permits only declared, authorized social organizations, all of which contribute to the socialization of its citizens and are inspired by Soviet ideology. In the Caucasus, with half a million adepts, among whom many of the most highly educated classes, the young, and women are included—the Tariqats are actually mass organizations totally alien to the ideology of the Soviet system. They are an instrument for socialization competing with the officially recognized social organizations. They possess as much authority as these, and probably a wider influence in the surrounding society. Their work is spiritual, but also temporal. Wherever the Tariqats exist, the real authority in the social group is held by them. And the problem of authority in Moslem society is very extensive.

The Soviet government has often had to admit that the structures it has set up—soviets, parties, and the like—have been placed in a difficult position in facing the traditional authorities of Moslem society, primarily the Elders. There are many reports of decisions made outside of the official authorities by the councils of wise men called the *Aksakal* (white beards), who, for example, decide on the amount of the *Kalym* and impose their decisions on the community. Again in this connection, the Soviet government, after first resisting, has now gone along with tradition by allowing the existence of these councils of wise men, which function all over Central Asia.[48] The regime claims that their activity is limited to dispensing moderating advice, but their moral authority goes far beyond this framework; many disputes have been settled by them, and their judgment is accepted because Moslem society believes in the wisdom of old age and of men. Equality of the sexes and the Party's supreme wisdom carry little weight with this traditional authority.

That Moslem society forms a cohesive bloc different from the rest of the USSR becomes clear when we consider how few mixed families there are, the weight of tradition in all areas of life, and the extensive network of authority alien to the Soviet system.

This socio-cultural homogeneity is maintained despite a campaign of propaganda at every level concentrating on the common traits of Soviet society, and not on the differences existing within it. In this regard, the use of the media and the influence they can exercise raise an interesting question.

As noted by one Soviet author,[49] "In the last ten years ... the press, the radio, and television have been utilized on an increasing scale to shape the ideological-political thinking of Soviet citizens, and have focused on the development of internationalism (that is to say, on weakening nationalistic consciousness)." This writer carried out a comparative study of Russian-language Communist Party newspapers in the Moldavian, Georgian and Uzbek republics.[50] Analyzing the content—articles, news, essays—on two themes, economic cooperation between Soviet nations and cultural cooperation, the author makes several observations. First of all, regarding terminology, he says that the word "national," whether it refers to economics or to culture, is much less frequently used than the term "republican." The economy is said to be "republican," four times out of five; and the culture is qualified as being "republican" twice as often as being "national." The newspapers endeavor to link the economy and culture to the administrative framework, not to an ethnic framework.

As for informing readers about anything that has to do with the economic relations of their national group with the other nations of the USSR, one reaches the conclusion that while in Moldavia and Georgia the emphasis is placed on the contributions of these republics to the economy of sister republics and the creation of an economy reaching beyond republican boundaries, in Uzbekistan the news is slanted toward the aid received by Uzbekistan and its dependence on the Soviet Union for its development. Likewise, with regard to cultural contacts, the focus of the Uzbek press is primarily on outside aid received and on cultural cooperation in the USSR. It should be pointed out that the Uzbekistan newspaper was chosen as being typical of the whole Central Asian press.

It is striking that what the author of this excellent study refers to as "the reader's internationalist education"[51] is the insistence on the Uzbek's dependence compared to the other Soviet nations, a dependence which is both economic and cultural, and the Uzbeks' marked inferiority in this domain as compared to the Moldavians and the Georgians. The mobilization of the media to prove to the Uzbeks and, by extension, to all the Moslem peoples, that they cannot live on their own economic and cultural resources, is striking on two counts. First in its extent, and secondly in its ineffectiveness. Developments in Moslem Central Asia and the Caucasus give evidence of great imperviousness to such pressures and an astonishing capacity to preserve the personality of the ethnic group.

In the USSR today there is a Moslem society which is united by the bonds of history, culture, and tradition. The fact that Homo Islamicus asserts himself in Daghestan or Tashkent, in the city or the country, raises a serious problem for the Soviet regime. This Homo Islamicus has in effect behind him more than a half-century of cultural revolution intended to create a Homo Sovieticus. He has gone through the standardizing mold of schools and youth organizations. As a preschooler he was an "Octobrist"; then he proudly wore the red neckerchief of the Pioneers and learned the rudiments of socialist morality and socialist behavior, which a whole lifetime was to reinforce. And now having come of age, this citizen, in whom the regime has invested so much, spontaneously rediscovers the authority of the father and the Elders, the disparaged traditions, the pre-eminent solidarity of the national cultural group from which he sprang.

The lifestyles and traditions of Homo Islamicus are often—though not always—based on religion. The peoples of Central Asia and the Caucasus have seen civilizations come and go, have witnessed the superimposition of different cults, great religions, and borrowed traditions at every phase of a long and turbulent history. In this area, Islam has assimilated the migratory flows that preceded it, and this syncretism emerges in the variety and power of the traditions which exist today. But whether the ways of these people are of pagan or Moslem origin, they have long since been incorporated in a culture which all the peoples of the borderlands feel as being common to them and as separating them from those who do not belong to their spiritual world.

Homo Islamicus is not an adversary. He does not set himself up as an enemy of the Soviet system, which he does not even criticize. But simply by his existence, by his presence in the whole area where the Moslem civilization has existed, he bears witness that the Soviet people has at least two components: the Soviets and the Soviet Moslems. He demonstrates that the human prototype which socialist society was to shape does not exist—or does not exist everywhere. Above all, he demonstrates that while it is relatively easy—on condition of paying the price—to change the structures of society, it is extremely difficult to alter minds.

The resistance of the spiritual and material culture of the Moslems introduces an element of undeniable pluralism in a Soviet system based on uniformity. But can the system adapt to it, this system which has never accepted competition with other ideologies or other organizations? And now, without being attacked in any way, the Soviet system sees another social system, one founded on another ideology, being maintained, even expanding, within its borders. And this rival system has in its favor that it comprises more than one-fifth of the Soviet population. It can no longer be classified in the category of ethnographic curiosities.

Conclusion

N ational diversity and intensity of national feelings characterize the Soviet political scene. In this respect the regime's
nationality policy constitutes a resounding success—and a
no less resounding failure. It qualifies as a success inasmuch as the
regime originally set its sights at permitting and aiding nations and
nationalities, even the smallest ethnic groups, to develop, the idea
being to exhaust their national aspirations within the freedom granted. Everything points to Moscow's success in attaining this goal in a
preliminary phase. But the second phase of the Bolshevik plan,
namely the obliteration of national differences and their fusion in a
new and superior historical community—the Soviet people—has not
succeeded.

It hardly matters if the Soviet leaders declare that this "Soviet
people" exists. Their repeated assertions sound more like incanta-
tions. But words cannot change a social reality. And the reality is
that the nationalities are expressing themselves vigorously. No magic can make them suddenly disappear for the benefit of the "Soviet
people." One is confronted here with the ambiguity of the Soviet
idea of a nation.

In its plan for nationalities the Soviet regime merges two concepts
of a nation and its vitality, which are far from being compatible.[1]
One of them has long been adopted by Western European society
and can be summarized in Renan's formula: "A nation is the will to
live together." According to this concept, adherence to a national
community is a matter of individual, reflective choice.

The other idea has prevailed in Eastern Europe where ethnic boundaries have been so difficult to establish. It is a more sociological concept stressing the permanent elements of nationality, in the forefront of which stand language and culture. According to the Soviet timetable, these two approaches were to succeed each other. The concept that could be termed "East European" prevailed in the first phase when the nations, defined by specific conditions, were urged to develop and assert themselves. Following that, however, the stage involving their integration into the Soviet people was to feature the Western concept. It is on this point that the regime and the people under its administration hold divergent views.

For the Soviet leaders, adopting a modern concept of the nation comes under the heading of modernization. In one way, they share the views of Karl Deutsch and other theoreticians of integration who hold that modernization modifies national consciousness. The nations of the USSR, on the other hand, cling to the idea of what can be called the "permanence" of the nation, in which the "intangible character" of the group prevails over individual consciousness. For them, nationality is a permanent factor transcending political plans and changes in the environment.

The noteworthy feature about this growing national conflict lies precisely in its connection with the modernization of society. To some degree, all the elements favorable to a progressive integration of the nations are present in most of the national minorities, namely the economic equality of nations, urbanization, the progressive equalization of cultural levels, the slow but undeniable penetration of a common language, and in a number of cases, cultural assimilation. Yet, far from paving the way towards integration, this modernization serves as a framework for a nationalism that is being asserted more than ever before and above all more knowingly.

Admittedly, national feelings do not have the same power or the same impact everywhere in the USSR. For the sake of simplification, these can be classified in three groups. The first group includes the national communities that show a tendency to grow weaker, and are obviously being assimilated or are assimilable. Many small ethnic groups fall into this category, notably those lost in the Siberian expanse which were promoted to the rank of viable nationalities and granted the attributes of national existence, primarily a language and culture of their own. The rapid drop in the number of declared nationalities, from one census to the other, points to the mounting assimilation of these communities by more dynamic nations. The Belorussian nation can probably be placed in this category, in spite of the fact that at different times in Soviet history it has shown particularist tendencies. But, having been set up artificially and given a language without historical justification, and being too close to Russia in its effort to differentiate itself from Poland and Lithuania, Belorussia has been more subject to Russian influence than other nations.

A second group is comprised of nationalities having a high degree of national consciousness, but condemned by circumstance to weakness, or even to extinction. This is especially the case of the Baltic nations, particularly the Estonians and Latvians. Despite the strength of their national feeling, despite everything distinguishing them historically and culturally from the other peoples of the USSR, these nationalities are headed not toward assimilation, but toward physical extinction. The possible disappearance of nations endowed with such strong personalities is an historic tragedy of which every Balt is conscious, and yet no one seems able to prevent it. Faced with this fate, the Baltic nationalities seem not even able to react by forming a Baltic bloc. Each becomes weaker still by isolating itself in its particularism and the things which separate it historically from the other nations in the region. This isolation and withdrawal heighten the extreme vulnerability of this part of the USSR, which from every point of view is the most modern, the most impregnated with outside influences, the least Sovietized. Yet, apparently, none of this can impede the Baltic people from advancing toward the annihilation of their nations.

Equally conscious of their national existence, but showing the promise of a totally opposite destiny, the third group comprises the peoples of the Caucasus and Central Asia, and to a lesser degree, of the Ukraine. In Central Asia and the Caucasus, ethnic consciousness and demographic vitality go hand in hand, assuring these nationalities an increasingly important place in the family of Soviet peoples. Even the Ukrainians, who are less well placed demographically, seem to have realized that the survival of a group depends on a growing population and the capacity to perpetuate itself.

In these varied situations, a distinction should be made between "nationalities" and "cultural areas." The USSR is the proving ground for national entities that declare themselves vital and eager to maintain their existence as individual nations. But besides these nationalities there are also the Moslems who form a supranational group, just as loudly affirming a marked "specificity." This represents a definite deviation from the multinational model accepted by Bolshevik leaders in 1917 for resolving the problems involved in the peaceful coexistence of different ethnic groups. The Soviet regime has never wanted cultural areas or a community of cultures, and has systematically tried to destroy them. The re-emergence of this community of cultures is a basic factor in Soviet evolution in the last part of this century. It adds to the seriousness and deep significance of the nationality problem.

The affirmation of nationalism in the USSR takes on a special character that must be emphasized. It is not a question of ethnic dissidence freely expressed and intended to assure the independence of the groups concerned. Nationalism in the USSR develops within a special context, that of Soviet ideology and its institutions, so it is futile to interpret it as a movement for national independence.

For the moment, belonging to Soviet society is a fact that no one seriously questions. But within that society, in the very name of its ideals, each nationality seeks to organize itself as best it can to ensure its own continuance. What the national minorities demand in diverse ways is not the destruction of the existing system, but the broadening within this system of their national privileges and the advantages that may be derived from them. The goal of every nation is the strict application of federalism, real autonomy of power within each republic and equal participation for all the republics in the decision-making at the federal level. Their aim is to "freeze" the political framework of the Soviet system, federalism, and broaden their powers within this framework so that the national level becomes the principal level of the whole system.

The conflict between this static concept of federalism and the transformist vision of the Soviet regime resides in the fact that federalism and the survival of nationalities have been considered by Moscow as nothing more than a temporary concession. Everyone is aware of the misconception, but the nations intend to exploit it by insisting on the concepts of coexistence which had been offered to them at the dawn of the Soviet era. In substance, their position seems more defensible than the regime's. By demanding an ideology that has been specifically enunciated—and actually appears in the Constitution—the nations sometimes succeed in making the regime accept their positions and retreat in its efforts to shift into the second stage, namely the obliteration of nationality status. Some excellent examples of this can be cited.

In reaffirming the principle of territorial nations in the 1977 Soviet Constitution, an unmistakable step backwards in the process of setting up a socialist nation is evident. When presenting the Constitution, Leonid Brezhnev clearly acknowledged that the problem of suppressing the Soviet national states had been considered, but that such a change would be premature at this point because it would run counter to social consciousness in the various national territories.[2] On the other hand, to maintain a territorial framework means maintaining the conditions in which nationalism can develop. If the Belorussians maintain a certain degree of national consciousness under unfavorable conditions, it is simply because they exist as a nation. The Soviet government does not dare suppress the national states because the nationalities are not ready to accept the political and cultural integration such a change implies. But by maintaining national status, the regime permits nationalist movements to affirm themselves and grow. In the same way, the regime never stops repeating that a common language is necessary for the progress of internationalism in the USSR, yet it had to back down before the determination of the Caucasian peoples to maintain the preferential place of their languages in their constitutions.

National mentalities and loyalties, the importance of which Moscow implicitly recognizes, are also characterized by highly contradictory ways of expressing them, which confuses the observer. Sometimes this national thinking is manifested in rigidly conservative positions that suggest nostalgia for the past rather than any viable plan. This is the purely superficial interpretation which can be applied to the success of the Tariqats in Central Asia and the Caucasus; or again to explain the quasi-fanatic continuance of certain social practices. A hasty analysis of the kind made by Soviet political cadres, not by experts, concludes that these manifestations are "survivals," on the verge of dying out. But the more knowledgeable scholars seek to distinguish what is pure nostalgia from the desire to identify with a group and prevent being absorbed in the overall Soviet society. It should be noted, however, that these manifestations of nationalism, dismissed as "survivals," represent only part of the picture. There is also an ostentatious type of nationalism, assumed by Soviet elites mainly in urban society, which poses the problem of national life in modern terms, i.e., economic priorities and cultural development.

While the Soviet regime may challenge the upholders of traditions, which they relegate to the area of mere folklore, how can it oppose the cadres it has trained and which, imbued with Soviet egalitarian ideology, are simply asking for the implementation of the Party's program as defined by Lenin? This modern aspect of nationalism and its defense by the most advanced segment of the Soviet population is what Moscow finds most disconcerting, and prompts Soviet leaders to re-examine an issue they thought should have been settled long ago.

Significantly, just when the USSR leaders have triumphantly announced the birth of the Soviet people, the conferences and researches on the problem of nationality are taking on considerable importance. Since the late 1960s the USSR Academy of Sciences has included an agency specializing in questions of nationality. This body lay dormant for several years but since 1976 it has become a very important research center. In addition, the Twenty-fifth Congress called on Soviet ethnographers to focus their attention on ethnic developments in the USSR.[3] In December 1976, at the conference on nationality problems held in Tallin,[4] the extent of Soviet perplexity in this regard was quite clear. On the one hand, the Vice-Chairman of the USSR Academy of Sciences, Fedoseev, insisted on the integration of the nationalities and the emergence of a pan-Soviet culture in which the Russian language was presented as an essential means of communication. But at the same time, J. Bromlei, whose studies in this domain have shed considerable light on interethnic relations, after having carefully paid lip service to the theory of integration ("Soviet people," "Soviet culture," "Soviet consciousness"), proceeded to stress the fact that "the spiritual cultures of the peoples of the USSR preserve—to a significant degree—a national coloring." He underscored even more the fact that ethnic peculiarities, while often manifested by the language, may well be independent of it.

The concept of "national character," a concept that Lenin vigorously opposed, now has acknowledged supporters in the USSR[5] who attempt to show the complexity of the elements which make up national consciousness, and point to spiritual elements totally independent of the socio-economic environment, and even of the linguistic context. The vehemence with which Moscow refutes these theories bears witness to the highly charged atmosphere surrounding any discussion of this problem.

The question is no longer whether or not the nationality problem exists in a USSR at the stage of "advanced socialism." Clearly, the problem does exist—overwhelmingly so. At issue is the very nature of the phenomenon facing the Soviet regime. The men in Moscow thought they knew what constitutes a nation and how it changes. But the development of the nations, and the manifestations of their existence and aspirations in the USSR, prove how elusive the nationality question is and how difficult it is to define it precisely.

For a long time, political anthropology had tried to interpret the national problem as a social manifestation linked with the general social context and evolving within that context. What is actually happening in the USSR suggests that the nationality issue and the relations between nationalities fall into a particular historical field, which must be considered in the light of its specific features. Just what exactly is this national consciousness? What is it that prompts an individual to identify himself with a national group? Soviet society gives evidence that there is a wide range of possible answers to this question. Certainly language is one of them. But then there are the Jews who, for the most part, speak neither Yiddish nor Hebrew, but Russian, and yet identify themselves more and more as Jews. To that it would be logical to reply that they feel themselves discriminated against and that this feeling of oppression prompts them to identify with a Jewish group. Perhaps.

But then how does one explain the fact that in Daghestan where the penetration of Russian—to the detriment of some national languages—is incontestable, there is, alongside of a certain cultural Russification, a growing national sentiment, as revealed in the social organization of the peoples there? The Daghestanis are not subject to any discrimination, yet they assert that they are different. In Daghestan, the Russified elites call for the adoption of Arabic as a common language, instead of Russian, because they claim that Arabic is "the Latin of the East."

For some people, religion, not language, serves as the common denominator. The Buddhist Kalmyks, despite their long period of deportation to Siberia, followed by their being a definite minority in their national territory—which has led to a faster spread of Russian—call themselves Buddhists and therefore feel deeply what separates them from those around them. While religion constitutes one of the most powerful determinants of identity, its content may vary from one nation to another. Mari and Tcheremiss paganism and the forms of worship connected with it, as well as the Buddhism of the Kalmyks, are certainly focused on religious beliefs. But Moslem solidarity is more subtly shaded and has a double significance. On the one hand, there is the Turkish solidarity generating a pan-Turkism which expresses itself clearly at times. On the other, there is the broader solidarity of all who belong to the cultural world of Islam. Within these two loyalties, fidelity to the small linguistic group is less important. It is significant in this connection to note that the national demands of the Crimean Tatars or the Mskhetian Turks[6] find greater support among the Russian intelligentsia than among their Central Asian brothers. For the Moslem peoples, it makes little sense to fight for a Crimea lost centuries ago, while the Turkish or Moslem nation is the real framework of existence of the Tatars or Mskhetians.

But regardless of the language spoken by a national group and regardless of which element of identification prevails with them, it is safe to say that the consciousness of identity with the group has become infinitely greater than in the past, because of advantages resulting from progress. There is a tendency to think that national consciousness is a survival of the past because it involves older and less educated people. This notion, which Moscow encourages, distorts the problem. It is true that elderly people and those whose education is incomplete, especially in the countryside, cultivate national nostalgia out of habit and inertia. But alongside the generations that are dying out are rising younger, better educated generations that have—thanks in fact to Soviet policy—access to their own culture and history, to everything that enables them to identify with their own nationality. It is an advantage which was not available to the older generation.

To understand the difference, one need only look at the mass of newspapers, magazines, and books published in each republic, and see the titles. Everything that constitutes the past glory of each Soviet people in the cultural sphere now finds its way into print. This heritage, formerly within reach only of a tiny elite, is now accessible to all. That is one of the undeniable achievements of the Soviet system, which was expanded by the Twentieth Congress and its liberal tendencies on nationality questions. It represents a perilous achievement, for every nationality has begun to reveal a growing eagerness to learn about its own heritage, with which it can become identified.

Among the Turkish peoples there is even a name to describe this quest for the heritage peculiar to each group—*mirasism* (from *miras*, meaning heritage). And precisely because national feeling thrives on the past and on culture, because it is built on them, it is possible to understand what distinguishes the Soviet nationalities in the process of integration from those which the regime must accept as being different. The thing that differentiates them is the weight of history.

Those nationalities that have a cultural past, even if the culture is limited, can derive support from it to assert their own existence: Even though weak and deprived of such essentials as language, they can if need be invoke their past in order to survive and enjoy a rebirth. But when history is lacking, the national minorities are entirely dependent on the environment, changing with it and having no means of turning back. Marx, who seriously overestimated the part played by economic and social factors in the development of nations, saw clearly on one point: that the so-called "historic nations" have nothing in common with the "nations without history." Clearly, the former have a vitality of their own, while the latter are carried along in the overall dynamism of the society around them.

It should also be noted that Russian nationalism is not exempt from this tendency to assert itself, and hence to maintain its integrity. Russia is not only, through its language, the vehicle of internationalism and the melting pot of a new society. From the very beginning of the Soviet regime, many features of historical tradition and Russian culture have impregnated the Soviet interpretation of Marxism. At the present time, Russian nationalism is moving in two opposite directions. One of these, characterized by defensive nationalism, is marked by a return to Slavophile ideals and orthodoxy. Frightened by the rise of the Eastern nationalities and by an ideology that robs Russia herself of part of her historic-cultural heritage, the more intellectual segment of the Russian population is turning back to its own values.[7] On the other hand, the Kremlin, aware of the weak response to its internationalist ideology, tends to return to an idea rooted in pre-Revolutionary Russian political tradition: the civilizing and protective role of the Russian people, the "elder brother" of the other Soviet peoples. It is no accident that in the space of a few months two national Communist cadres have re-established this concept, which in the general equality of the Soviet nations makes the Russian nation the most equal of all.[8]

Like the Soviet people, the "elder brother" concept falls under the heading of intention more than reality. The Russian people is unquestionably the elder brother of the peoples that it can assimilate; for the others, it is a partner, not a guide. But the resurrection of the "elder brother" concept attests to Moscow's impatience and distress. Confronted with the nationality problem, the regime resorts to the most contradictory ideas. How can the Soviet people, a homogeneous community gradually replacing the fraternal family of peoples of the USSR, coexist with the idea of an "elder brother"? How can the "elder brother" idea be reconciled with the egalitarian principle?

The reappearance of this "elder brother," whose demise had been decreed by the Revolution, makes us wonder about Soviet progress since 1917. By the late nineteenth century the czarist regime had embarked on a program of rapid modernization. The one sphere with which the czars had been unable to cope was that of the relations with the various nations living in Russian territory. The czarist regime's vulnerability in World War I had been multiplied ten-fold by its vulnerability in the borderlands and by the rapid crumbling of the colonial empire. In sixty years, the Soviet regime has considerably transformed its society. Without question, the Kremlin is running into many problems. But one thing is clear: of all the problems facing Moscow, the most urgent and the most stubborn is the one raised by the national minorities. And like the Empire that it succeeded, the Soviet State seems incapable of extricating itself from the nationality impasse.

NOTES

INTRODUCTION

1. There were 194 of them in 1926; 126 in 1959; 91 today.

2. The Soviet citizen's passport indicates both the individual's *citizenship* (Soviet) and *nationality* (Russian, Uzbek, etc.).

CHAPTER 1

1. For Lenin and the Bolsheviks, cf. H. B. Davis, *Nationalism and Socialism—Marxist and Labor Theories of Nationalism to 1917* (New York, 1967); and H. Carrère d'Encausse, "Unité prolétarienne et diversité nationale—Lénine et la théorie de l'autodétermination," *Revue française de science politique* 21, no. 2, (April 1971): 221–256.

2. *Pervyi s'ezd narodov vostoka Baku, 1–8 sentiabr' 1920,* (Petrograd, 1920), pp. 31–179; and *Zhizn' natsional'nostei, no. 46(54) (December 20, 1919), and 47(55) (December 27, 1919).*

3. *F. Conte, Christian Rakovski—1873–1941* (Paris, 1975), vol. 1, pp. 212–217.

4. In 1913, Stalin wrote "Marxism and the Question of Nationality and Colonialism," in *Sochineniia* 2: 290–367, at Lenin's request. Just after the revolution, Stalin was appointed Commissar of Nationalities.

5. R. Pipes, *The Formation of the Soviet Union* (Cambridge, Mass.: Harvard University Press, 1954); and E. H. Carr, *The Bolshevik Revolution* (Harmondsworth, 1966), vol. 1, pp. 292–368.

6. R. Tucker, *Stalin as Revolutionary* (New York, 1973), pp. 250–252.

7. Cf. M. Lewin, *Le Dernier Combat de Lénine* (Paris, 1967), pp. 145–146.

8. Ibid., pp. 55–74.

9. Ibid., pp. 146–150.

10. At that time, the problem facing the Georgians lay in the fact that they were being urged to join the Federation via the device of a Transcaucasian Federation (comprising Armenia, Azerbaijan, and Georgia) and not directly as the Ukraine had joined. The Georgians refused to accept this dissolution of their statehood.

11. *Autonomization* was Stalin's plan. Cf. Lenin in *Polnoe sobranie sochinenii,* vol. XLX, pp. 211–213, 356 and 559.

12. For further information on the Soviet State's juridical organization, cf. H. Carrère d'Encausse, *Bolchevisme et Nation,* (forthcoming publication) p. 222 ff.

13. The concept of *korenizatsiia* and the program go back to the 10th Congress in 1921. Cf. *K.P.S.S. v rezoliutsiiakh i recheniakh* 2 (Moscow, 1970): 252.

14. For the program of the cultural revolution in the 1920s and its application, cf. V. A. Kumanev, *Revoliutsia i prosveshchenie mass* (Moscow, 1973), pp. 148–183. In addition, the works devoted to each republic's history include cultural sections that make an analysis of

the situation possible—in particular, T. P. Kalandadze, *Kul'turnaia revoliutsia v Gruzii* (Tbilisi, 1963), p. 15. For cultural institutions, cf. I. Grochev, *Istoricheskii opyt KPSS po osushchestvleniiu Leninskoi natsional'noi politiki* (Moscow, 1967), pp. 99–100.

15. P. A. Azimov and J. D. Decheriev, *Sovetskii opyt razvitiia natsional'nykh na base rodnykh iazykov* (Moscow, 1972), p. 9.

16. Ibid. p. 10.

17. S. L. Guthier, "The Bielorussians: National Identification and Assimilation—1897–1970," *Soviet Studies* 24, no. 1 (January 1977): 52–53. Also, N. Vakar in *Bielorussia, The Making of a Nation* (Cambridge, Mass.: Harvard University Press, 1956), pp. 75–92, reports the problems involved in shifting from spoken languages to written ones.

18. Regarding the role of linguists, cf. *Mladopismenye iazyki narodov S.S.S.R.* (Moscow-Leningrad, 1959), p. 4. On the exaggerated assigning of languages to tiny groups, cf. Kumanev, *Revoliutsia,* p. 190.

19. E. & S. Dunn, "The Transformation of Economy and Culture in the Soviet North," *Arctic Anthropology* 1, no. 2 (1963): 2; as well as Kumanev, *Revoliutsia,* p. 189.

20. On the correlation between language and cultural areas, cf. Kumanev, *Revoliutsia,* p. 183.

21. A. Bennigsen, *Soviet Nationality Problems,* ed. E. Allworth (New York: Columbia University Press, 1971), pp. 178–179.

22. *Torzhestvo Leninskoi natsional'noi politiki* (Moscow, 1963), pp. 291–292, in which V. Kostomarov discusses the general concept of the linguistic compromise and Stalin's idea of "zonal" languages.

23. This is particularly important for the Moslem area, in which institutions bound up with a special system of values were suppressed. Cf. Suleimanova in *Sovetskoe Gosudarstvo i Pravo* 3 (March 1949): 69, regarding the reform of the judicial system.

24. Guthier, "The Bielorussians," p. 27.

25. *Bol'chevik* 4 (1935): 24–26, regarding the national crisis in Belorussia in 1933.

26. For further information on the Basmachis, cf. J. Castagné, *Les Basmatchis—le mouvement national des indigènes d'Asie centrale* (Paris, 1925), 88 pp.; in addition, cf. Jeyoun B. H. B., Observer in *The Asiatic Review* 27 (92) (London, 1931): 682–692. With regard to F. K. Hodjaev, cf. H. Carrère d'Encausse, *Central Asia, A Century of Russian Rule* (New York: Columbia University Press, 1967), p. 252.

27. This hierarchy is covered by Chapters VIII and IX of the 1936 Constitution; cf., in particular, Articles 70, 84–86.

28. Khansuvarov, *Latinizatsiia, orudie Leninskoi natsional'noi politiki* (Moscow, 1932), 38 pp. The contradictions involved in Latinization should be noted; i.e., before the revolution, the Kalmyks, who had a highly complex Mongol alphabet, were in the process of adopting the Cyrillic alphabet, which held sway until 1929 when authorities replaced it with the Latin one; Khansuvarov, p. 26.

29. L. Zak and M. Isaev, "Problemy pismennosti narodov v kul'turnoi revoliutsii," *Voprosy Istorii* 2 (1966): 13, concerning the shift to Cyrillization.

30. Cf. Lowell Tillet, *The Great Friendship* (Chapel Hill: University of North Carolina Press, 1969), 322 pp.

31. With regard to this trend, cf. Pachukanis, "Mezhdunarodnoe Pravo" in Entsiklopedia i prava (Moscow, 1925), vol. 2, p. 857 ff; Pachukanis, *Ocherki po mezhdunarodnomu prava* (Moscow, 1935), pp. 14–15, 20, 78; and Kozhevnikov, *Sovetskoe gosudarstvo i mezhdunarodnoe pravo, 1917–1947* (Moscow, 1948), p. 32 (continuity of the State) and p. 180 (territory).

32. K. F. Shteppa, *Russian Historians and the Soviet State,* (New Brunswick, 1962), p. 133 ff.; A. Popov in *Protiv antimarksistkoi kontseptsii M.N. Pokrovskogo* (Moscow, 1940), vol. 2, p. 320 ff.

33. Curiously enough, this theory was revived in 1977 by E. Chevarnadzé in "Internatsionalistkoe vospitanie mass," *Kommunist,* no. 13 (Sept. 1977): 46–47. Chevarnadzé even rejects the idea of a lesser evil, writing on p. 46, "Evil is evil, regardless of whether it is lesser or greater. In the final analysis, the term *lesser* alters nothing. It would therefore be fairer for us to give up this term."

34. R. Portal in *Russes et Ukrainiens* (Paris, 1970), pp. 118–126, discusses the scope of the agreement and the part played by B. Khmelnitski.

35. On this policy, cf. H. Carrère d'Encausse, *L'Union soviétique de Lénine à Staline* (Paris, 1972), pp. 309–328.

36. Ibid., pp. 329–351.

37. R. Conquest, *The Nation Killers—Soviet Deportation of Nationalities* (London, 1970), 222 pp.; and A. M. Nekrich, *The Punished Peoples* (New York, 1978), 244 pp.

38. Speech by Stalin in *Pravda* (25 May 1945); and F. Barghoorn, "Stalinism and the Russian Cultural Heritage," *Review of Politics* 14, no. 2 (April 1952): 178–203.

39. *Bakinskii Rabochii,* 8 July, 1950.

40. A. Bennigsen, "The Crisis of the Turkic National Epic, 1951–1952: Local Nationalism or Internationalism?," *Canadian Slavonic Papers* 17, nos. 2 and 3 (1975): 463–475.

41. Beginning with the 20th Congress, the history review *Voprosy Istorii* set up a conference at which six hundred historians revised the "chauvinist concepts" that had prevailed until then.

42. Cf. in *Voprosy Istorii,* December 1956, the entire November 1956 debate.

43. M. Lavigne, *Les Economies socialistes soviétiques et européenes* (Paris, 1970), pp. 54–58.

44. On the development of republican rights, *Sovetskii narod, novaia istoricheskaia obshchnost' lyudei: stanovlenie i razvitie* (Moscow, 1975), pp. 349–350, is remarkable for its brevity.

45. Cf. the explanation of this given in ibid., p. 355, emphasizing the existence of "considerations of foreign policy."

46. This anxiety would be expressed in plainer language by leaders of Moslem republics in the Party's theoretical review; cf. *Kommunist,* October 1959, pp. 39–53 (the article by Rachidov), and ibid., December 1959, pp. 30–44 (the article by Djandildin.)

47. *Programma kommunisticheskoi partii sovetskogo soyuza* (Proekt) (Moscow, 1961), proclaims from the first page the withering away of social classes.

48. *XXII s'ezd kommunisticheskoi partii sovetskogo soyuza* (Moscow, 1961), pp. 362, 402.

49. Ibid., and Kaltchakian, "O natsii," *Voprosy Istorii,* June 1966, pp. 24, 43.

50. On this concept, see two recent works: *Natsional'nye otnocheniia v razvitom sotsialisticheskom obshchestve* (Moscow, 1977), 385 pp.; and *Sovetskii narod . . .* (op. cit.), 520 pp.

CHAPTER II

1. *Izvestia,* 22 July 1978, p. 3 (the figures are from 1 July 1978).

2. B. Kerblay, *La Société soviétique contemporaine* (Paris, 1977), p. 30.

3. Throughout this chapter we use data from the censuses of 1897, 1959 and 1970 (cf. Bibliography), and the study of F. Lorimer, *The Population of the Soviet Union* (Geneva, 1946), 289 pp.

4. Based on Lorimer, *Population,* and census data.

5. M. Maksudov, "Pertes subies par la population de l'U.R.S.S., 1918–1958," *Cahiers du monde russe et soviétique,* March 1977, pp. 223–266; and Lorimer, *Population,* pp. 133–137.

6. Maksudov, "Pertes subies," pp. 228–232. The figure 26 million has been advanced by the Soviet economist Strumilin. Kerblay, *La Société soviétique,* p. 31, emphasizes that these population losses represent the equivalent of seven years' national income, according to Strumilin.

7. Kerblay, *La Société soviétique,* p. 32; and Maksudov, "Pertes subies," pp. 227, 245.

8. Kerblay, *La Société soviétique,* p. 32.

9. Comparing Maksudov, "Pertes subies," pp. 243–244, with Lorimer, *Population* (1914–1926), and V. V. Pokchichevskii, *Geografiia naseleniia S.S.S.R.* (Moscow, 1971), p. 34 (World War II losses), we find that figures for losses range from 40–60 million.

10. *Bol'shaia Sovetskaia Entsiklopedia, Ezhegodnik* (1977 ed.), p. 13.

11. *Naselenie S.S.S.R.: Spravochnik* (Moscow, 1974), p. 21.

12. Ibid., p. 9.

13. The recovery is even more marked if calculated over several years and not year by year. Thus, *Vestnik Statistiki,* December 1973, p. 71, gives the following mortality rates:

1937–1940 : 17.9%	1951–1955 : 9.1%	1956–1960 : 7.5%
1961–1965 : 7.2%	1966–1970 : 7.8%	1971–1972 : 8.4%

    The influenza epidemics of 1957, 1959 and 1962 should be taken into consideration; without them, the very low mortality rates for those years would have been lower still.

14. According to Boldyrev, *Itogi perepisi naseleniia S.S.S.R.* (Moscow, 1974), p. 18, the forecasts made by the Central Board for Statistics at the start of the 1960s were as follows: 1970: 248 million; 1975: 263 million; 1980: 280 million.

15. *Naselenie S.S.S.R.,* p. 28.

16. Ibid., p. 29.

17. I. Belov, *Affaires d'habitude* (Paris, 1969), 289 pp., translated from the Russian and with a foreword by J. Cathala.

18. Boldyrev, *Itogi perepisi,* p. 18.

19. V. I. Kozlov, *Natsional'nosti S.S.S.R.* (Moscow, 1975), p. 62.

20. R. A. Lewis, R. H. Rowland, and R. S. Clem, *Nationality and Population Change in Russia and the USSR* (New York, 1976), p. 278.

21. *Naselenie S.S.S.R.,* p. 56.

22. During a Moscow conference in 1975 on demographic trends since the census, a participant noted the steady demographic decline in Central Chernoziom where the birth rate is below the national average. Nevertheless, it is a rural area. Cf. *Voprosy Ekonomiki,* August 1975, pp. 149–152.

23. For the period 1959–1970: *Demograficheskoe razvitie Ukrainskoi S.S.R.* (Kiev, 1977), pp. 12–16; for the period of the Empire: A. Rachin, *Naselenie Rossii za sto let 1811–1913* (Moscow, 1956), pp. 217–218, and Lorimer, *Population,* p. 81.

24. Lorimer, *Population,* and Rachin, *Naselenie Rossii.*

25. Rachin, *Naselenie Rossii,* pp. 101, 167, 168, 176 and 188; and Tönu Parming in *Nationality Group Survival in Multi-Ethnic States,* ed. E. Allworth (New York, 1977), pp. 33–40.

26. A. Nove and J. Newth, *Les Juifs en Union soviétique depuis 1917* (Paris, 1971), p. 198.

27. Lewis, Rowland, and Clem, *Nationality and Population Change,* p. 301.

28. Nove and Newth, *Les Juifs,* p. 179.

29. Kozlov, *Natsional'nosti,* p. 220.

30. *Vestnik Statistiki,* December 1973, p. 79.

31. Lewis, Rowland, and Clem, *Nationality and Population Change,* pp. 223–238.

32. Source: G. A. Bondarskaia, *Rozhdaemost' v S.S.S.R.* (Moscow, 1977), p. 96.

33. Kozlov, *Natsional'nosti,* p. 144.

34. Boldyrev, *Itogi perepisi,* p. 27.

35. *Naselenie S.S.S.R.,* pp. 90–93.

36. The following tables have been compiled on the basis of censuses: Tsentral'noe Statisticheskoe Upravlenie Pri Sovete Ministrov SSSR, *Itogi vsesoyuznoi perepisi naseleniia 1959 goda;* and idem, *Itogi vsesoyuznoi perepisi naseleniia 1970 goda,* vol. 4.

37. G. A. Bondarskaia in *Rozhdaemost': Sbornik statei* (Moscow, 1976), pp. 106–107. See also, by the same author, *Rozhdaemost' v S.S.S.R.* (op. cit.), pp. 43–45.

38. Bondarskaia, *Rozhdaemost' v S.S.S.R.,* pp. 121–122.

39. Boldyrev, *Itogi perepisi,* pp. 9–10; and V. A. Borisov, *Perspektivy rozhdaemosti* (Moscow, 1976), p. 74.

40. Table compiled on the basis of Bondarskaia, *Sbornik statei,* pp. 87–93.

41. V. A. Belova, *Chislo detei v. Semie* (Moscow, 1975), p.151.

42. Ibid., p. 127, gives comparative data on the replies of urban and rural women when queried about the number of children that they planned to have.

43. Kerblay, La Société soviétique, p. 107.

44. Bondarskaia, *Rozhdaemost' v S.S.S.R.,* p. 58.

45. Ibid., p. 93.

46. Ibid., p. 101. Cf. also the conclusions of Borisov, *Perspektivy,* pp. 219–233.

47. M. Feshbach, *Prospects for Massive Out-Migrations from Central Asia During the Next Decade* (Washington, D.C., Working Document, 1977), p. 23.

48. Kerblay, *La Société soviétique,* p. 38.

CHAPTER III

1. For the chapter as a whole, the recent statistical data come from the 1970 census and, in particular, from volume 7 devoted to population migrations; for the foregoing figures, cf. B. Kerblay, *La Société soviétique contemporaine* (Paris, 1977), pp. 33–34.

2. M. Feshbach and S. Rapawy, *Soviet Population and Manpower, Trends and Policies,* U.S. Congress—Joint Economic Committee (Washington, D.C., October 1976), p. 131.

3. M. Feshbach, *The Structure and Composition of the Soviet Industrial Labor Force,* NATO Colloquium 1978, Conference Paper (Washington, D.C., 1978) p. 6. On this point cf. a recent Soviet analysis: V. Kostakov, *Trudovye resursy piatiletki* (Moscow, 1976), pp. 7, 8.

4. M. Feshbach, *Structure and Composition,* p. 6.

5. M. B. Mazanova, *Territorial'nye proportsii narodnogo khoziaistva S.S.S.R.* (Moscow, 1974), pp. 63–67 and 194.

6. V. F. Pavlenko, *Territorial'noe planirovanie v S.S.S.R.* (Moscow, 1976), p. 254.

7. M. Feshbach and S. Rapawy, *Labor Constraints in the Five-Year Plan,* U.S. Congress—Joint Economic Committee (Washington, D.C., June 1973), pp. 497–501. Cf. also the general correlation between Soviet labor requirements and education: K. Nojko et al., *Educational Planning in the USSR* (Paris: UNESCO, 1968), p. 256.

8. Feshbach and Rapawy, *Soviet Population and Manpower,* p. 128.

9. M. Lantsev, *Sotsial'noe obespechenie v S.S.S.R.—Ekonomicheskii aspekt* (Moscow, 1974), p. 137.

10. Feshbach and Rapawy, *Soviet Population and Manpower,* p. 128.

11. Ibid., p. 146.

12. This is basically the position held by Perevedentsev in *Komsomol'skaia Pravda,* 28 January 1976; and J. A. Zaiontchkovskaia and D. M. Zakharina, "Problemy obespecheniia Sibiri rabochei siloi" in *Problemy razvitiia vostochnyh raionov S.S.S.R.* (Moscow, 1971), p. 55 ff.

13. V. I. Perevedentsev, *Metody izucheniia migratsii naseleniia* (Moscow, 1975), pp. 43–51.

14. *Narodonaselenie stran mira* (Moscow, 1974), p. 403.

15. Compiled on the basis of vol. 7 of the census, table 2, p. 8.

16. Ibid., tables 18 ff., pp. 158–163.

17. G. M. Maximov, ed., *Vsesozhuznaia perepisi naseleniia 1970 goda* (Moscow, 1976), p. 200.

18. S. Bruk, "Natsional'nost i iazyk v perepisi naseleniia 1970 g.," *Vestnik Statistiki* 5 (1972): 42–54.

19. In 1959, there were 3,359,000 Ukrainians; in 1970, they numbered 3,344,000.

20. *Naselenie S.S.S.R.: Spravochnik* (Moscow, 1974), p. 90–91; and *Uroven' obrazovania, natsional'nyj sostav, 1959* (Moscow, 1960), pp. 14–15.

21. *Naselenie S.S.S.R.*, pp. 90–91.

22. Compiled on the basis of V. I. Kozlov, *Natsional'nosti S.S.S.R.* (Moscow, 1975), p. 124.

23. Ibid.

24. B. S. Khorev and V. M. Moiseenko, *Sdvigi v razmeshchenie naseleniia S.S.S.R.* (Moscow, 1976), p. 56.

25. This graph was set up on the basis of data from *Narodnoe khoziaistvo S.S.S.R. v 1974 g.* (Moscow, 1975), p. 9, and *Naselenie S.S.S.R. v 1973 g.* (Moscow, 1975), pp. 14–25.

26. Feshbach and Rapawy, *Soviet Population and Manpower*, p. 125.

27. Ibid.

28. Ibid.

29. Kerblay, *La Société soviétique*, p. 22.

30. *Migratsionnaia podvizhnost' naseleniia v. S.S.S.R.* (Moscow, 1974), pp. 58–59.

31. Ibid., p. 55.

32. *Narodonaselenie i ekonomika* (Moscow, 1967), p. 104.

33. *Narodnoe khoziaistvo S.S.S.R. v 1970 g.*, p. 300.

34. R. A. Lewis, R. H. Rowland, and R. S. Clem, *Nationality and Population Change in Russia and the USSR* (New York, 1976), p. 356.

35. *Narodnoe khoziaistvo, 1970*, p. 348.

36. Mazanova in *Territorial'nye proportsii*, p. 171 ff., raises the question of the economic redistribution needed.

37. M. Feshbach, *Prospects for Massive Out-Migrations from Central Asia During the Next Decade* (Washington, D.C., Working Document, 1977), pp. 6, 7.

38. Ibid., and Mazanova, *Territorial'nye proportsii*, pp. 65–67.

39. *Migratsionnaia podviznost'*, p. 16 ff.

40. A. V. Topilin, *Territorial'noe pereraspredelenie trudovykh resursov v S.S.S.R.* (Moscow, 1975), p. 3.

41. Ibid., p. 129.

42. Ibid., p. 124.

43. Ibid., p. 128, and *Demograficheskie aspekty zaniatnosti* (Moscow, 1975), pp. 94–103, on the use of student volunteers.

44. Feshbach and Rapawy, *Soviet Population and Manpower*, p. 129. In addition, F. Levcik, *Migration und Ausländerbeschäftigung in den RGW-Ländern und ihre Probleme*, no. 32 (December 1975), p. 14.

45. *The New York Times*, 19 December 1973.

46. Fesbach and Rapawy, *Soviet Population and Manpower*, pp. 129–130. Cf. also Feshbach and Rapawy, *Labor Constraints*, p. 503.

47. Cf. supra, chapter 6.

48. *Sobranie postalnovlenii pravitel'stva S.S.S.R.* 13 (1973): 266–280.

49. *Sovetskaia Torgovlia,* September 1977, pp. 27–33, shows the share of non-food purchases used as cost-of-living indicators. These data are broken down by economic region. The USSR average: 46.42%; RSFSR: 43.84%; Ukraine: 49.14%; Belorussia: 47.45%; Baltic republics: 49.04%; Central Asia: 52.43%; Kazakhstan: 47.63%; Caucasus: 50.64%; Moldavia: 56.31%.

50. G. Schreder, cited by Feshbach in *Prospects for Massive Out-Migrations,* p. 3.

51. Feshbach, *Prospects for Massive Out-Migrations,* pp. 3, 4.

52. E. Wädekin, "Income Distribution in Soviet Agriculture," *Soviet Studies* 1 (January 1975): 327; table, p. 13.

53. Ibid., p. 11.

54. Grey Hodnett, *Soviet Politics and Society in the 1970s,* ed. H. W. Morton and R. L. Tökes (New York, 1974), p. 93; Grey Hodnett uses the kolkhozniks of Uzbekistan as an example, and works on the basis of a Soviet study.

55. On the consumption of alcohol in the USSR, cf. W. Treml, "Production and Consumption of Alcoholic Beverages in the USSR," (Durham, N.C.: Duke University, 1974), 52 pp.

56. Kerblay, *La Société soviétique,* p. 86.

CHAPTER IV

1. Russian text published in Moscow, Politizdat, 1977, 62 pp.

2. In particular, articles published in: *Voprosy Istorii,* no. 3, 1967, pp. 82–96; July 1967, pp. 87–104; February 1968, pp. 99–112; March 1968, pp. 83–91; *Voprosy Filosofii,* no. 9, 1967, pp. 26–36; February 1969, pp. 26–31; *Kommunist Tatarii,* no. 1, 1967, pp. 12–18; *Kommunist Uzbekistana,* no. 8, 1968, pp. 72–79. A good summary of the discussion appears in G. Hodnett, "What's a Nation?" *Problems of Communism,* September–October 1967, pp. 2–14.

3. Cf. also *The Program of the CPSU,* Russian edition (Moscow, 1976), p. 113.

4. Article 74 of the Constitution contradicts somewhat article 72, in stating that "the territory of the Union of Soviet Socialist Republics shall be integral and shall comprise the territories of the Union Republics."

5. *Kommunist,* no. 15 (October 1977): 5–20.

6. Cf. Article 1 of the Constitution and Leonid Brezhnev's commentary on the draft, *Pravda,* 5 June 1977.

7. Cf. Article 13 of the 1936 Constitution and Article 70 of the 1977 Constitution.

8. *Kommunist,* no. 15 (October 1977): 10–11.

9. See the reaction of Usmanov, Chairman of the Tatar ASSR Council of Ministers, on the viability of the federal system, *Pravda,* 24 June 1977.

10. In the Soviet Union, deputies were elected by equal population constituency (300,000 inhabitants for one deputy) in 1936; the number of inhabitants per constituency has not been specified in the new constitution. In the Soviet of Nationalities, there are 32 deputies per SSR, 11 per ASSR, 5 per AR and 1 per autonomous district.

11. The Supreme Soviet meets in ordinary session twice a year for sessions ranging from two to three days—hence, roughly one week a year in all.

12. M. Rywkin, *Russia in Central Asia* (New York, 1963), pp. 125 and 130. The most accurate analysis of the KGB's position is given by Y. Bilinsky in "The Rulers and the Ruled," in *Problems of Communism* September–October 1967, p. 22.

13. Articles 18a and b: *Sbornik zakonov S.S.S.R. i ukazov presidiuma verkhovnogo soveta 1938–1967* (Moscow, 1968), vol. 1, pp. 138–139.

14. *Handbook of Major Soviet Nationalities*, ed. J. Katz (Boston: M.I.T., 1975), p. 30.

15. Decision of the Presidium of the Supreme Soviet of the USSR, *Radio Moscow*, 17 August 1976.

16. It was no accident that, just a few days before the announcement of this change, *Pravda Vostoka* (Uzbekistan), 7 August 1976, pp. 2 and 3, published two articles on the urgency of the employment problem and the need for major solutions. The chairman of the new State Committee, G. Lomonossov, had been Second Secretary of the Uzbek CP until then.

17. The judicial sphere is marked by the same imbalance. It was discussed at the time of the constitutional debate, the republics trying to put the nomination of republican procurators within their sphere of competence. Cf. *Izvestia*, 24 and 30 August 1977; *Kommunist Tadjikistana*, 31 August 1977.

18. R. C. Tucker, *Stalin as Revolutionary* (New York, 1973), p. 151.

19. Except in the RSFSR.

20. "K.P.S.S. v tsifrakh," *Partiinaia zhizn'*, October 1976, p. 16.

21. Table compiled on the basis of: *Partiinaia zhizn'*, no. 1, 1962, p. 44; no. 19, 1967, p. 14; and no. 10, 1976, p. 16.

22. H. Righby, *Communist Party Membership in the USSR (1917–1967)* (New York: Columbia University Press, 1967), p. 375.

23. *Sotsialnyi sostav VKP* (b), p. 117.

24. *Partiinaia zhizn'*, October 1976, p. 16; and *Narodnoe khoziaistvo S.S.S.R. v 1973 g.*, pp. 35–38.

25. *Sovetskaia Latvia*, 16 February 1977. We should note the presence at this meeting of N. S. Perun, in charge of organization problems in the CC of the CPSU and who seems to have attended all meetings of this kind in the republics at the start of the 1970s. Cf. also *Bol'shaia Sovetskaia Entsiklopedia, Ezhegodnik* (1976 ed.), p. 1.

26. *Bakinskii Rabochii*, 30 January 1976. On the Azerbaijan CP in general, cf. *Kommunisticheskaia Partiia Azerbaidjana v tsifrakh* (Baku, 1970), 160 pp.

27. A number of indices suggest that this gap also exists in the Ukraine—*Pravda Ukrainy*, 11 February 1976—and in Moldavisa—*Sovetskaia Moldavia*, 30 January 1976.

28. Cf. the make-up of the Central Committee following the 25th Congress.

29. On this point, cf. A. Nove, "Y a-t-il une classe dirigeante en U.R.S.S.?" in *Revue des études comparatives Est-Ouest* 6, no. 4 (1975): 5–44.

30. For an analysis of the problem as a whole, cf. the fine study by Y. Bilinsky, "The Rulers and the Ruled" (art. cit.), pp. 16–27.

31. Such was the case in the late 1950s for I. Naidek who was listed in the directory of the Supreme Soviet of the USSR for 1958 as Secretary, whereas the Party's local newspaper, *Pravda Ukrainy*, gave him as *Second* Secretary on 27 December 1957; quoted by J. H. Miller, "Cadres Policy in the Nationality Area," *Soviet Studies* 29, no. 1 (January 1977): 3–36.

32. Ibid., p. 7.

33. J. Hough, *The Soviet Prefects* (Cambridge, Mass.: Harvard University Press, 1969), p. 173.

34. Miller, "Cadres Policy."

35. Ibid., table, p. 12.

36. Belorussia did not come under this heading until 1956. The Abkhaz ASSR had a Russian Second Secretary in 1955.

37. R. Sullivan, "The Ukrainians," *Problems of Communism*, September–October 1967, pp. 52–53.

38. *Pravda* 2 March 1972 and 30 September 1972.

39. Cf. the decree of the Central Committee of the CPSU criticizing the action of the Tbilisi Party's committee, *Pravda*, 3 March 1972.

40. "V tsentral'nom komitete K.P.S.S.," *Pravda*, 27 June 1976; and *Zaria Vostoka*, 4 November 1976, 24 December 1976, and 16 February 1977.

41. *Kommunist* of Erivan, 1 February 1975, 15 March 1975, and 23 May 1975.

42. Rywkin, *Russia in Central Asia*, p. 127 and Miller, "Cadres Policy," p. 27.

43. Miller, "Cadres Policy," p. 29.

44. *Sovetskaia Estonia*, 12 February 1971.

45. Bilinsky, "The Rulers and the Ruled," pp. 21–22.

46. *Voina i revoliutsia*, May 1927, pp. 114–115.

47. A. Bennigsen and C. Quelquejay, *Les Mouvements nationaux chez les musulmans de Russie: le Sultangalievisme au Tatarstan* (Paris, 1960), pp. 118–119.

48. Colonel P. Rtishchev, "Leninskaia natsional 'naia politika i stroitel'stvo sovetskikh vooruzhenykh sil," *Voennyi Istoricheskii Zhurnal*, June 1974, pp. 4–5.

49. G. Haupt and J. J. Marie, *Les Bolcheviks par eux-mêmes* (Paris, 1969), pp. 200–212.

50. I. Dziuba, *Internationalism or Russification?* (London, 1968), p. 136, note 2.

51. Ibid., note 3.

52. Bennigsen and Quelquejay, *Les Mouvements nationaux*, p. 167.

53. Rtishchev, "Leninskaia natsional'naia," p. 6.

54. M. V. Frunze, *Izbrannye proizvedeniia* (Moscow, 1957), vol. 2, pp. 269–270.

55. Rtischev, "Leninskaia natsional'naia," p. 7.

56. Ibid., p. 8; and Lepechkin et al., *Kurs sovetskogo gosudarstvennogo Prava* (Moscow, 1962), part 2, p. 157.

57. On the role of Russian in the army: *Zaria Vostoka*, 24 October 1976, p. 2 (on the conference held in Tbilisi, 20–22 October 1976).

58. Leonid Brezhnev, *O piatidesiatiletii soyuza sovetskikh sotsialisticheskikh respublik* (Moscow, 1972), p. 23.

59. Rtishchev, "Leninskaia natsional'naia," p. 9.

60. Herbert Goldhammer, *The Soviet Soldier: Soviet Military Management at the Troop Level* (New York: Crane, Russak & Co., 1975), p. 28.

61. M. Feshbach and S. Rapawy, *Soviet Population and Manpower, Trends and Policy,* U.S. Congress—Joint Economic Committee (Washington, D.C., October 1976), p. 149.

62. Rtishchev, "Leninskaia natsional'naia," p. 7.

63. Quoted by T. Rakowska-Harmstone, "Sur l 'armée et les nationalités" (unpublished conference paper), who compiled the following ethno-sociological data.

64. While there are many Ukrainians in the military hierarchy, they seem to serve outside the Ukraine for the most part; thus, the commander of the Kiev military region is now a Russian, Ivan Gerassimov. He was also appointed to the Politburo of the UCP in 1977.

65. Rakowska-Harmstone, "Sur l'armée."

66. I. Dziuba, *Internationalism or Russification?,* p. 137.

67. *Razvitie natsional'nogo dvuyazichiia* (Moscow, 1976), particularly p. 30.

68. *Krasnaia Zvezda,* 15 April 1971; 10 December 1972; 3 April 1974; 29 September 1974; 31 March 1976, and 26 September 1976. Many examples of criticism against "exemption scandals" could be cited.

CHAPTER V

1. Without going back to Stalin and his theory of the nation, we should note that contemporary Soviet writers constantly stress the importance of language in defining the nation. Cf. V. I. Kozlov, *Natsional'nosti S.S.S.R.* (Moscow, 1975), p. 207.

2. National language is defined in *Bol'shaia Sovetskaia Entsiklopedia,* 3rd ed. (1974), vol. 17, p. 374.

3. Russian text published in Moscow, 1977, Art. 36, Para. 2.

4. This hierarchy appears in *Sovetskii narod, novaia istoricheskaia obshchnost lyudei: Stanovlenie i razvitie* (Moscow, 1975), p. 450. As this work was published by the Academy of Sciences, it can be considered an official source.

5. *Razvitie natsional'no russkogo dvuyazichiia* (Moscow, 1976), p. 8.

6. Lenin, *Polnoe sobranie sochenineii,* vol. 24, p. 295: "We are for every inhabitant of Russia being able to learn the Russian language. But there is one thing that we don't want: obligation."

7. In the late 1970s, a Kirghiz estimated that Russian words incorporated into the Kirghiz language represented 25% of the total vocabulary.

8. Drawn up on the basis of the table compiled by Kozlov, *Natsional'nosti,* pp. 211–212.

9. In this category were 4,541,000 Ukrainians, 1,733,000 Jews, 1,212,000 Belorussians, 392,000 Germans. Cf. ibid., p. 218.

10. Among the myriad works devoted to bilingualism and the concrete aspects of its develop-

ment, cf. the work cited in footnote 5, *Razvitie natsional'no russkogo dvuyazichiia,* 368 pp., directed by a leading Soviet expert, I. Decheriev. In this connection, cf. also the works of S. Bruk and M. Guboglo in *Sovetskaia Etnografiia,* nos. 4 and 5 (1975), which attempt to analyze the census.

11. *Narodnoe khoziaistvo S.S.S.R. v 1972 g.,* p. 32.

12. In the Tatar ASSR, 54.8% of the Tatars are bilingual, while 65.5% of those living outside speak two languages. This second group is preponderant, for 74.1% of the Tatars live outside their own republic. Cf. Tsentral'noe Statisticheskoe Upravlenie Pri Sovete Ministrov SSSR, *Itogi vsesoyuznoi perepisi naseleniia 1970 goda,* vol. 4, tables 20, 144. The Tatars often form the subject of sociological studies.

13. The change is slight (0.3%), but contrasts with the increase in Belorussian migration (+2%).

14. *Zaria Vostoka,* 8 May 1971.

15. This becomes clear when we take the comparable position of the Baltic group as an example. The Estonians hold last place for their knowledge of Russian; nevertheless, they are the most urbanized: 55.1%, against 52.7% for the Latvians and 46.7% for the Lithuanians. These percentages reflect the ethnic group, not the republic. If we take the percentage on a republican basis, Estonia as a whole holds first place for urbanization (66%); Latvia, third place (64%); Lithuania, seventh (53%). Cf. *Narodnoe khoziaistvo,* 1972, p. 499.

16. S. L. Guthier, "The Bielorussians: National Identification and Assimilation—1897–1970," *Soviet Studies* 29, no. 1 (January 1977): 59.

17. An excellent survey of developments in educational policy affecting the nationalities is Y. Bilinsky, "Education of the Non-Russian Peoples in the U.S.S.R., 1917–1967," *Slavic Review,* 27, no. 3 (1968): 411–437.

18. This is article 19 of the 1958 Law. On this reform, cf. Y. Bilinsky, "The Soviet Education Laws of 1958–1959 and Soviet Nationality Policy," *Soviet Studies* 14, no. 2 (1962): 138–157.

19. V. Malantchuk, "Dvi Kontseptsii mynduloho i suchasnoho Ukrayiny," a long article published in 1972 in a Ukrainian review and quoted by R. Szporluk in *Handbook of Major Soviet Nationalities,* ed. Z. Katz (Boston: M.I.T., 1975), pp. 35–36.

20. Jan Zaprudnik, in ibid., p. 61, gives the Russian and Belorussian programs, such as they were published in the Belorussian *Teachers Journal* of April 8, 1979.

21. A great effort was made in Belorussia to make complete secondary school education the general rule. A law adopted on June 23, 1972 by the Belorussian Supreme Soviet called for such a program in the immediate future.

22. At the time of the census, 27% of the pupils enrolled in the schools attended urban schools. Cf. *Narodnoe obrazovanie,* 1971, p. 644.

23. *Ekonomika Litvy,* 1970, p. 358. It should be pointed out that Polish is also a language of instruction in Lithuania where 4% of the pupils are enrolled in schools using Polish.

24. A. Danilov, "Mnogonatsional'naia shkola R.S.F.S.R.—Prakticheskoe voploshchnie Leninskoi national'noi politiki," *Narodnoe obrazovanie,* December 1972, p. 23.

25. *Narodnoe obrazovanie,* 1971, p. 196.

26. *Uchitel'skaia gazeta,* August 18, 1972.

27. This is the case in Azerbaijan, but this measure does not solve anything, inasmuch as the Azeris—especially, the girls—leave school after eight years of compulsory education and, often, sooner. *Bakinskii rabotchii,* 5 November 1972, reports that the percentage of students leaving school before completing the required eight years is 23%.

28. *Kommunist Tajikistana,* 1 and 2 June 1973, underscores the fact that a knowledge of Russian isn't compulsory, but rather, desirable.

29. Brian Silver, "The Status of National Minority Languages in Soviet Education: An Assessment of Recent Changes," *Soviet Studies* 26, no. 1 (1974): 28–41.

30. Ibid., p. 33.

31. Based on data from the table compiled by Brian Silver, ibid. The figure 0 indicates the existence of pre-school education in the national language.

32. It should be noted that these data, compiled by Brian Silver, are based on official Soviet sources, as they come from A. Danilov, RSFSR Minister of Education, who uses them in *Narodnoe obrazovanie,* December 1972, p. 23.

33. Kozlov, *Natsional'nosti,* pp. 219–220. The data for 1970 are hard to establish, but we may assume that they scarcely change.

34. Silver, "Status of Minority Languages," p. 37.

35. Reported by A. Bennigsen and B. Silver at the colloquy on the nationalities held in Chicago in March 1977.

36. Thus, for example, in Estonia the Russian word *Lunokhod* was used at first to describe lunar probes. Gradually, however, the Estonian press replaced that term by one of its own invention, *Kuukulgur.* Quoted by Rein Taagevera in *Handbook of Major Soviet Nationalities,* p. 80.

37. The congress was reported briefly by *Zaria Vostoka* on 24 April 1976. Djaparidzé was attacked by the Third Plenum of the CC of the Georgian CP. See *Zaria Vostoka,* 25 and 27 July 1976.

38. *Zaria Vostoka,* 25 August 1976.

39. *Zaria Vostoka,* 27 July 1976.

40. This experiment, which took place at the Zugid boarding school, was reported by the Georgian Minister of Education in *Uchitel'skaia gazeta,* 10 January 1976.

41. *Pravda Vostoka,* 24 January 1976.

42. *Pravda Vostoka,* 9 December 1975, in an article entitled "Second Mother Tongue," wrote: "Russian has been, is and will be the second mother tongue of all the Soviet Union's nations and nationalities."
   Kommunist (of Erivan), 13 November 1976; *Turkmenskaia Iskra,* January 21, 1976.

43. *Pravda Vostoka,* 21 and 24 October 1975.

44. *Sovet Mektebe,* January 1970, p. 33.

45. Ibid. and *Kazan Utlary,* April 1973, pp. 164–169.

46. For the first conference, cf. *Sovet Mektebe,* July 1973, p. 25; for the second, ibid., June 1975, pp. 17–19.

47. In 1974, there were 1,571 teachers of language and literature in the Tatar republic. Of this number, 62% had university diplomas; 20% had an incomplete college education; and 18% had no actual university training. On this problem, cf. also *Sovet Mektebe,* June 1975, pp. 17–19.

48. *Sovet Mektebe,* January 1972, p. 5; January 1973, p. 16; August 1975, p. 7.

49. *Sovetskaia Rossiia,* 16 August 1975.

50. *Sovetskaia Estonia,* 30 November 1976.

51. Töny Parming in *Nationality Group Survival in Multi-Ethnic States,* ed. A. Allworth (New York, 1977), pp. 108–109.

52. The czarist government, which had no specific doctrine on Russification, was determined to Russify the Tatars owing to their historical role with regard to Russia and to their hold on Central Asia. The Orthodox missionaries made systematic efforts to Christianize (and, in so doing, to Russify) the Tatar country.

53. This reasoning is based on the work of Uriel Weinreich: *Languages in Contact: Findings and Problems* (The Hague, 1950), p. 94, quoted by Silver, "Status of Minority Languages," p. 35.

CHAPTER VI

1. Crises have erupted in most of the Soviet nations in the last few years. But some of these crises are more directly related to the movement fighting for human rights and the democratization of the Soviet system. We have cited only those crises specifically related to these issues. We have also discussed what was specifically national within broader movements. Accordingly, the various groups set up in the borderlands to respect the Helsinki agreements have not been covered in this study. In a general way, this also explains why the Balts are missing from the analysis.

2. Cf. in particular the resolution of the Central Committee of the CPSU of 21 February 1972, "O podgotovke k 50-letii obrazovania soyuza sovetskikh sotsialisticheskikh respublik" (Moscow, 1972), p. 17, and the speech of Brezhnev on December 21, 1972 in the Kremlin, "O piatidesiatiletii soyuza sovetskikh sotsialisticheskikh respublik" (Moscow, 1973), p. 19.

3. General Grigorenko took a position in favor of the Tatars on 17 March 1968 during the 72nd birthday celebration for writer A. Kosterin in Moscow. In May 1969, he came to Tashkent to testify in their defense and was then arrested.

4. There were 5,931,000 in 1970 as opposed to 4,968,000 eleven years earlier. Tsentral'noe Statisticheskoe Upravlenie Pri Sovete Ministrov SSSR, *Itogi vsesoyuznoi perepisi naseleniia 1970 goda,* vol. 4.

5. This figure was given by the Tatars in a petition to the Supreme Soviet of the USSR in July 1972; cited in *Handbook of Major Soviet Nationalities,* ed. Z. Katz (Boston: M.I.T., 1975), p. 390. There were 188,000 Tatars in 1897.

6. Their secular presence goes back to the 13th century. In the 15th century, an independent Tatar Khanate was set up in the Crimea. It resisted Russia until its annexation by Cather-

ine II in 1783. Cf. A. Fischer, *The Russian Annexation of the Crimea, 1772–1783* (Cambridge, 1970), 180 pp.

7. At the time they represented 25% of the republic's population, which stood at 714,000 persons in the 1926 census.

8. The Tatar language is an official language on an equal footing with Russian.

9. Seven peoples were labelled "collaborators": the Chechen, Ingush, Karachais, Balkars, Kalmyks, Crimean Tatars and Volga Germans (the latter had been deported by 1941). In all, one million persons were involved.

10. Decree in *Izvestia,* 26 June 1946.

11. Decision of 19 February 1954.

12. In spite of these publications, volume 2 of the classic publication of the Academy of Sciences on the languages of the Soviet peoples says that Crimean Tatar is an "unwritten language."

13. *Lenin Bayragi* (Lenin's flag).

14. The autonomous territories of the deported Caucasian peoples were restored in January 1957.

15. At the 22nd Congress of the CPSU, the Tatars submitted a petition bearing 25,000 signatures.

16. The first known Tatar lawsuit goes back to 1961.

17. Between 1964 and 1968, 4,000 Tatar delegates were sent to Moscow by their countrymen.

18. Articles 191–4 (dissemination of news slandering the Soviet regime), and 191–6 (organizing or participating in group action disturbing the peace).

19. *Pravda Vostoka,* 9 September 1967.

20. *Pravda Vostoka,* 16 September 1967.

21. In May 1971, on behalf of the Human Rights Committee, Sakharov and Tchalidze raised the issue of the fate of the Tatars with the Soviet authorities.

22. In 1967, of the 6,000 Tatars who had tried the Crimean venture, three unmarried men and two families managed to win the right to live there.

23. A Bennigsen and C. Quelquejay, *Les Mouvements nationaux chez les musulmans de Russie: le Sultangalievisme au Tatarstan* (Paris, 1960), 260 pp.

24. Tsentral'noe . . ., *Itogi . . . 1970,* vol. 4.

25. In addition to the ASSR, the 17 German nationality districts (6 in the RSFSR, 1 in Azerbaijan, 1 in Georgia and 9 in the Ukraine) were eliminated. The deportation affected 800,000 persons, 400,000 of whom lived in the republic.

26. The Germans have been authorized to elect their compatriots in the local soviets. In 1957, *Neues Leben* (which was to become a weekly with a circulation of 300,000) reappeared in Moscow. By 1956 German programs were being broadcast over Radio Moscow. Kazakh radio made its appearance in 1957, while Kirghiz stations began operation in 1962. Since 1957, in any school having at least 10 German pupils, parents may request that a German-language course be instituted.

27. *Vedomosti verkhovnogo soveta S.S.S.R.,* 28 December 1964.

28. Receiving a delegation of Germans on 7 June 1965, Mikoyan acknowledged that the restoration of a national territory would be the best solution but that, without German participation, the clearing of virgin land was doomed to failure.

29. Three Germans were elected to the Supreme Soviet in 1970. One of them became Minister of Food Industries for the USSR. German political representation in all local soviets is geared to numerical size.

30. The restoration of the national territory is championed primarily by those who used to live there. On the other hand, the Germans who used to live in the region of the Black Sea are more interested in the possibility of leaving the Soviet Union.

31. Figures from the three censuses, supplemented by *Sovetskii Kazakhstan,* 1971, pp. 25–26.

32. Cf. *Narodnoe khoziastvo Tajikistanskoi, S.S.R.,* 1970, p. 293, where we find that the German-speaking Germans of Tajikistan went from 88.7% (1959) to 81.4% (1970).

33. Cf. the Tajik trend which goes from 99.3% (1959) to 99.4% (in 1970); in the whole republic, the percentage of those speaking *their* mother tongue went from 96.7 (1959) to 97.2 (1970).

34. In the 1950s, The German Red Cross determined that 43,000 German families in the Soviet Union could avail themselves of the family-reunion clause.

35. In 1965, this agreement was supplemented in Vienna by an agreement between the Soviet Red Cross and the German one. As a result, 984 Germans returned to Germany in 1966, while 836 went back in 1967. But by 1968 this movement seemed to have come to a halt.

36. *The New York Times* of 9 March 1977 reports a demonstration of Germans on Red Square—the first demonstration at that place since 1968.

37. *Nordwest Zeitung,* 20 May 1977.

38. To such a degree that, unlike Stalin, the Imperial regime neither moved the Germans nor placed them under special surveillance during the First World War, considering them loyal subjects. And, in fact, they created no security problem.

39. *Nordwest Zeitung,* 20 May 1977. Cf. also the letter of A. Sakharov to President Scheel and to Chancellor Schmidt, *Frankfurter Neue Presse,* 22 February 1978.

40. *Sovetskaia Kirgizia,* 13 May 1977.

41. On this point, both the articles published in the USSR and in Germany refrain from emphasizing that there may be a link between economic policy and the exit of Germans.

42. This connection becomes apparent when we see that, in 1972, three weeks before the German general elections, 2,000 Germans received their exit visas. Likewise, in 1976, a German election year, emigration hit its highest level.

43. "Weltpolitik mit fanfarenstössen," *Die Zeit,* 4 March 1977; or, as another possibility, "Predigt oder Politik," *Die Zeit,* 8 July 1977.

44. On the Bolsheviks' attitude, the study by Annie Kriegel, "La question juive en Union soviétique," can be read with profit; in *Les Juifs en Union Soviétique,* no. 23 (July 1976), pp. 14–28 (published by la Bibliothèque juive contemporaine).

45. M. S. Belenkii, *Judaism*, 2nd ed. (Moscow, 1974), p. 232.

46. The census reports 2,150,707: Tsentral'noe ... *Itogi* ... *1970*, vol. 4, pp. 9–19. But the census gives figures that contradict other Soviet sources. *Atlas narodov mira*, 1964, p. 158 lists the number of Jews in the USSR as 2.5 million, whereas the 1959 census reported only 2,268,000. A. Kriegel ("La question juive," p. 14), believes that, based on many sources, the actual figure probably falls between 2,400,000 and 3,400,000.

47. Such as Tati, the Crimean Jewish variant, etc.

48. Tsentral'noe ..., *Itogi* ... *1959*, pp. 184–188.

49. Ibid., *1970*, vol. 4, p. 20; *Narodnoe khoziaistvo S.S.S.R. v 1972 g.*, p. 32.

50. Z. Gitelman, "The Jews," *Problems of Communism*, Sept.–Oct. 1967, pp. 92–102.

51. L. Hirszowicz, "Jewish Cultural Life in the U.S.S.R.—A Survey," *Soviet Jewish Affairs* 7, no. 2 (1977): 11.

52. We should also add to this number some *minyan* (prayer groups gathering informally at a believer's home). Cf. also on the number of houses of worship open in the USSR, A. Yodfat, "Jewish Religious Communities in the USSR," *Soviet Jewish Affairs* 2, (1971): 61–67.

53. According to Hirszowicz, ("Jewish Cultural Life," p. 11) despite official Soviet estimates which reported 56,000 religious Jews in the USSR in 1976, the actual number of practicing Jews is much higher. Z. Gitelman, in a survey carried out among Soviet Jewish émigrés in Israel, finds that 9% of the émigrés describe themselves as religious. See Gitelman, "Soviet Political Culture: Insights from Jewish Emigrés," *Soviet Studies*, October 1977, p. 549.

54. The Jews have the highest urbanization rate in the USSR: 78.5%. From 1897 to 1970, they registered the most spectacular trend and, in each census, they led all the nationalities in terms of urbanization.

55. Kriegel, "La question juive," p. 19; on the difficult problem of Russianization, Russification and assimilation, cf. the analysis of A. Kriegel cited earlier.

56. In 1970, there were 11,542 Jews in Birobijan, against 14,269 in 1959. At the present time, only 1,970 speak Yiddish. *Narodnoe khoziaistvo*, 1972, p. 32; Tsentral'noe ..., *Itogi* ... *1959*, pp. 184–188; idem, *Itogi* ... *1970*, vol. 4, p. 76.

57. The census gives no overall statistics for the education of Jews, but merely statistics per republic. Thus, in the RSFSR, the Jews have an educational level eight times higher than the Russians. Cf. Tsentral'noe ..., *Itogi* ... *1970*, vol. 4, p. 405–449.

58. H. Salisbury cited by Hirszowicz, "Jewish Cultural Life," p. 4.

59. Two publications appear in Yiddish in the USSR: the *Sovetish Heimland* [Soviet Homeland] published in Moscow since 1961 and having a circulation of 25,000. The magazine is headed by Aron Vergelis. In Birobijan there is also the *Birobijaner Stern* [Star of Birobijan] with a circulation of 12,000 and appearing 260 times a year. Unlike the Sovetish Heimland which tries to be the organ of the Jewish community, *Birobijaner Stern* is—like most of the regional organs—a translation of the Russian organ for the region.

60. Hirszowicz, "Jewish Cultural Life," p. 13.

61. In 1971, Jews attempted to announce programs of Hebrew studies—the law allows this—and thereby win legal status. After a period of hesitation and contradictory decisions, private Hebrew instruction was forbidden late in 1972 since it conveyed ideas that conflicted with Soviet interests. The authorities also found technicalities to justify their decision to ban private Hebrew lessons.

62. Emigration followed a rising curve until 1973 when it began a sharp decline: 1967: 480 emigrants; 1968: 231; 1969: 3019; 1970: 999; 1971: 12,832; 1972: 31,652; 1973: 33,477; 1974: 17,373; 1975: 8,531; 1976: 7,274. (Figures from the Israeli Ministry for the Integration of Immigrants, cited by Z. Gitelman, "Soviet Political Culture," p. 545.) This figure is actually lower than the number of Jewish emigrants, but some of them do not go to Israel; for this reason, the statistics on arrivals in Vienna are considerably higher. Annie Kriegel, *Le Figaro,* 16 January 1978, estimates Jewish emigration since 1968 at 150,000 persons. According to W. Frankel, *The New York Times,* 12 May 1977, 135,000 Jews had emigrated since the same date.

63. In 1972, 71% of the emigrants were under 45 years of age and 50% under 30. On the other hand, the under-30 group among Jews in the RSFSR represents 26% of the whole community.

64. Along with the problems involved in emigration, it should be noted that the Jews are subjected to special procedures regarding the financial conditions of their exile. The taxes accompanying an exit visa were lowered in 1976 to 300 rubles. Notwithstanding this, Jews must pay 500 supplementary rubles to give up Soviet citizenship. The solidarity of the international Jewish community enables them to surmount this obstacle. On the other hand, every applicant for emigration is on his own when facing such problems as loss of employment which often follows the visa request; worse still, in the event his application is rejected, Soviet Jews are branded as *otkazniks* (those who have not received their visa but who find themselves outside the Soviet community for having applied for one).

65. The most explicit manifestation of anti-Semitism is the anti-Zionism that took the form of a real press campaign at the very moment when the will for emigration began to be manifested on a large scale. Cf. J. Frankel, "The Anti-Zionist Press Campaigns in the U.S.S.R. 1969–1971, Political Implication," (research paper, Hebrew University of Jerusalem, 1972), 62 pp.

66. *The New York Times,* 12 May 1977; cf. also D. Harris, "A Note on the Problem of the Noshrims," *Soviet Jewish Affairs,* February 1976, pp. 104–114.

67. These are official figures given by the CPSU organ, *Partiinaia zhizn',* no. 10, 1976, p. 16.

68. *Literaturnaia Gazeta,* 24 January 1973.

69. Out of 1,000 people over 10 years of age, 73 have received a higher education. The Soviet average is 42 for 1,000, the Russian average is 44. The lowest average is held by Moldavia and Tajikistan: 29 for 1,000. Tsentral'noe . . ., *Itogi . . . 1970,* vol. 3 (Education), pp. 6–30.

70. On illegality in the economic sphere, cf. A. Katsenelinboigen, "Colored Markets in the Soviet Union," *Soviet Studies* 29, no. 1 (January 1977): pp. 67–85.

71. *Pravda,* 3 March 1972.

72. *Pravda,* 27 June 1976.

73. *Trud,* 5 June 1976.

74. *Zaria Vostoka,* 4 November 1976; the same censure appeared in *Zaria Vostoka,* 24 December 1976.

75. *Zaria Vostoka,* 16 February 1977.

76. *Zaria Vostoka,* 4 November 1976. Cf. also in the same organ of 24 December 1976, the insistence on the weight and prestige to be given to the militia; cf. also *Zaria Vostoka,* 11 November 1975.

77. *Zaria Vostoka,* 8 February 1977 and 16–17 February 1977.

78. The official version says that somebody had given them 50,000 rubles, but the courts hardly seemed concerned about finding out who had paid them 50,000 rubles to burn down the theater. In addition, the defendants retracted their statements at the trial and declared that their confessions had been obtained by force.

79. *Zaria Vostoka,* 3 March 1977.

80. *Zaria Vostoka,* 8 February 1977.

81. *Zaria Vostoka,* 10 January 1976.

82. *Zaria Vostoka,* 9 January 1976.

83. *Zaria Vostoka,* May 1978.

84. Estimates regarding the number of demonstrators varied. Unofficial Georgian sources put them at about 30,000; *The New York Times* reported about 20,000; the *International Herald Tribune* of 5 May 1978, 5,000. Whatever figure is used, the incident remains very important, given the political conditions of the USSR where only social organizations have the right to call for demonstrations.

85. Published in *Zaria Vostoka,* 16 April 1978.

86. *Uchitel'skaia Gazeta,* 18 July 1972 and *Bakinski Rabochii,* 4 and 6 January 1973.

87. Bribes are very often depicted as a sign of backwardness in the socialization process. Cf. the constant attacks on bribery in Azerbaijan, *Bakinskii Rabochii,* 11 February 1972 and 11 December 1976.

88. In Georgia, the authorities take great pains to root out traditions that promote particularism. Cf. for example *Zaria Vostoka* of 4 November 1972, 27 April 1973, and 27 October 1976; for Azerbaijan, cf. *Pravda,* 26 June 1972.

89. This becomes quite apparent from the speech of Armenian CP First Secretary Karen Demirchian before the CC plenum in December 1974 and published in the *Kommunist* of Erivan, 2 February 1975. Cf. also Demirchian's criticism of Armenian political cadres in the *Kommunist* of Erivan, 21 January 1976; on the purge in Armenia, *Kommunist,* 10 January 1975, 1 February 1975, 28 February 1975, and 23 May 1975.

90. J. A. Armstrong, *Ukrainian Nationalism 1939–1945* (New York, 1955), pp. 14–32. The book as a whole sheds light on the most dramatic aspects of Soviet–Ukrainian relations.

91. The Politburo of the CC of the CPSU had been converted into a Presidium at the 19th Congress (1952). It became a Politburo once more at the 23rd Congress in 1966.

92. I. Dziuba, *Internationalism or Russification?* (London, 1968), 239 pp.

93. V. Chornovil, *The Chornovil Papers* (New York: McGraw-Hill, 1968), 246 pp.

94. I am grateful for everything concerning the Chelest case to Y. Bilinsky of the University of Delaware whose in-depth analysis of the situation in the Ukraine, during our talks at the University of Chicago in 1977, taught me a great deal about the Ukraine and about nationality problems as a whole.

95. *Ukraina nasha radianska* (Kiev, 1970), 58 pp.

96. Ukrainian National Communism existed at the start of the Soviet regime. For the best understanding of the facts, cf. a pamphlet written in 1919 by two Ukrainians—V. Chakhrai and S. Mazlakh—entitled *Do Khvyli*. It was published in English under the title *On the Current Situation in the Ukraine* (Ann Arbor, 1970), 220 pp.

97. Y. Bilinsky, "Politics, Purge and Dissent in the Ukraine Since the Fall of Chelest," in I. Kamenetsky, ed., *Nationalism and Human Rights: Processes of Modernization in the U.S.S.R.* (Littleton, Colorado, 1977), pp. 168–185.

98. *Narodnoe obrazovanie,* March 1974, p. 9. Reference thanks to Y. Bilinsky and I. Dziuba, *Internationalism or Russification?,* p. 157.

99. Dziuba, *Internationalism or Russification?;* and Bilinsky, "The Communist Party of the Ukraine after 1966," in *Ukraine in the Seventies,* ed. P. Potychnyi (Oakville, Ontario, 1975), p. 246.

CHAPTER VII

1. For example, this was affirmed by the Chairman of the Council on Religious Matters under the USSR Council of Ministers in "reply to Western criticism on the freedom of conscience." In an article entitled "Sovetskii zakon i svoboda sovesti," *Izvestia,* 31 January 1976, p. 5.

2. *Nauka i Religiia* gives a fairly complete view of official reactions to the religious issue.

3. Thus, early in 1974 during a Moscow conference on "scientific atheism" which brought together the leading experts in this field, a report on research (institutions, activities, publications) was drawn up. Cf. "Koordinatsiia ateisticheskoi raboty: opyt, perspektivy," *Nauka i Religiia,* August 1974, pp. 21–27.

4. Cf., for example, the long editorial in the *Kazakhstanskaia Pravda,* 24 April 1976, p. 1: "Ateisticheskoie vospitanie shkol'nikov."

5. Ibid.

6. A good example of this more uneasy and sophisticated attitude with regard to religion appears in the work by V. I. Nosovitch, *Nauchnyi ateizm o religioznoi psikhologii* (Moscow, 1975), 134 pp.

7. V. Maslinkov, "Veshchi nesovmestnye," *Znamia Yunosti,* 28 November 1975, p. 3.

8. F. Protasov and D. Ugrinovitch, "Issledovanie religioznosti naseleniia i ateisticheskoe vospitanie," *Politicheskoe Samoobrazovanie,* 1975, pp. 109–116.

9. Y. Kasperavicius, "Muzli idet k liudiam," *Sovetskaia Litva,* 20 May 1974, p. 4, even announces the creation of a special journal, *Informatsia—metodika,* organ of the Lithuanian Museum of Atheism, the first publication to raise the question of the concrete, militant work of the atheism museums scattered through the republics. Cf. also A. Martulis,

"Tiesa yra tikviena—Ave Vita," *Komiaunimo Tiesa,* 20 May 1975, p. 2, which gives a detailed report on the activity of the Lithuanian club Ave Vita devoted to the propagation of atheism and to atheist education. This article proposes Ave Vita as a model.

10. J. Gailums, "Zinotniski ateistisko va i antereligisko?," *Skolotaiu Avize,* 7 April 1976, p. 3.

11. The most reliable statistics go back to the period of independence. The situation in the/ 1930s can be taken as a basis for understanding the present period. According to Royal Institute of International Affairs, *The Baltic States* (London: Oxford University Press, 1938), p. 38, the religious makeup of the Baltic population was as follows: Estonia: 7.8% Lutheran; 19% Orthodox; 1% Jewish. Latvia: 5.7% Lutheran; 24% Catholic; 9% Orthodox; 5% old believers; 5% Jewish. Lithuania: 81% Catholic; 9% Lutheran; 3% Orthodox; 1% Jewish.

12. T. Parming and E. Järvesoo, eds., *A Case Study of a Soviet Republic: The Estonian S.S.R.* (Boulder, Colorado: Westview Press, 1978), pp. 376–453.

13. *Nationality Group Survival in Multi-Ethnic States,* ed. E. Allworth (New York, 1977), p. 169. These figures are based on Soviet data.

14. A document published by the Lutheran World Federation, "Lutheran World Federation President Visits Lutherans in the U.S.S.R.," *Religion in Communist Dominated Areas* 11, no. 7–9 (July–Sept. 1972): 130–131. It should also be noted that the average age of students at the Tallin Lutheran Academy was much lower in 1972 than during the previous decade.

15. At the present time, nearly 3,000 propagandists work in the countryside and in factories. The 36 universities of "scientific atheism" scattered through the republic had 3,500 students in 1975.

16. The most important provisions are the texts supplementing article 142 of the Republic's Penal Code, which were adopted by the Supreme Soviet on 12 May 1966 and supplement the list of "acts violating art. 143" (on the separation of Church and State) and the complementary decrees of 1968 and 1969. All these measures are aimed at preventing religious cultural activities among teenagers and, in particular, those activities required for preparing them for confirmation.

17. *Kazakhstanskaia Pravda,* 27 August 1972.

18. E. Allworth, ed., *Nationality Group Survival,* p. 175.

19. On the number of signatures that can be brought in on a petition, cf. the report made by V. Krasin to the CESES (Venice Colloquium), August 1975 (unpublished working document).

20. This organ entitled *Lituvos Kataliky Bažnyčios Kronika* [Chronicle of the Lithuanian Catholic Church] appeared 24 times from 1972 to 1977.

21. Number 4 carries a protest against the ban on local national costumes in religious ceremonies. In this issue, we also find a prayer for "the Lithuanian homeland." Number 6 focuses on the insufficient study allotted to local national history in the schools. Number 20 in 1975 was devoted largely to the government's pressure to promote Russian-language instruction in the schools, etc.

22. The symbol of such a link is the personality of the great Lithuanian writers Antanas Baranauskas (1835–1902) and Maironis (1862–1932), who played a decisive role in the 19th-

century Lithuanian national movement despite being clerics like so many of their counterparts.

23. K. Khaliarov, "Partiinye organizatsii i bor'ba s religioznymi perezhitkami," *Politicheskoe Samoobrazovanie,* June 1975, pp. 74–78.

24. Ibid.

25. The scarcity of clergy nowadays is especially remarkable in view of the fact that there was an overabundance of clergy before the revolution. In 1917, there were 26,000 mosques in the Russian Empire and 45,000 persons capable of officiating at services, i.e., one for each 700 to 1,000 Moslems. *Zhizn' natsional'nostei,* 14 December 1921.

26. K. I. Koichumanov, "Nekotrye osobennosti ateisticheskoi propagandy v Kirghizii," *Voprosy Istorii partii Kirghizii,* 1969, pp. 340–341.

27. S. M. Abramzon, *Kirghizia i eë etnogeneticheskie i istoriko-kul'turnyie sviazi* (Leningrad), p. 302 ff.

28. *Handbook of Major Soviet Nationalities,* ed. Z. Katz (Boston: M.I.T., 1975), pp. 70, 71, 244; J. Bazarbaev, *Sekularizatsiia naseleniia sotsialisticheskoi karakalpakii* (Nukus, 1973), p. 61; and U. G. Pivovarov, *Na etapakh sotsialisticheskogo issledovaniia Gruzii* (1974), p. 158 ff.

29. Moreover, the Sunnites of the USSR are divided into two groups. The majority practise the Hanafite rites, while in Daghestan the Shafi'ite rites prevail. The Shiites, separated from the Sunnites on the problem of the Prophet's succession, are followers of his son-in-law, Ali. On this score as well, variety predominates in the USSR. The majority of Shiites belong to the duodecimal branch of Shiism (for whom the succession broke off after the disappearance of the twelfth Imam) but we also find in this branch Isma'ilis who recognize the authority of the Aga Khan, etc.

30. It should be noted, however, that this system was not uniform throughout the Russian Empire. While the bulk of the Moslems came under the Shari'a law, the unwritten laws (*Ada*) were applied in some Islamic regions.

31. This remark is often made in Soviet studies, whether sociological or ideological. Accordingly, in an analysis of religious attitudes in the Tatar ASSR, the growth of religious activity in the Tatar communities was stressed. *O nauchnom ateizme i ateisticheskom vospitanie dlya partiinogo aktiva i organizatorov ateisticheskoi raboty* (Moscow, 1974), 287 pp. Cf. pp. 72–75.

32. P. Mavliutov, "Molitva," *Nauka i Religiia,* October 1976, p. 60.

33. Sermon delivered in the Allan mosque of Tashkent by Imam N. Kutbedinov, cited by N. Achirov, *Evolzhutsia Islama v S.S.S.R.* (Moscow, 1972), p. 135.

34. Sermon delivered in the Baku cathedral-mosque by the Mufti Ahmed Bozgaziev on 13 December 1968, cited in ibid., pp. 135–136.

35. Achirov, *Evolzhutsia Islama.*

36. *Kommunist Tadjikistana,* 4 September 1976, p. 3. The article is entitled: "He doesn't fast, but . . ."

37. Achirov, *Evolzhutsia Islama,* p. 143; and R. Mavliutov and G. Kerimov, "Mavlud," *Nauka i Religiia,* February 1976, pp. 66–67.

38. M. Gaudefroy-Demombynes, in *Les Institutions musulmanes* (Paris, 1966), p. 91, notes that, in this case, the *hadj* is only valid for the person who commissions another to make the pil-

grimage in his stead, not for his replacement. In practice, however, it seems that the Moslem authorities of the USSR consider that the handful of pilgrims who actually leave the country do so in the name of all their co-religionists.

39. On 21 March 1969, Ismail Satiev, proxy for the Mufti of Tashkent, coming home from Mecca, made this problem the theme of his sermon at the Moscow cathedral-mosque: Achirov, *Evolzhutsia Islama*, p. 144.

Cf. also in *Izvestia*, 20 May 1976, the account of Jordan's Minister of Religious Affairs visiting the USSR. He was accompanied by a delegation of Moslem dignitaries. The news article describes their reception at the spiritual directorate of the Moslems of European Russia and Siberia by Mufti Abdul Bori Isaev.

40. Snesarev, "Chamany i Sviatye," *Nauka i Religiia*, December 1976, pp. 31 to 36.

41. In *Nauka i Religiia*, July 1976, pp. 41–43, S. Umarov makes a systematic study of the growth and effects of the cult of saints on the collective thinking. He emphasizes that the cults have not only produced isolated movements but "powerful popular movements" as well. On Central Asia, cf. G. Snesarev, "Chamany i sviatye," particularly p. 31.

42. V. N. Basilov, "Tachmat Bola," *Sovetskaia Etnografiia*, May 1975, pp. 112-124. Basilov, in "Chamany Segodnia," *Nauka i Religiia*, April 1976, p. 52, covers diverse sources and reveals the extent of this phenomenon.

43. In *Musulmani Sovetskogo Vostoka*, March 1970, p. 35.

44. Ibid.

45. Speech of the Mufti Ahmed Habibullah Bozgoziev, proxy for the Mufti of Transcaucasia, ibid.

46. Speech of M. Hazaev in Tashkent, October 1970, ibid.

47. Reply made during a press conference organized in Paris by the newspaper *Le Monde*. In addition, cf. D. Chigaev, "Islam i Sovremennost'," *Agitator*, October 1975, pp. 47–48. Furthermore, this tendency has been observed for all religions. Cf. N. Krasnikov, "Posle pomestnogo sobora," *Nauka i Religiia*, December 1975, pp. 38–40, which notes the same characteristics in the Orthodox. *Kazakhstanskaia Pravda*, 24 April 1976, p. 1, notes the difficulty of teaching atheism in these conditions.

48. H. Carrère d'Encausse, "Politische Sozialisation in der U.S.S.R.—Unter besondeer Berücksichtigung der nichtrussischen Nationalitäten," *Ehrziehungs und Sozialisations Probleme in der Sowjet Union, der DDR und Polen*, ed. O. Anweiler (Hanover, 1978). On parents' responsibility in the area of religious instruction, cf. *Moskovskii Komsomolets*, 11 July 1976 and 11 August 1976. These articles call on teachers to combat and observe the harmful influence of families. *Nachal'naia Shkola*, September 1975, pp. 25—30, makes suggestions concerning more vigorous control over religious instruction received in the home and, in particular, suggests that teachers set up a "daily journal" noting all information concerning "the believing child."

49. *Sovetskaia Kirgiziia*, 17 June 1976, p. 4.

50. *Kommunist Tadjikistana*, 13 December 1974, p. 2.

51. Cf. *Komsomol'skaia Pravda*, 4 September 1975, p. 2, on religious survivals in Dagestan.

52. Commemoration of the martyrdom of Hussain, eldest son of Ali, son-in-law of the Prophet, in Kerbela in 680.

53. This type of commemoration has been strictly forbidden in Turkmenia, Azerbaijan and Georgia since 1929. Cf. R. Mavliutov and G. Kerimov, "Achura," *Nauka i Religiia,* December 1975, p. 42; and N. Achirov, "Islam i natsional 'nye otnocheniia," *Nauka i Religiia,* February 1974, p. 35.

54. Mavliutov and Kerimov, "Achura," p. 40: the author of the study notes how much this type of play "particularizes" Moslem children and isolates them in their historical background.

55. N. Achirov, "Islam i natsional'nye otnocheniia," *Nauka i Religiia,* December 1973, p. 46.

56. Khaliarov, "Partiinye organizatsii," pp. 74–78. Cf. *Komsomol'skaia Pravda,* 4 September 1975, which tells how a woman, only recently an active member of Komsomol, becomes a militant Moslem; and *Nauka i Religiia,* January 1976, p. 2, on the situation in Uzbekistan: "Religion is a barrier between young people of different nationalities." See also the same organ of November 1976, pp. 2–9. *Turkmenskaia Iskra,* 23 November 1976, p. 3, and *Pravda,* 1 June 1976, note that the problem was discussed by the Turkmen Party's Central Committee during its last plenum. *Kommunist Tadjikistana,* 7 July 1976, p. 2, notes that the organs of the Party and the State tolerate Islam and its practices.

57. An article illuminating this point was published by the Uighur-language organ, *Kommunist Tughi,* 27 September 1975. This article reports that during the month of Ramadan, in the Talgir district, a special commission of twelve persons was set up by the Party's district committee to collaborate with existing propaganda agencies in the struggle against religious practices. This is clearly a case of combating the various ways of observing Ramadan.

58. *Kommunist Tughi,* 23 September 1975.

59. *Karmannyi Slovar'ateista* (Moscow, 1975), p. 159.

60. *Isläm va hazirgi zäman* (Tashkent, 1972). This publication directed by A. Artikov collects fourteen educational posters—all of them aimed against Islam).

61. Khaliarov, "Partiinye organizatsii."

62. N. Achirov, "Islam i natsional'nye otnocheniia," *Nauka i Religiia,* December 1973, pp. 43–44.

63. Ibid., p. 41.

64. Ibid., p. 46.

65. G. A. Bondarskaia, *Rozhdaemost': Sbornik statei* (Moscow, 1976), p. 114; and Vagabov, *Islam i zhenshchina* (Moscow, 1968), p. 38.

66. Achirov, "Islam i natsional 'nye otnocheniia," *Nauka i Religiia,* February 1974, p. 37.

67. A. Bennigsen and C. Quelquejay, *Les Mouvements nationaux chez les musulmans de Russie: le Sultangalievisme au Tatarstan* (Paris, 1960). It is interesting to note that, after decades of silence on Sultan Galiev, a clear-cut attack has been made against him—namely: *Tatarstan Kommunisty,* January 1975, p. 67. It should be noted here that, unlike his closest rivals, the Uzbek Faizullah Khodjaev, rehabilitated in 1966 and the Kazakh Ryskulov, rehabilitated two years earlier, Sultan Galiev remains a political "non-person."

CHAPTER VIII

1. Leonid Brezhnev, *O piatidesiatilettii soyuza sovetskikh sotsialisticheskikh respublik* (Moscow, 1972) p. 21.

2. On the notion of political culture and the use of the concept of culture in political anthropology, cf. Tucker, "Culture, Political Culture and Communist Society," *Political Science Quarterly* 2 (June 1973): 170–190.

3. A. Khartchev, *Brak i sem'ia v S.S.S.R.* (Moscow, 1964) and *Sovetskaia Kirgizia,* 14 October 1976: the author notes with regard to mixed marriages in the USSR that "international-ism has become a conviction and a standard of behavior" (p. 3).

4. L. Tchuiko, *Braki i razvotly* (Moscow, 1975), p. 76.

5. S. M. Abramzon, "Otrajenie problemy sblijenii natsii na semeino-by-tovom uklade naro-dov Srednei Azii i Kazakhstana," *Sovetskaia Etnografiia,* March 1962, pp. 18–34.

6. Khartchev, *Brak i sem'ia,* p. 195, confirms this hostility.

7. V. I. Kozlov, *Natsional'nosti S.S.S.R.* (Moscow, 1975), writes on p. 243: "No such studies exist for Central Asia but, looking at the data available, the situation there is similar to the one in the Caucasus on many points."

8. J. Evstingeev, "Natsional 'nye smechannye braki v makhachkale," *Sovetskaia Etnografia,* April 1971, pp. 80—85.

9. A. Kozenko and L. Monogarova, "Statisticheskoe izuchenie pokazatelei odnonatsional 'noi i smechannoi brachnosti v Duchanbe," *Sovetskaia Etnografiia,* June 1971, pp. 112–118.

10. Ibid., p. 113.

11. N. Borzykh, "Rasprostranenie mezhnatsional'nykh brakov v respublikakh Srednei Azii i Kazakhstana v 1930 khgodakh," *Sovetskaia Etnografiia,* April 1970, pp. 94–95.

12. A. I. Ismailov, "Nekotorye aspekty razvitiia mezhnatsional 'nykh brakov v S.S.S.R.," *Izvestia Akademii Nauk Kirgizskoi S.S.R.,* April 1972, p. 87.

13. M. Djunusov, "O nekotorykh natsional'nykh osobenostiakh obraza zhizn' v usloviiakh sotsializma," *Sotsiologicheskie issledovania,* February 1975, table 1, p. 65, for comparative ur-banization; p. 68 for education.

14. L. M. Drobijeva, "Sotsial'no-kul'turnye osobennosti lichnosti i natsional'nye ustanovki," *Sovetskaia Etnografiia,* March 1971, pp. 3–15.

15. G. A. Sergueeva and I. S. Smirnova, "K voprosu o natsional'nom samoznanii gorodskoi molodëjy," *Sovetskaia Etnografiia,* April 1971, pp. 86–92; and Evstingeev, "Natsional'nye smechannye braki," p. 84.

16. *Sovetskaia Etnografiia,* March 1976, p. 45 reports the results of a survey carried out among the Kazan Tatars in an industrialized milieu where migration was not uncommon.

17. Evstingeev, "Natsional'nye smechannye braki," p. 84.

18. Cf. Sergueeva and Smirnova, "K voprosu o natsional'nom," on attitudes to inter-ethnic contacts in general. Cf. also L. M. Drobijeva, "Sotsial 'no-kul 'turnye osobennosti lich-

nosti i natsional'nye ustanovki," *Sovetskaia Etnografiia,* March 1971, pp. 3–15.

19. G. V. Starovoitova, "K issledovaniiu etnopsikhologii gorodskikh tatar," *Sovetskaia Etnografiia,* March 1976, p. 53.

20. *Nauka i Religiia,* December 1975, p. 42. *Turkmenskaia Iskra,* 14 July 1976, says that parents should stop giving children names that have religious meaning.

21. Starovoitova, "K issledovaniiu etnopsikhologii," p. 53.

22. *Literaturnaia gazeta,* 17 November 1976, p. 11, and R. K. Kereitov, "Novye cherty v svadebnom obriade kubanskikh nogaitsev," *Sovetskaia Etnografiia,* March 1973, p. 85.

23. Kereitov, "Novye cherty."

24. *Literaturnaia Gazeta,* 28 May 1975, p. 12. On marriages of pre-pubescent girls, cf. also *Turkmenskaia Iskra,* 14 July 1976.

25. *Nauka i Religiia,* August 1975, p. 92; *Turkmenskaia Iskra,* 14 July 1976, p. 2.

26. O. Umurzakova, *Zakonomernosti sblizheniia byta i traditsii sotsialisticheskikh natsii* (Tashkent, 1971), p. 209. *Sovetskaia Rossiia,* 9 October 1976, p. 4, says that 2,000 rubles were paid for the *Kalym* in Daghestan.

27. Umurzakova, *Zakonomernosti sblizheniia byta,* p. 210.

28. Kereitov, "Novye cherty," p. 89.

29. Ibid., p. 88.

30. Starovoitova, "K issledovaniiu etnopsikhologii," p. 54.

31. Achirov, "Islam i natsional'nye otnocheniia," *Nauka i Religiia,* February 1974, p. 35.

32. H. Smith, in *The New York Times,* 22 November 1972.

33. Umurzakova, *Zakonomernosti sblizheniia byta,* p. 204.

34. Achirov, "Islam i natsional'nye."

35. Cf. *Sem'ia i semeinye obriady u narodov Srednei Azii i Kazakhstana* (Moscow, 1977), 272 pp.

36. H. Smith, *The New York Times,* 22 November 1972.

37. Umurzakova, *Zakonomernosti sblizheniia byta,* p. 218.

38. N. P. Lobatcheva, *Formirovanie novoi obraidnosti Uzbekov* (Moscow, 1975), pp. 80–81. The same author had published an article in *Sovetskaia Etnografiia,* March 1973, pp. 14–24.

39. Umurzakova, *Zakonomernosti sblizheniia byta,* p. 173.

40. Ibid., p. 130.

41. Lobatcheva in *Voprosy Etnografii,* February 1967, p. 20.

42. Quite involuntarily, a recent work gave an inkling of the contradictory results of this policy: K. Esbergenov and T. Atamuratov, *Traditsii i ikh preobrazovanie v gorodskom bytu Karakalpakov* (Nukus, 1975), 211 pp.

43. On Soviet women and the career world, cf. "Zhenshchiny v S.S.S.R.," *Vestnik Statistiki,* 1975; on women deputies in Central Asia, *Pravda,* 21 June 1975. Detailed information by

republics on working women appears in the republican editions of *Narodnoe khoziaistvo*.

44. G. P. Vasilieva, "Zhenshchiny respublik Srednei Azii i Kazakhstana i ïkh rol' v preobrazovanie byta sel'skogo naselenia," *Sovetskaia Etnografiia,* June 1975, p. 26.

45. V. N. Basilov, "Tachmat Bola," *Sovetskaia Etnografiia,* May 1975, pp. 112–124; "Chamany segodnia," *Nauka i Religiia,* April 1976, p. 52; and G. Snesarev, "Chamany i sviatye v Srednei Azii," *Nauka i Religiia,* December 1976, pp. 31–35.

46. G. Snesarev and V. Basilov, eds., *Domusul'manskie verovaniia i obriady v Srednei Azii* (Moscow, 1975), 340 pp.

47. On this problem and sources, cf. A. Bennigsen and C. Lemercier-Quelquejay, "Muslim Religious Conservatism and Dissent in the U.S.S.R.," *Religion in Communist Lands,* vol. 6, no. 3, Autumn 1978.

48. Vasilieva, "Zhenshchiny respublik Srednei Azii," p. 26.

49. V. K. Mal'kova, "Primenenie kontent-analiza dlya izuchenia sotrudnichestva sovetskikh narodov," *Sovetskaia Etnografiia,* May 1977, pp. 71–80.

50. The newspapers involved were the *Sovetskaia Moldavia* for Moldavia, the *Zaria Vostoka* for Georgia and the *Pravda Vostoka* for Uzbekistan.

51. Mal'kova, "Primenenie Kontent-analiza," p. 75.

CONCLUSION

1. Another fruitful approach to the problem of nationality has been advanced by E. Kedourie, *Nationalism* London, 1-60. This approach has not been used here, for the simple reason that it does not apply to Soviet developments.

2. *Kommunist,* no. 15 (October 1977): 10.

3. *Sovetskaia Etnografiia,* March 1976, pp. 3–9.

4. *Sovetskaia Estonia,* 30 November 1976.

5. Cf. the work of N. Djandil'din, *Priroda natsional'noi psikhologii* (Alma Ata, 1971), and its review in *Sovetskaia Etnografiia,* February 1973, pp. 69–83; cf. also the article by S. Gurvitch, "Sovremennye napravleniia ethnicheskikh protesessov v S.S.S.R.," *Sovetskaia Etnografiia,* April 1972, pp. 16–34.

6. The Mskhetians, a Moslem group of 150,000 persons of mixed origin in the south of Georgia, were also deported in 1944; less is known about their fate than that of the Tatars.

7. On the general evolution of Russian ideology, an interesting study was written by M. Agursky, "The Soviet Legitimacy Crisis and its International Implications," a report submitted at the Chicago conference: "What is Communism?" (Conference Report, 1977), 95 pp.

8. Refer to the article by E. Chevarnadzé, "Internatsionalisticheskoe vospitanie mass," *Kommunist,* no. 13 (September 1977): 45, 46.

BIBLIOGRAPHY

(This bibliography does not contain all of the books referred to in this work, but only the most important titles published in the USSR or in the West, and used here.)

I. POPULATION PROBLEMS

Bogarskii, I., *Naselenie S.S.S.R. za 400 let—The Population of the USSR in the Last Four Hundred Years.* Vols. 16–20. Moscow, 1973, 159 pp.

Borisov, V. A., *Perspektivy rozhdaemosti—Birth Rate Perspectives.* Moscow, 1976, 274 pp.

Dunn, S. and E., *Introduction to Soviet Ethnography.* 2 vols. Berkeley, 1974, 362 and 363 pp. respectively.

Kozlov, V. I., *Dinamika chislenosti narodov: Metodologiia issledovaniia i osnovnye faktory—The Dynamics of the Peoples' Numerical Strength: Research Methods and Basic Factors.* Moscow, 1969, 408 pp.

Kozlov, V. I., *Natsional'nosti S.S.S.R.—The Nationalities of the USSR.* Moscow, 1975, 262 pp.

Lewis, R. A.; Rowland, R. H.; and Clem, R. S., *Nationality and Population Change in Russia and the USSR: An Evaluation of Census Data, 1897–1970.* New York, 1976, 456 pp.

Lorimer, F., *The Population of the Soviet Union: History and Prospects.* Geneva, 1946, 289 pp.

Narodnoe khoziaistvo S.S.S.R. v 1959 g.—The National Economy of the USSR in 1959. Moscow, 1960. Statistical almanac.

Narodnoe khoziaistvo S.S.S.R. v 1961 g.—The National Economy of the USSR in 1961. Moscow, 1962.

Narodnoe khoziaistvo S.S.S.R. v 1970 g.—The National Economy of the USSR in 1970. Moscow, 1971.

Narodnoe khoziaistvo S.S.S.R. v 1972 g.—The National Economy of the USSR in 1972. Moscow, 1973.

Narodnoe khoziaistvo S.S.S.R. 1922–1972: Yubileinyi statisticheskii ezhegodnik—The National Economy of the USSR, 1922–1972: Jubilee Statistical Almanac. Moscow, 1972.

Naselenie S.S.S.R.: Spravochnik—The Population of the USSR: A Guidebook. Moscow, 1974, 191 pp.

Perevedentsev, *Metody izucheniia migratsii naseleniia—Methods of Studying Population Migration.* Moscow, 1974, 231 pp.

Pokchichevskii, V. V., *Geografiia naseleniia S.S.S.R.—Geography of the Population of the USSR.* Moscow, 1971.

Rachin, A., *Naselenie Rossii za sto let 1811–1913—The Population of Russia from 1811 to 1913.* Moscow, 1956, 352 pp.

Slesarov, G. A., *Metodologiia sotsiologicheskogo issledovaniia problem narodonaseleniia S.S.S.R.— Methodology of the Sociological Study of Population Problems in the USSR.* Moscow, 1965, 160 pp.

S.S.S.R.: Administrativo-territorial 'noe delenie soyuznikh respublik, 1971—The USSR: Administrative-Territorial Division of the Federated Republics, 1971. Moscow, 1971, 688 pp.

Tokarev, S., *Etnografiia narodov S.S.S.R.: Istoricheskie osnovy byta i kul 'tury—Ethnography of the Peoples of the USSR: The Historical Bases of Their Way of Life and Culture.* Moscow, 1958, 615 pp.

Tsentral'noe Statisticheskoe Upravlenie Pri Sovete Ministrov SSSR, *Itogi vsesoyuznoi perepisi naseleniia 1959 goda—Results of the USSR Population Census of 1959.* 16 vols. Moscow, 1962–1963.

Tsentral'noe Statisticheskoe Upravlenie Pri Sovete Ministrov SSSR, *Itogi vsesoyuznoi perepisi naseleniia 1970 goda—Results of the USSR Population Census of 1970.* 7 vols. Moscow: Statistika, 1972–1974.

II. NATIONALITY PROBLEMS

Allworth, E., ed., *Soviet Nationality Problems.* New York, 1971, 296 pp.

Allworth, E., ed., *Nationality Group Survival in Multi-Ethnic States: Shifting Support Patterns in the Soviet Baltic Region.* New York, 1977, 299 pp.

Arutiunian, I. V.; Drobijeva, L. M.; and Chkaratan, O. I., *Sotsial'noe i natsional'noe: Opyt etnosotsiologicheskikh issledovanii po materialam tatarskoi A.S.S.R.—The Social and the National: Testing Ethno-Sociological Research on the Basis of Materials from the Tatar Republic.* Moscow, 1973, 330 pp.

Barghoorn, F., *Soviet Russian Nationalism.* Vol. 12. New York, 1956, 330 pp.

Bennigsen, A., and Lemercier-Quelquejay, C., *L'Islam en Union soviétique.* 1968, 264 pp.

Carrère d'Encausse, H., *Bolchevisme et Nation 1917–1929.* (forthcoming publication)

Conquest, R., *The Nation Killers—Soviet Deportation of Nationalities.* London, 1970, 222 pp.

Decheriev, I. D., *Razvitie obshchestvennykh funktsii literaturnykh iazykov—The Development of the Social Functions of Literary Languages.* Moscow, 1976, 430 pp.

Directory of Soviet Officials, Union Republics. Vol. III. Washington, D.C.: Central Intelligence Agency, May 1975.

Goldhagen, E., ed., *Ethnic Minorities in the Soviet Union.* New York, 1968. Collective anthology.

Karpov, ed., *Razvitie sotsialisticheskoi kultury v soyuznykh respublikakh—The Development of Socialist Culture in the Federated Republics.* Moscow, 1962, 610 pp.

Katz, Z., ed., *Handbook of Major Soviet Nationalities.* New York-London, 1975, 481 pp.

Kerblay, Bernard, *La Société soviétique contemporaine.* Paris, 1977, 304 pp.

Pipes, R., *The Formation of the Soviet Union—Communism and Nationalism 1917–1923.* Cambridge, Mass.: Harvard University Press, 1954, 355 pp.

Sovetskii narod, novaia istoricheskaia obshchnost' Lyudei: Stanovlenie i razvitie—The Soviet People, A New Human Community: ANSSSR. Moscow, 1975, 519 pp.

S.S.S.R., Velikoe Sodruzhestvo narodov-bratiev—The USSR, A Great Community of Brother-Peoples. Moscow, 1972, 332 pp.

Sujikov, M., and Demakov, G., *Vliyanie podvizhnosti naseleniia na sblizhenie natsii—The Influence of Population Mobility on the Rapprochement of Nations.* Alma-Ata, 1974, 199 pp.

Umurzakova, O. P., *Zakonomernosti sblizheniia byta i traditsii sotsialisticheskikh natsii—The Laws Governing the Convergence of Mores and Traditions of Socialist Nations.* Tashkent, 1971, 239 pp.

Valiev, A. K., *Sovetskaia natsional'naia intelligentsia i ee sotsial'naia rol'—The Soviet National Intelligentsia and Its Social Role.* Tashkent, 1969, 288 pp.